D1201246

# LABBY

Photo

Elliott & Fry

"LABBY" in 1887

# Labby

## (The Life and Character of Henry Labouchere)

*by*

## HESKETH PEARSON

*published by*

**HAMISH HAMILTON**

**90 Great Russell Street London**

| First Published - | - | *April* 1936 |
| *Reprinted* - | - | *May* 1936 |
| *Reprinted* - | - | *October* 1936 |
| *Reprinted* - | - | *September* 1937 |
| *Reprinted* - | - | *October* 1945 |
| *Reprinted* - | - | *March* 1948 |

TO

## DOUGLAS JEFFERIES

PRINTED IN GREAT BRITAIN BY
BISHOP & SONS, LTD.
NICOLSON SQUARE, EDINBURGH

'That horrible lying Labouchere.'
— Queen Victoria.

'One of the very few quite honest M.P.s who always told the truth and was always amusing.'
— Wilfred Scawen Blunt.

'That viper Labouchere.'
— King Edward VII.

'A kinder-hearted man never lived.'
The Earl of Dunraven.

# ACKNOWLEDGMENT

I GRATEFULLY acknowledge the help given me by Mr. Thomas Colsey, Mr. J. V. Kitto, the Right Hon. George Lambert, Mr. Walter Legge, Mr. Sydney Maiden and Mr. Thomas Thornely.

My thanks are due to the editors of the *News Chronicle* and *Truth* for allowing me to quote from their columns, to the proprietors of *Punch* for permission to print a poem by Sir Frederick Bridge, to Messrs. Macmillan and Co. Ltd. for leave to quote from a poem by Alfred Austin, and to Messrs. Constable and Co. Ltd: and Mr. Algar Thorold for letting me make a few quotations from the latter's *Life of Henry Labouchere* (1913).

Mr. Thorold's work, to which I am also indebted for many facts, is indispensable to those who are interested in late Victorian politics. I have concentrated on the character of Labby.

# CONTENTS

# CONTENTS

# LABBY

## CHAPTER I

### AN ENGLISH EDUCATION

A YOUNG French clerk in the house of Hope at Amsterdam was sent to England by his firm in order to negotiate certain business with Sir Francis Baring, fell in love with the financier's daughter and asked permission to marry her. The answer was not encouraging.

'Would it make any difference to your decision if you knew that Mr. Hope was about to take me into partnership?' queried the young French clerk.

'Well – yes – certainly it would,' replied Sir Francis Baring.

The young French clerk, whose name was Pierre-César Labouchere and who was descended from a family of Huguenot cloth-merchants, returned to Amsterdam and expressed a wish that he should be given a partnership. Mr. Hope's reply was unfavourable.

'Would it make any difference to your decision if you knew that I was engaged to the daughter of Sir Francis Baring?' asked Pierre-César.

Mr. Hope thought it would make a lot of difference.

Whereupon Pierre-César sat down and wrote a letter to Sir Francis Baring, explaining that he was about to become a partner in the house of Hope and reminding Sir Francis of his promise. The marriage took place and Pierre-César began to make a fortune, most of which, together with much of his character, was inherited by his grandson, Henry Labouchere, the subject of this book.

After the Napoleonic wars, the house of Labouchere and Baring placed France financially on her feet, at a handsome profit to themselves, and Pierre-César was able to consider the future of his two sons with equanimity. The elder boy became an eminent politician of the conventional whig type, occupying several posts in the cabinet and ending up as Baron Taunton. The younger boy, John, went into the family business, married the daughter of a Buckinghamshire squire named Du Pre, bought Broome Hall in Surrey and a town house at No. 16 Portland Place, and begat nine children. John Labouchere was a professional puritan and a pillar of Exeter Hall, then the great temple of British intolerance, or religion as it was called. He was an earnest sorrowful man, who subscribed heavily to earnest and sorrowful movements, such as temperance, the conversion of the heathen and the distribution of the Bible. It added greatly to his sorrows that his eldest son Henry should have displayed from childhood a marked disinclination to sobriety of thought or behaviour and even appeared to read the Bible for pleasure not profit.

Henry Du Pre Labouchere first appeared at 16 Portland Place, London, on November 9, 1831. Somehow no one ever associated him with such commonplace occurrences as birth, marriage or death. To those who knew him in after-life it seemed that he had always been alive; they could not imagine a world without 'Labby'; he was the comic conscience of the universe; and just as he was different from all other men, so was he different from all other children, even his birth taking on the quality of a visitation.

Certainly he was born with his wits about him

because at a very early age he noted the effects of puritanical suppression in the strange behaviour of an aged relative. He used to visit his grandfather, whose house in Hamilton Place was frequented by the famous and wealthy, and there one day he observed an upright and godly grand-uncle, who had never danced in his life, taking part in a quadrille. To his amazement this solemn and decorous person suddenly caught the infection of unaccustomed motion, abandoned all restraint, flung his legs about like a ballet dancer and pranced around like a young and skittish colt. On the whole a stimulating exhibition, from which the child was able to infer that whenever sober people break out they rush into excesses. He also picked out from his grandfather's visitors the languid figure of Talleyrand, who earned his lifelong interest by presenting him with a magnificent box of dominoes.

The excitement of London and the charm of Broome Hall were not allowed to operate for long on the infant's fancy. It was a stern world, inhabited by stern and forbidding fathers, and when Queen Victoria came to the throne he was packed off to a private school at Brighton. Here he produced his first witticism, which, like many a one in later life, was expensive. Ranged in a row the morning after their arrival, the new boys were subjected to the usual dental catechism. Had they washed their teeth? The answers were satisfactory, as anticipated: 'Yes, sir' from all except Henry, who said 'No.' The sinful boy was lectured at length on the crime of unwashed teeth and was finally asked why he had failed to wash them.

'Because I haven't got any,' was Henry's triumphant retort as he opened his mouth to provide the evidence. His baby teeth, at the age of six, had just disappeared and the new ones had not yet taken their place.

His triumph was premature, and from that moment to the end of his days at the Brighton school he was never able to sit down with comfort. 'My skin,' he declared, 'was in a permanent state of discolouration owing to the kind attentions of the master.' Though the school had a considerable reputation, mainly because the owner 'had the effrontery to charge a high price for the privilege of being at it', the master, according to this pupil, was 'one of the most ill-conditioned ruffians that ever wielded a cane'. If the boys did not know their lessons or committed the least fault, they were made to stand up on a bench. Then the headmaster, who suffered from lumbago, which afforded some consolation to his pupils, would crawl in almost on all-fours, straighten himself suddenly and thrash them to his heart's content, doubtless in the belief that the exercise was good for his lumbago. Those were the days of the bull-dog breed, when Britons were men, or at least Victorians; for if any boy squealed when he was thrashed, his companions cuffed and kicked him after school-hours. Labby (it is a mental strain to call him anything else, for he was to be known by no other name throughout the two hemispheres) never became a true Victorian. The beating and bullying of his school-days made such an unfortunate impression on him that, sixty years later, he refused to vote for a bill that gave magistrates the power to have youthful offenders flogged.

Having learnt very little and suffered very much and developed a strong taste for gambling by playing innumerable games of pitch-and-toss, he left the private school and went to Eton at the age of thirteen. Very small for his age, he determined to make up for lack of inches by vigorously cultivating all the more popular British sports, such as bullying. When another boy was being pummelled and sat upon, he engaged in the pastime, realising that the only way to survive early school-life without personal injury was to be a sportsman, one of the hunters not the hunted. Another passport to popularity and personal safety was to score off the masters, and he did not fail to apply his mind to the problem. One of his successes in this field revealed a keen sense of drama. During service in chapel a boy was seen to faint; four others sprang forward, lifted him up and carried him out; Labby followed with their hats. Safely outside, all six craved instant refreshment and made a bee-line for the nearest supply. This drama would have been repeated but for the fact that the next boy who fainted aroused the sympathy of a master, in whose charge he recovered almost as quickly as he would have done if left to the care of his friends.

Although the headmaster at Eton did not enter into the spirit of the thing with that whole-hearted enjoyment which distinguished his Brighton contemporary, he flogged about twenty boys a day as a mere formality, doing the job with the utmost politeness and in an amiable frame of mind. That he felt no personal animosity is proved by the fact that a brisk trade in vicarious birchings was carried on among the boys. The par price for which one boy would consent to be beaten for another was five shillings, and according to the state of his exchequer Labby was a constant buyer and seller on those terms. The headmaster was shocked if a boy was ill-mannered enough to howl during the proceedings and encouraged the other boys to punish him for such a grave breach of etiquette. The other boys required no encouragement and the culprit was subjected to a pretty severe kicking then and thereafter.

Like most fags, Labby objected to the system of fagging, which taught him 'all the tricks and dodges of the slave'. For example, he stole the milk and gravy of his 'master' and watered the remainder to make up for the deficiency. In after-life he remarked, as proof that women were in many respects more sensible than men, that no woman could have invented the monitorial system, in which the strong boys were able to tyrannise over the weak. 'Delightful as the little fellows are in the main,' he said, 'their mothers find it necessary, next to hindering them from self-destruction by fire, gunpowder, chemical experiments and gymnastic feats, to devote the most watchful care to keeping every living thing, from their sisters to the cat, as far as possible out of the sphere of their activity.'

When his fagging days were over, he made up for earlier delinquencies by championing the weak and making life less easy for the bullies. Indeed he seems even to have befriended the brute creation, fighting a bargee who was tormenting a cat and then taking on another bargee who came to the rescue of his friend. His career at Eton was not distinguished, though he made some reputation as an underhand bowler and in his last year won the school sack-race in a canter; but his boisterous high spirits made him popular with some and his sardonic humour gained him the respectful enmity of those who could not compete with him in conversation or knock him down. He left Eton with the firm conviction that 'an English education, for the time and money that it consumes, is the worst that the world has yet produced'. It had however one advantage in his opinion: the religious teaching was entirely undenominational. Once a week his class studied the Greek Testament. When his turn came to read aloud, the master shuddered and said:

'What Greek is that? What would Thucydides have said?'

Labby had to confess that he did not know what Thucydides would have said. But the subject was not one to detain him, especially as it occurred to him that the value of Christ's teaching was not dependent on the proper pronunciation of Greek.

Apparently his father was dissatisfied with his prowess at Eton, because he was removed from school at the age of sixteen and placed in the hands of clerical tutors. The first of these was the only man who ever managed to teach him anything. The conduct of this clergyman was perfectly arbitrary, and he gave no reason for it, but his pupils either learnt a lot or left him quickly. Labby both learnt a lot and left quickly, because he refused to teach children in a Sunday-school. Then he went to another clergyman, who flattered instead of teaching him, and with whom he amused himself until he went to Cambridge.

From 1850 to 1852 he resided at Trinity College, Cambridge. It cannot be said that he used the College for any other purpose than a race-course residence. Probably his father had not realised that Newmarket was within easy driving-distance. At any rate Labby attended every meeting at Newmarket and spent his evenings in a tavern with sportsmen and tipsters. It is true that at first his ambitions were of a higher order, for he spoke at the Debating Society and had a shot at a prize poem; but as, to his astonishment, he broke down in the middle of his speech in favour of the regicides, and as, to his further astonishment, he could not get beyond the first line of his poem, he decided to win distinction in the less arduous sphere of betting. Although he despised the prizes and positions sought for by most ambitious men, he was always anxious to become known and to be talked about. 'I would rather be deformed than unnoticed,' he once let out. And since he could not gain the attention of book-learners without a great deal of tedious labour, he challenged the attention of book-makers. Here he was on surer ground, achieving such marked success that by the time he left Cambridge he had lost well over £6,000.

When there was no racing at Newmarket and life was slow, he used to visit London for gambling of another kind, putting up at Evans's, a well-known hotel and night-club in Covent Garden, the original of Thackeray's 'Cave of Harmony', where he could talk and bet and listen to bawdy songs and watch his

companions getting more and more drunk (he did
not care for drink himself) and generally speaking
enjoy himself in the mode of the moment. During
one of these visits he was strolling light-heartedly
through the streets, feeling that life was extremely
pleasant, when suddenly he came face to face with
his father. After the first gasp of amazement, his
father addressed him sternly:

'What! Henry! How is this? Why are you not at
Cambridge?'

But Labby was equal to the occasion. Making a
slight readjustment of his features, he asked:

'Who are you? and what business is it of yours that
I am walking in the Strand?'

Labouchere senior exploded:

'What business, eh? What the devil do you mean,
sir! Aren't you my son?'

'My dear old gentleman,' said the other, shaking
his head sadly and speaking in a strained tone of voice,
'you must be mad. I your son? Too ridiculous!'
and he brushed his parent aside.

Anxious to avoid a misunderstanding, he caught
the next train to Cambridge, noting with interest that
his father, labouring under the same anxiety, had
caught it too. On arrival at Cambridge he was well
down the platform before the train had come to a stop
and lost no time in repairing to his College, where
he was soon to be seen, gowned and among his books.
In a little while his studies were interrupted. There
were a series of imperative knocks, and Mr. John
Labouchere was disclosed, panting and fuming.

'Why, dad! This *is* a pleasure!'

Astonishment and delight fought for possession of
the son's features. Explanations followed, incredulity
was properly registered, and, in the words of the
rehabilitated student, 'I was carried to the Lion and
given a most excellent dinner, of which after my
adventure I stood in real need.'

It is perhaps unnecessary to add that he was not popular with the College authorities. He was a born rebel, hated discipline in any shape or form, and when there was nothing better to do he passed the tedious hours with the time-honoured sport of 'don-baiting'. Whewell, the Master of Trinity, once stopped him and asked:

'Is that a proper academic costume, Mr. Labouchere?'

'I must refer you to my tailor,' was the reply.

During an examination he was seen to be looking at regular intervals at something underneath his blotting-paper. He was asked to show it, and refused. When ordered to do so, he produced the photo of a music-hall 'star', declaring that he was inspired by her beauty to persevere with his paper.

It is hardly surprising that his career at Cambridge should have ended abruptly and in odium. Not having attended a single lecture since his arrival at College and having done nothing to prove his recognition of the purpose for which the College was endowed, it was naturally assumed that he would obtain unlawful assistance in the examinations. At any rate one of the proproctors, Mr. Barnard Smith, kept a wary eye on him from the very beginning of the examination in the Senate House, and Labby, having finished the exam and always ready to justify the worst suspicions of his conduct, wrote a note to a friend asking him how he was getting on. Instantly Mr. Smith, suspecting that the note was a crib, asked to see it. But Labby had thrown it away at the approach of Mr. Smith, and after denying that it was a crib said that it was somewhere on the floor. Another examiner now joined in and ordered Labby to search for the piece of paper. Labby resented his manner, explained what the note was about, declined to look for it, handed in his examination papers, and left the Senate House. He then wrote out a complaint of the treatment he had received, which he sent to the authorities; Mr. Smith lodged a counter-complaint, the case came before a court, and in the end Labby was 'admonished and suspended from his degree for two years'.

He missed his Newmarket friends when he left Cambridge, and, since his father paid all his debts with promptitude, his Newmarket friends missed him.

# CHAPTER II

## AN AMERICAN EDUCATION

H E returned home but did not stay there long. The whole family was steeped in religion and the house was as dull as a mausoleum. Few things are more irritating to a young man than the consciousness that he has erred in the sight of others, without feeling a personal conviction of sin, and after enduring the long faces of his relatives for a day or two he decided that Evans's was his spiritual home and went to live there. In the 'fifties this place was the chief resort of Bohemian men-of-letters: Thackeray, Edmund Yates, Douglas Jerrold, George Augustus Sala and John Leech were regular visitors, and though Labby chiefly prided himself on his winnings and losings at gambling, and preferred argument to discussion, he privately studied Boswell's *Life of Johnson* and Chesterfield's *Letters to his Son* in order to qualify for the society of the writers he met. The 'Cave of Harmony', as readers of *The Newcomes* will remember, was not exactly a haunt of vice, but the writers who frequented it were at least free to discuss what they dared not print and to live in a manner that would have scandalised some of their readers. Occasionally Labby found their society a little slow and went in search of faster company. There was a notorious house in Panton Street where, in the decorous phrase of T. P. O'Connor, 'Venus and Bacchus equally presided'; it was, in short, a brothel and beer-house; and when the wits of Evans's were being less witty than they supposed, Labby would forsake literature in Covent Garden for love in Panton Street.

After some months of happiness spent in this manner, he was heavily in debt and was forced once again to appeal to his father. He did not like his father, and his father strongly disapproved of him, but there was something galling to a puritan to have a son misconducting himself almost within a stone's throw of Exeter Hall, and the upshot was that the father agreed to pay his son's debts if his son would in future misconduct himself at a more respectable distance. It was not, of course, put precisely in those words, but that was roughly the feeling behind the transaction. Labby was 'rescued' from Evans's and sent abroad under the guidance of a bear-leader. He was sorry to leave Evans's, especially the chief character of the place, Paddy Green, who as head waiter was on excellent raillery-terms with everyone. Labby was fond of Paddy, while Paddy mourned Labby in these words: 'Loboocheer, Loboocheer, poor young man! He was always his own worst enemy.'

At a dangerously early stage in their continental trip Labby and his mentor found themselves at Wiesbaden, then a famous gambling resort. 'There was a vague notion that, somewhere or other, there were waters,' said Labby, 'but where precisely they were, and what they cured, very few knew.' The visitors were more interested in roulette than in health, and on the first day of his arrival Labby won £150. This sum his mentor took back to the hotel, but on the following morning would not surrender it unless Labby promised to stop playing. Labby refused and they separated. The mentor, who wished to study still nature, went on to the Carpathian Mountains. Labby, who wished to study human nature, remained at Wiesbaden. At the end of two months he was in serious need of funds and wrote to propose a reconciliation. It was finally agreed that they should meet in Paris, where Labby went to receive his money, which naturally disappeared in a few days.

They returned to England and Labby spent a month in the frowning formality of Broome Hall, sometimes escaping to Evans's for a little relief. It was now clear to his father that the Continent was not much safer than Covent Garden, and John Labouchere decided that nothing less than an ocean should be placed between his firstborn and himself. The family firm had many commercial interests in the southern portions of America, and it was arranged that Labby should go there with letters of introduction. The same mentor accompanied him and on November 2, 1852, they left in the steam packet *Orinoco* for Mexico. For ten days Labby suffered from seasickness and had a jaundiced view of the ocean. When they came within sight of Vera Cruz a mosquito stung him in the eye, and as he spent the first two days on shore bathing it in hot water he failed to appreciate the chief Mexican port. On the third day they left for Mexico City in a diligence, and an angry discussion arose among the passengers when they were told that no one could take more than twenty-five pounds of luggage, since each of their portmanteaus weighed more than fifty. While the storm was raging Labby slipped his portmanteau, much the largest of the lot, under the coachman's seat and a dollar into the coachman's hand. When his action became known the tempers of the other passengers, who were travelling with little more than their tooth-brushes, did not improve.

The three-days' journey to the city was altogether unpleasant because the roads were abominable and the heads of the passengers came into contact with the roof of the diligence about once every minute. Labby envied Cortes, whose journey to the capital was on the whole more comfortable.

Arrived in the city he and his companion put up at

a good hotel, and Labby was soon losing his money in the way that was most agreeable to him. In two months he was without a penny, owed £250, and announced his intention of retiring into the country, where he would remain until his mentor paid his debts. He carried out the threat and spent a solitary month in an inn at Quotla di Amalpas, where he reviewed his past life and took himself seriously to task. After careful reflection he came to the conclusion that he was an unpolished, unaccomplished, ignorant, conceited liar and gambler. He determined to mend his ways, to give up gambling, to be more reserved, to learn how to dance and pay compliments, to engage in as many love-affairs as possible, to cultivate self-command and to cease bragging. Having thus consulted his conscience and overhauled his character, he raised some money from somewhere, paid his debts, parted finally from his bear-leader, said farewell to his English friends, and with a light heart and a light purse began a series of adventures up and down the country of Mexico, losing touch with family, friends and civilisation for eighteen months.

As Labby was gifted with a singularly picturesque imagination, it is not easy to separate fancy from fact in the various accounts of his Mexican adventures which he gave in later life. But as he also had a born reporter's eye, we are on fairly firm ground whenever he describes anything in detail; and of course, since character does not greatly change, we can always arrive at the truth when he records his own behaviour in any given circumstances. At the outset he took the precaution to be inoculated against snake-bite by an old Indian crone, and was then told by the local experts that no snake could harm him; he was careful, however, not to put his immunity to the test. He was much struck by the happy and contented lives of the Mexicans, and came to the conclusion that the so-called blessings of civilisation were much overestimated, since they did not produce as much comfort of mind and body as was enjoyed by people who lived on the bounty of Nature. A good deal of his political life was spent in telling a mechanised nation to leave the 'backward' peoples alone in their primitive happiness. Guns, top-hats, and chartered companies were not, in his opinion, superior to peace, nudity and antiquated agriculture.

His quenchless curiosity led him to strange places and into the company of strange people. For weeks he roamed the mountains with a notorious robber, and once he became involved in local politics. There was a quarrel between two districts through which he happened to be passing and hostilities had already broken out. By nature a man of peace, he suggested that as an impartial neutral he should discover a basis for friendly negotiation. His offer was accepted and for some time he passed from one party to the other in a spirit of reconciliation. His character, in one important respect, was thoroughly Boswellian. There were few things he enjoyed more than to watch the reaction of human beings to different suggestions. Though his motives were on the whole altruistic, his relish for the comedy in all human situations was, now and always, the dominant influence in his political intrigues. Later we shall see the effect on English political life of his detached curiosity. In Mexico it nearly cost him his life, for one of the parties to the dispute began to suspect that he was being much too friendly with the other and arranged to have him shot when next he appeared with a further batch of quaint suggestions. Somehow he got wind of the arrangement; his interest in the business at once became exclusively personal; and he decamped without further ado.

Although he had made up his mind never to gamble again, he changed it the moment he saw reason to do so, and once more was lucky to escape with his life.

Finding himself at a place called Tacubaya, not far from the capital, where a Mexican gentleman had inaugurated a monte bank, he sat down and played all the afternoon, evening and night, rising from the table at five the following morning. He had smashed the bank; his pockets were bulging with gold 'ounces'; and he went downstairs into the courtyard where his horse was tied by a lasso to a manger. A number of gentlemen from whom he had won money descended the stairs with him and intimated in the friendliest fashion that they would accompany him back to the city. His heart sank within him. All of them had guns, swords, lassoes, and all of them were well-mounted. Moreover he knew that, while it was a question of honour with Mexicans to pay their gambling debts, while they would not hesitate for a moment to rob a church in order to do so, at the same time their social code permitted them to recover by force the debts they had paid; and if in the course of the struggle the lucky winner was murdered, that was all part of the game.

Feeling that he was already a dead man, Labby had serious thoughts of handing over his complete winnings, but remembered in time that he had one of the best horses in the country. This inspired him with a certain amount of confidence and he replied that he would be delighted to ride with them to the city. Then, just to show that he was in no hurry to start, he ordered chocolate all round. While they were busy drinking and making certain whispered arrangements, Labby jumped on his horse, slipped the lasso which attached it to the manger, clattered out of the courtyard and galloped for dear life along the road to Mexico City. The rest of the party did not stop to finish their chocolate and were soon making a commotion behind him. As they rode they fired, but their guns were old-fashioned and the bullets went wide. Their only hope now was to get within lassoing distance, and Labby was sufficiently aware of their proficiency in that art to realise that his only hope was speed. Several times they threw their lassoes, but always just short of him, and when they reached the outskirts of the city they abandoned the chase.

Labby's Mexican adventures were fitly rounded off with a love-affair. The object of his affections was a circus-girl, and he used to go night after night to watch her perform. Soon he began to haunt the more private portions of the establishment and one day the proprietor asked him impolitely what he meant by trespassing. He answered that he had formed an honourable attachment for one of the circus-riders and the reason for his presence in that particular spot was that he wished to kiss the hem of her garment as she passed by.

'Get to hell out of this, you damned loafer!' said the circus proprietor.

Labby never made the mistake of arguing a point when his opponent was not in a frame of mind to appreciate the point of an argument, and lost no time in getting to hell out of that. But a little later he contrived to present himself in a more favourable aspect before the proprietor by begging for an engagement, and, when asked what his line was, replying that he specialised in 'standing jumps'. Having passed the necessary tests, he was taken on the strength of the troupe, dressed in pink tights with a fillet round his head and billed as the 'Bounding Buck of Babylon'. He also took the money at the door, or rather the payment-in-kind, for money was scarce in the smaller Mexican towns and the inhabitants secured their seats with oranges and maize. It was an idyllic episode and lasted for some months. He reviewed it from a distance of seventeen years:

'I was once in love. The object of my affections had many amiable qualities. I remember I thought her an angel; but when she was crossed, she used to go into her room and say that she would remain there without eating until I yielded the point at issue between us. As I was invariably right and she was invariably wrong, I could not do this; but, pitying the weakness of her sex and knowing its obstinacy, I usually managed to arrange matters in a way which allowed her to emerge from her retreat without any great sacrifice of *amour propre*.'

In some manner unrecorded, Labby found himself in California during the 'gold rush' of 1853, and had a taste of humanity at its worst. He was able to shock the British House of Commons a generation later by saying that he had sat on a jury and condemned a man to be hung by lynch law. Towards the end of the year he travelled eastwards to St. Anthony's Falls, where a go-ahead chemist strongly advised him to buy land. As the city of Minneapolis was soon to be built on the land that was then going for a song, he lived to regret his lack of interest in the proposal. At St. Paul he fell in with a number of Chippeway Indians, who were on their way home. Becoming friendly with their chief, known as Hole-in-Heaven, he accompanied them to their hunting-ground to the west of Lake Superior, remaining with them for some months and being waited upon by the chief's sister. He witnessed the ritual of physical torture whereby the young men of the tribe were transformed into 'braves'. They qualified for this honour by enduring without a murmur the pain of having sharp sticks thrust through the flesh on their breasts, and the agony of having thongs bound so tightly round their ankles and wrists that the leather cut to the bone. He also saw an Indian war-dance; but as Hole-in-Heaven hinted that during this ceremony the sight of a white face might remind the warriors of their tomahawks, he saw it through a slit in his wigwam.

Having had enough of 'nature red in tooth and claw' to go on with, he traversed Lake Superior in a canoe and took his way by easy stages to New York, where he made a close study of the manners, customs and institutions of the white community. It was during this period that he became a convinced radical and republican, and for the rest of his life he never tired of comparing the class-conscious upbringing and antiquated opinions of Englishmen with the equalitarian education and rational outlook of Americans. Every single aspect of American life – laws, customs, constitution, character – was in his opinion vastly superior to its English parallel. 'How different,' he once exclaimed, 'American diplomatists are to the prim old women who represent us abroad, with a staff of half a dozen dandies helping each other to do nothing, who have been taught to regard all who are not of their craft as their natural enemies.' That reflection was the outcome of ten years in the diplomatic service, which he was now about to enter.

His family were beginning to feel that it was high time he should settle down, but as they were not anxious for him to return home they cast about for some means of keeping him in America. The chief difficulty was to place him in a position of social responsibility, in which he would have to behave himself and from which he could not easily break away and run riot. The diplomatic service seemed to meet the difficulty, especially as it was not necessary for him to pass an examination. Unaware that his relations were busying themselves over his future career, Labby was again enjoying the simple life west of the Great Lakes when he received the information that he had been appointed attaché at Washington. He raised no objection and took up his duties at the legation in the middle of 1854. One of his main characteristics was an intense interest in anything new that came his way, followed by a marked apathy when the novelty had worn off. So eager was he to serve his country that when, morning after morning, he arrived punctually and showed a keen disposition to be employed, the minister checked his enthusiasm with: 'If you fancy that you are likely to get on in the service by hard work you will soon discover your error; far better will it be for you if you can prove that some relation of yours is the sixteenth cousin of the porter at the Foreign Office.' This was of course broadly true, though sometimes it happened that exceptional personal qualities in a candidate of good family were recognised. For example:

'I had a chum,' Labby stated, 'who obtained a nomination under rather peculiar circumstances. The younger son of a peer, he thought he might as well get a berth in the diplomatic service, understanding that there was little to do and a pretty fair allowance to get. There was the preliminary difficulty of the nomination. Of the questions upon which it was based he knew absolutely nothing. However, there was at least the prospect of a lark, so he went in for the exam. The result exceeded his wildest expectation. As far as he could make out, he did not supply a single correct answer to the long catechism. Not accustomed to be taken aback by an unexpected turn of events, he, to his breathless surprise, found he had not only passed but was placed at the head of the list. Meeting one of the examiners at dinner a few days later, he ventured to ask how the thing came about. "We at once saw you knew nothing," said the examiner, "but your manner was so free from constraint under what to most people would have been peculiarly embarrassing circumstances that we agreed you were the very man to make a diplomatist. So we gave you a start on your career." '

Labby soon learnt that to be a successful diplomat

one had to attach enormous importance to trifles. During the discussions in some Virginian hotel on the Reciprocity Treaty between Canada and the United States, the American Secretary of State, Mr. Marcy, usually a most genial man, was very bad-tempered and would agree to nothing that the English minister proposed.

'What on earth is the matter with your chief?' Labby asked Mr. Marcy's secretary.

'He does not have his rubber of whist,' said the secretary.

Thereafter the English minister and Labby played whist every night with the American minister and his secretary, and every night the Englishmen lost. The stakes were trifling, but Mr. Marcy got so much pleasure out of 'beating the Britishers at their own game' that his good humour returned; with the result that every morning when the details of the Treaty were being discussed, the Englishmen had their revenge and 'scored a few points for Canada'.

Whenever the British Government wished to interfere in Central American politics, it was necessary to fix up some sort of commercial treaty in the State concerned. For this purpose the English minister would call in a seedy-looking wastrel, who spent his time loafing about the pothouses and who was known at the legation as the King of Mosquito. For a new coat or a bottle of brandy His Majesty would sign any treaty that was placed before him, and with the flourishing of this document in the faces of the United States authorities England's right of intervention in Central American affairs was secured. It was a valuable lesson for Labby, who was often in the years ahead to profit from a well-played game of bluff. Another experience taught him the futility of red-tape, on which he was to pour ridicule for the rest of his life. An Englishman without friends or relations died in the State of New York and it became a question whether the legation at Washington or the consulate at New York ought to bury him; so the body was placed in a wooden box and spent a considerable period in journeying between the two cities. 'I myself,' said Labby, 'directed it at least a dozen times to the consulate "This side up – with care". Whether this uneasy corpse has found a grave or whether it is still lurking in the luggage vans of an American railroad company, I do not know.'

The English minister of that time, Mr. Crampton, became very unpopular with his American associates, and brought about a diplomatic crisis between the two countries by attempting to raise a foreign corps for service in the Crimea. When his action was made public he was removed from Washington, 'though what became of the troops,' Labby confessed, 'was a mystery I was never able to fathom.' Crampton's frank cynicism appealed to Labby and they remained on friendly terms in spite of the latter's occasional liberties. One morning Labby arrived at headquarters and found a letter from Crampton addressed to him. As he had arranged to leave Washington that day for a holiday, which would have to be postponed if the letter contained instructions, he put it in his coat-tail pocket and did not open it until he was enjoying himself many miles away. Then, finding that his apprehensions were verified, he wrote an apology to Crampton commencing with the perfectly truthful statement, 'Your letter has followed me here.'

On another occasion he was sent on a mission to Boston, gambled away all his money on the night of his arrival, dispatched an urgent appeal to Washington for more, spent two nights on a bench on the common, and would have eaten nothing during his stay in the city but for the fact that he was mistaken for a well-known Irish patriot by the manager of a restaurant, who, for the sake of Ireland and Freedom, would not charge him for a dinner that he had eaten and for which (though the manager was unaware of this) he could not pay. 'From a man like you, who has suffered in the good cause, I can take no money,' said the manager; 'allow a brother-patriot to shake you by the hand.' Labby allowed not only the manager but all the waiters to shake him by the hand, and then left the restaurant for his bench on the common with the stern and dismal air he had seen assumed by exiled patriots.

A further episode that would have annoyed a more strait-laced official than Mr. Crampton occurred during that minister's temporary absence. An American citizen, swelling with matters of secrecy and importance, called at the legation and demanded an interview with His Excellency.

'Say, I want to see the boss,' was his way of putting it.

'You can't,' replied Labby; 'he's not here; you'd better see me instead.'

But the American knew all about diplomats and was not going to be put off by idle subterfuge.

'Not here, ain't he? Then I'll wait for him.'

'Very well,' said the courteous Labby; 'pray take a seat.'

The American sat down grimly and Labby went on with his writing. An hour passed by.

'Say, d'you expect the boss back?' suddenly barked the American.

'Oh, certainly!' Labby answered politely.

There was another long silence, broken only by the scratch of the attaché's pen. At last the American's patience gave way.

'Say, stranger, I've been fooling around here for two hours. Has the boss come in yet?'

'No.'

'When shall I know he's back?'

'You'll see him drive up to the front door.'

'How long d'you reckon he'll be?'

'About six weeks, I should fancy. He left for England yesterday.'

A man after Labby's own heart was sometimes to be seen at social gatherings in Washington and they became great friends. This was James McNeill Whistler, who was struggling with poverty but trying to look respectable, a feat which he accomplished by pinning back the skirts of his frock-coat to make it pass for a dress-coat at evening parties. Labby was always more interested in personalities than in policies, and though he heard one of Daniel Webster's greatest speeches he was more impressed by the number of drinks that kept the orator going than by the fervour and eloquence of the oratory.

Having failed to keep his resolution not to gamble, he made up for it by constant adherence to another resolution made in the inn at Quotla di Amalpas, and engaged in as many love-affairs as he could manage with comfort.

'I have a great weakness for the American girl,' he confessed; 'she always puts her heart in what she is about. When she flirts she does it conscientiously – besides, as a rule, she is pretty, a gift of nature which I am very far from undervaluing.'

He never troubled to cast a halo of romance over his amorous adventures, and his description of them would have seemed tame to Romeo:

In America young ladies are accustomed to sit all day in darkened rooms in order to bleach themselves, and this habit accounts for the paleness of Americans. Years ago I passed a winter at Washington. The prettiest girl was a Miss Becky. One day I called upon her and was shown into a room which seemed to me to be quite dark. "Sit down," said a voice which I recognised as that of Becky, and I sat down upon an arm-chair against which I had stumbled. I felt myself propelled in the air, and a second voice cried out, "Take care what you are doing." "Why, you've sat down on pa. You get out, pa!" observed Becky, and this was followed by a scuttling which was produced by pa leaving the room. This was the only occasion I ever had of making the acquaintance of Becky's parent, although for many months I nursed a despairing affection for her. . . . From Becky I transferred my blighted affections to Maria. We used to ride together *more Americano*. One day I came to the conclusion that I would propose to her. Having meditated over the speech in which I would offer her my hand and heart, I blushingly commenced "Maria," when my horse kicked. Again I commenced "Maria," when the steed reared. I felt that these movements of the quadruped were a warning, like that which Balaam received from his ass – and held my peace.'[1]

[1] *Truth*, March 8, 1877.

# CHAPTER III

'I SHOULD be curious to know how many years it would take to reduce the intelligence of an ordinary banker's clerk to the level of a Foreign Office bureaucrat,' Labby once wrote. His official correspondence at the various legations to which he was attached convinced him that bureaucracy was a euphemism for imbecility.

In December, 1855, he left Washington and joined the legation at Munich. Old King Ludwig of Bavaria was still alive, though his affair with Lola Montes had caused his subjects to depose him, and he used frequently to stop Labby in the streets to inquire after the health of Queen Victoria. At length Labby felt impelled to tell him that Queen Victoria did not make it a rule to send daily bulletins of her health to all the attachés in her service. Throughout his diplomatic career Labby went on the principle that he had joined the service to see the world, and whenever he could absent himself from duty he allowed Fate to dump him where it willed. Once he visited Cairo, and having heard from Shepheard, the founder of the famous hotel, that he intended to ride to Suez, spending one night in the open on the way, decided to accompany him. Another time he rode with Lady Ellenborough and her Bedouin husband from Damascus to Palmyra. On a third occasion he was lounging about a hotel at Venice when he saw an old gentleman with long white hair tipping the porters before leaving the place.

'Where are you going?' asked Labby on the spur of the moment.

'To the Holy Land.'

'Wait five minutes and I'll come with you.'

He rushed upstairs, pitched his clothes into a portmanteau, and joined the picturesque old gentleman. On their way to Jerusalem his companion gave him a manuscript sermon to read every night, from which he inferred that the old gentleman was a clergyman. At one place they found themselves by several small streams.

'This,' said Labby, pointing to one of them, 'is the Jordan.'

'You are mistaken,' returned the old gentleman, pointing to another, 'that is the Jordan.'

'No one can doubt that this is the Jordan,' affirmed Labby.

'No one but an idiot can deny that that is the Jordan,' declared the other.

'It is really impossible to travel with a man whose ideas are so foolish,' said Labby.

'I really must decline to continue any longer with a person so bereft of sense as not to know a river when it is before his eyes,' said the old gentleman.

Whereupon each of them had his tent pitched by the side of his own particular Jordan, dined apart, and after dinner sat gazing with rapture at his chosen river and scowling defiance at the other. No sermon was pressed into Labby's hand that night, a fact which he lamented, for it gave the necessary elevation to his pillow. He awoke the following morning to find his companion by his side, pointing to a third stream.

'I begin to think that the Jordan is there,' he said.

'Obviously,' agreed Labby.

They mounted and finished the journey to Jerusalem the best of friends.

At Jerusalem the clergyman said that his name was

Bellew and that he was going to preach in the English Church in the presence of the Bishop. Labby felt it his duty to stand by his travelling-companion in such an emergency and, to impress the Bishop, he bribed a number of Arabs to attend divine service, their presence implying that the fame of Bellew had spread abroad in the land. The Bishop was duly impressed, but unfavourably.

There must have been something fishy about the condition of Labby's portmanteau when he returned to Germany after this trip, because the Custom House officer turned it inside out and began to inspect every item it contained with the closest care. This annoyed Labby, who calmly took a telegraph form from his pocket, wrote on it and handed it to an official who was superintending the inspection. The telegram was addressed to Prince Bismarck, Berlin, and ran:

'CANNOT DINE WITH YOU TO-NIGHT. MISSED TRAIN THROUGH A DAMNED ASS OF A CUSTOM HOUSE OFFICER. WILL LET YOU HAVE HIS NAME. LABOUCHERE. COLOGNE.'

No sooner had the official run his eye over this than the portmanteau was rapidly repacked and its owner was asked whether he would care for a special train. He had never, of course, seen Bismarck in his life.

In 1857 he was transferred to Stockholm, where he achieved considerable popularity with his superiors because he challenged an Austrian *chargé d'affaires* to a duel. Needless to say, the honour was thrust upon him; indeed it came as a result of his contempt for duels. The Austrian had spoken with derision of an Englishman who had refused to fight a duel with a Swede, and Labby had replied that the English were not such fools as to fight duels. The Austrian took this as an insult to his nation and, such was the code of the day, Labby was forced to issue a challenge, which he did in the devout hope that the Austrian would apologise. But a few hours later his seconds, a Prussian and a Frenchman, appeared and informed him cheerfully that the duel was arranged for the following morning with pistols. Looking a little dejected, they returned at seven o'clock the next morning.

'I have lost the mould for the bullets of my duelling-pistols,' said the Prussian dolefully, 'and we have had to borrow a pair of pistols. I cannot vouch for the accuracy of their aim.'

Labby's heart danced within him, but he had to pretend that he shared their regret. They sat down to breakfast.

'You are young, I am old,' said the Frenchman; 'would that I could take your place.'

Labby wished it far more ardently than the Frenchman, but with a grin and a shrug he managed to imply that nothing could now cheat him of his prey.

His opponent had not appeared when they reached the park, but the presence of a surgeon did not help to put him at his ease.

'An accident may happen,' remarked the Prussian in a sympathetic tone; 'do you wish to confide to me any dispositions that you may desire to be carried out in the event of – ?' The pause was eloquent.

'No,' replied Labby, thinking what an ass he was to fight a duel in order to establish an Englishman's right not to fight duels. To be killed was bad enough, he reflected, but to be killed paradoxically was still worse.

The arrival of the Austrian and his seconds was greeted by him with an inward groan and he noticed that the surgeon was already eyeing him as 'a subject'. The opponents stood apart while the seconds consulted. Then the Frenchman stepped out twelve paces. His legs, Labby thought, were remarkably short. While the pistols were being loaded it occurred to him that the seconds might leave out the bullets, but the comfort derived from this reflection was only momentary: the bullets were rammed down with gusto. The pistols were handed to the combatants, who faced each other across what seemed to one of them the twelve paces of a midget.

'I am to give the signal,' said the Prussian; 'I shall count one, two, three, and then at the word "fire", you will both fire. Gentlemen, are you ready?'

They both nodded.

'One, two, three – fire!'

The shots rang out, but the duellists remained unharmed. Labby could hardly suppress his joy and was breathing freely for the first time since the challenge was issued when the Frenchman approached him and said, to his horror:

'I think that I ought to demand a second shot for you; but mind, if nothing occurs again, I shall not allow a third shot.'

Labby made a croaking sound in his throat which was meant to convey strong approval of the first statement and disappointment with the second; another shot was fired; and again no harm was done. Knowing that the word of his French second was to be relied upon, Labby felt that he could now display his valour without danger to himself and demanded a third shot. There was an awkward moment while the seconds consulted, and he wished fervently that he had not taken the risk, but to his inexpressible relief they decided that honour had been satisfied with the discharge of two shots. He found it was much easier to look aggrieved after this decision than it had been to look pleased before it.

Much of his time at Stockholm was spent in ciphering and deciphering telegrams, which contained nothing of the least importance to anybody, and in receiving and sending absurd letters by Foreign Office messengers. A typical example of how his time was wasted in the service of the country may be given. The Duchess of Ostrogotha, afterwards Queen of Sweden, was delivered of a baby and a wire arrived from the Foreign Office conveying Queen Victoria's congratulations and expressing the wish that Her Majesty should be informed of the health of the mother and child. In the absence of the minister Labby called at the Palace to make the necessary inquiries, and was informed by a solemn-looking person that 'Her Royal Highness is as well as can be expected, but His Royal Highness is suffering a little internally, and it is thought that this is due to the milk of the wet nurse having been slightly sour yesterday evening.' Returning to the legation Labby carefully codified this important bulletin for the edification of Queen Victoria.

From Stockholm he went to Madrid, where, tired perhaps of being popular as a duellist, he decided to become unpopular by arranging duels of another kind. Finding that it was his job as junior attaché to pair off the guests at the big dinners, and that in Spain everybody was most punctilious about precedence, he sent down all the wrong people with all the wrong people. The dinner was a frightful fiasco; there was an unholy row; and Labby soon found himself at Frankfort. Here he passed the happiest months of his diplomatic career. The proximity of Homburg, with its roulette and its rouge-et-noir, gave a zest to life, and early every evening he galloped there, and early every morning he galloped back, with relays of horses both ways. There were private as well as public gaming-houses and he was soon a well-known figure at all of them. A smile of welcome went round the room as the chubby young man, with little slant eyes and an air of mock-modesty, appeared fresh and flushed from his ride; and a smile of satisfaction went round the room when, many hours later, a paler but still pleasant young man rose from the table with empty pockets and bade everyone a polite 'good morning'. When not on duty he passed all his time in the society of whores and croupiers and was considered far too disreputable for admission into Frankfort society. Occasionally he went out of his way to be charming to some highly respectable lady in the social world, who thought him so attractive that she did her best to reform him, but such lapses were only for his momentary amusement and he quickly slipped back into the freer atmosphere of brothels and casinos.

Of course he had to attend some of the Court functions, at which he became remarkably popular among his fellow-guests for a rather curious reason. On his first appearance he found himself sitting next to a grandee covered with stars and ribbons. The servant offered him champagne, which he disliked and so refused. The grandee nudged him and whispered, 'Let him pour it out,' explaining later that the guests were never given more than one glass, 'so you see if I drink yours I shall have two.' After that there was a tremendous struggle to sit near Labby at Court suppers.

His passion for gambling was intense and lasted many years. 'I have never more thoroughly enjoyed myself than when I have spent an entire night at this agreeable pastime,' he declared. Though he would carefully explain to all his friends that they were bound to lose in the long run, he could not resist the temptation himself, thus illustrating the difference between the principles of a philosopher and the practice of a human being. When at last he did give it up, he advanced the reason that he always won if playing for low stakes and always lost if playing for high stakes, which was contrary to sound economic principles; but he came nearer the truth in a later confession: 'When I was a young man, no sooner did I get any money than I played on until it was lost, and lost it always was, because a person who plays for the love of gambling must always lose against those who play for the love of money.' All the same he was luckier than most people, because he often paid the expenses of his holidays out of winnings at the tables, and he elaborated a method of playing at Monte Carlo which became famous as 'Labby's System'.

Bismarck was at Frankfort in the later 'fifties and spent his nights drinking beer in a garden overlooking the Main. Labby got to know him well and thought him the only agreeable Prussian he had ever met.

'All others with whom I have been thrown ... were proud as Scotchmen, cold as New Englanders, and touchy as only Prussians can be. I once had a friend among them. His name was Buckenbrock. I inadvertently called him Butterbrod. We have never spoken since.'

A few years after his residence at Frankfort Labby happened to be dining at Wiesbaden. A thin emaciated man who was sitting opposite leant forward and said: 'How do you do?' For a moment Labby was nonplussed:

'Then I remembered that he was Bismarck, and my recognition of him was owing to his hands. I never yet saw a man in respectable society with hands habitually so filthy.'

Labby had not been a year at Frankfort before the bureaucrats in London came to the conclusion that both he and the service would benefit by a change, and he received an order to join the Embassy at St. Petersburg. Part of the order he obeyed with alacrity, removing himself and his baggage from the legation at Frankfort. But he had not seen half enough of Homburg; indeed he had only seen it at night-time; and as it was a well-known beauty-resort, he determined to see all the beauties in it. He remained there for some months and would have remained there for many more if the minister at St. Petersburg had not noticed that his staff was under strength and telegraphed for information of the missing attaché. At length the Foreign Office located Labby and sent him a severe letter, to which he replied that as he was too poor to pay the railway-fare, which the Government did not provide, he had been forced to walk. Having got as far as Homburg, his legs had given out; but he was already convalescent and hoped in time to finish the journey on foot. The next letter from the Foreign Office was of so imperative a nature that he cut his losses and caught the next train to the Russian capital.

Having spent most of his time at Homburg in gambling and love-making, he appears to have spent most of his time at St. Petersburg in love-making and gambling. One of the ladies who took his fancy was the wife of a certain court-official. Unfortunately he had a French rival, who was making better progress in the lady's affections than himself. His big chance came in an unexpected manner. In his efforts to gain her attention he upset a cup of black coffee over her yellow satin train. She did not notice the accident, and after a pause, during which he hid the cup and saucer, he made an exclamation of horror and pointed at the stain on her dress. 'Who did it?' she demanded angrily. Labby glanced in the direction of his rival and replied: 'I know, but wild horses could not drag the knowledge from me.' The lady noted where his glance had rested, and Labby tasted the first-fruits of victory.

Another love-affair enabled him to combine business with pleasure. His laundress was very attractive, and he came to know her on what his official biographer describes as 'other than professional grounds'. Learning that her husband was a compositor in the Government printing-office and had access to the manuscript minutes of the Cabinet Council, he persuaded her to bring the sheets to him, backing his endearments with hard cash. The Foreign Secretary, Lord John Russell, was astonished at the accuracy and prevision of the information from Russia, made inquiries, learnt its source, and forbade the continuance

of such a method.  Labby was hurt: 'For what reason,
I wonder, does Russell imagine diplomacy was invented?' he asked.

The pompous airs of the Russian nobility did not
impress him, but he was always most polite and
accommodating.  One day, for instance, a fussy and
self-important aristocrat called at the legation and
asked to see the ambassador at once.

'Pray take a chair,' said Labby; 'he will be here
soon.'

'But, young man, do you know who I am?' and he
recited his distinctions in detail.

'Pray take two chairs,' came the quiet response.

The worst moment in Labby's gambling career
occurred at St. Petersburg.  He was playing a game
of three-handed whist with Khalil Pasha, the Turkish
Ambassador, and a Russian nobleman.  Khalil was
a terrific gambler.  He started life with an income of
£50,000 a year, almost all of which he lost in this way.
He always 'paid up like a gentleman', but his diplomatic career ended abruptly while he was Ambassador
at Paris, from whence he was recalled owing to his
being 'posted' at a club for 40,000 francs, which he
had dropped at écarté and could not pay.  He lost
millions of francs in Russia and he always played for
enormous stakes.  Labby did not quite appreciate
the possibilities of loss and gain when Khalil said to
him, '*Nous jouons avec le zéro?*' because he replied light-
heartedly, '*Comme vous voulez*'.  This meant that a zero
was added to every stake – 10 becoming 100 and so on
– and the consequence was that when Khalil and the
Russian had won their dummies, Labby discovered
to his horror that, allowing for the zero, he had lost
£4,000.  Then came his turn with the dummy.  He
started off well by winning a game; but the next game
was touch-and-go, because he scored six tricks to his
opponents' five, and everything depended on the last
two cards.  If he lost the odd trick he would be

£8,000 out of pocket. Khalil had the lead, and as he held the best trump and a thirteenth card – the only other trump being in dummy – all he had to do was to play his trump and then his thirteenth card in order to win the rubber. His fingers, however, were all thumbs, and in his excitement he let the thirteenth card drop. Before he could retrieve it, Labby pushed dummy's trump on to it and claimed the trick. His opponents howled with rage and accused him of sharp practice. He replied that whist was essentially a game of sharp practice and that his play was supported by the rules. An appeal was made to the onlookers, who had to give their judgment in his favour. But it was a near thing.

He left St. Petersburg at the end of 1860 and went to Dresden, where he made a closer study of German domestic life than he had been able to do at Homburg, and incidentally had his worst experience of red tape. His new chief thought that the ordinary official formalities were quite as important as the Ten Commandments and regarded the least irregularity as a crime of the first magnitude. At that time all the dispatches from the minister to the Foreign Secretary had to finish as follows:

> *I have the honour to be with the highest respect*
> > *My Lord*
> > > *Your Lordship's*
> > > > *Most humble*
> > > > > *Obedient Servant.*

But Labby so far forgot himself as to finish a dispatch with the words *Most humble obedient servant* in one line instead of two. The minister started back with horror at the sight of this appalling impropriety.

'Good heavens!' he cried; 'do you wish to ruin me? Look! *Look! !*' and he pointed at the offending passage.

'What's the matter with that?' asked Labby.

'Do you not know that it ought to be in two lines?' said the minister in a trembling voice.

'Why should it be?'

'There are no doubt good reasons,' the minister answered. 'If you treat with disrespect rules that have been laid down for our guidance, I am afraid you will never advance in your profession.'

Labby decided to profit by this advice. Shortly afterwards the chancery ran out of sealing-wax, and as every dispatch had to be sealed he asked for more.

'What I gave you a little time ago ought not to have been used so carelessly that none remains. I shall not give you any more before a month hence,' said the minister.

As he was in the habit of writing a dispatch on the slightest pretext or none at all, Labby had collected two or three dozen by the end of a month, when he again asked for sealing-wax, taking the opportunity of mentioning that the dispatches were accumulating. Before the minister had recovered from the shock Labby reminded him of their previous conversation concerning sealing-wax and the fact that there was a rule which forbade the sending of dispatches except in sealed envelopes.

'I did not feel justified in breaking this rule,' he added, 'after your valuable observations on obedience to orders.'

What really cut the minister to the quick was that no one at the Foreign Office had complained of his silence for a month or had shown any anxiety that it should be broken.

'If he realised that he had in me a model attaché, he did not express this opinion to me aloud,' was Labby's comment when relating the affair.

He was further annoyed during his Dresden days by the Court functions, at which King John of Saxony would progress slowly round the circle of diplomatic notabilities, suddenly fall fast asleep on his legs during the ceremony and keep everybody standing in solemn silence until he woke up and continued the round.

Labby's reputation as a lover must have followed him from St. Petersburg because King John's successor, Albert, chaffed him about it. He had given a *souper dansant* to some Maids of Honour, and a few days later met King Albert, who said in a strong Teutonic accent, '*Et pien, monsieur, qu'est qu'on me tit? Que vous tebauchez les temoiselles t'honneur!*'

While attached to the Dresden legation he went for a holiday to Italy, and owing to a landslide in South American politics he was able to extend this holiday from two to eighteen months. It happened in this manner. When on leave at Florence, he received a letter from the Foreign Office informing him that Her Majesty had graciously consented to his appointment as Secretary of Legation in the Republic of Parana. He had never heard of the Republic of Parana, but being of a curious disposition he inquired as to its whereabouts of every well-informed Italian in the district. No one could enlighten him, so he remained quietly in Italy, regularly drawing his salary, on the presumption that he had been promoted to the rank of a secretary *in partibus infidelium*. About a year later he received a second letter from the Foreign Office asking him why he had not gone to his post. Sensing a slight annoyance beneath the formality of the question, he instituted further inquiries over a larger area and was at length rewarded for his pains. Parana, he learnt from an expert in such matters, had once been a republic on the banks of the River Plate, but some months previously had been improved off the face of South America. He forwarded this information to headquarters, at the same time requesting the favour of any independent testimony as to the existence of the Republic which the Foreign Office might possess. Six months later he heard that the Foreign Office had been unable to trace the Republic.

During his stay in Florence he witnessed a revolution, met Cavour and Victor Emanuel II, and practised the art of flattery, in which he recorded his own proficiency. The Grand Duchess of Tuscany had a rather alarming maid of honour, aged about seventy-five, whose face was a study in artificial colours, who tripped when she moved and simpered when she spoke.

'How old do you think I am?' she once asked Labby in a way that made his blood freeze.

'Twenty,' he risked, after a slight hesitation.

'Flatterer!' she cried, tapping him playfully with her fan, 'I am twenty-five.'

Labby finished his diplomatic career at Constantinople, where he arrived towards the close of 1862. The minister there was Sir Henry Bulwer (Lord Dalling), whose curious habits used to amuse his subordinates. He was always taking medical advice, and as each doctor he consulted prescribed a different pill, he spent a fair portion of every day popping a large variety of pills into his mouth. Some of these could only be obtained from England, and as they were sent for by a Foreign Office messenger Labby calculated that each box cost the country anything from two to three hundred pounds, though he admitted that they were much more useful than most of the stuff sent out by the Foreign Office. Bulwer was invariably hard up, and it often happened that the wine at the official dinners was obtained from the Grecian islands and tasted of tar. This was gravely administered to the guests by a solemn steward with the words 'Château Lafitte, '48' or 'La Rose, '52', or some such vintage. For the sake of the others Bulwer pretended to enjoy it, drinking many glasses and swallowing dozens of pills to neutralise its effect on the system.

Labby, always anxious to make people happy, did strange things in Constantinople. Living in a Moslem world it struck him that there was no earthly or

heavenly reason why Her Majesty's subjects should
not enjoy amenities and distinctions denied them at
home. He therefore distributed certificates of nobility to seekers after titles (if a man really wanted to be
a baron, he argued, why shouldn't he be?) and celebrated marriages of doubtful validity. His philan-
thropic labours embraced the world of medicine and
he spent much time practising homoeopathy on the
poorer inhabitants of the city. While in Germany he
had learnt doctoring in order to learn German and
for the rest of his life he maintained a keen interest
in it, frequently offering to cure people gratis and
always disappointed when they declined his help. At
Constantinople he cured a Jew of the fever with
globules of aconite. His fame spread; he was invited
to try his skill on a woman in a harem; but though
she recovered he never felt quite certain that his
globules of something or other had done the trick.

During Bulwer's tenure of office, the Keeper of the
Archives, a Greek named Alexander Pisani, was made
head of the Chancellerie, to the disgust of the English
secretaries who belonged properly to the diplomatic
service. Pisani had obtained this post by the simple
method of threatening to resign and write his memoirs.
He took advantage of his position, made his authority
felt and aroused the strong resentment of all the
secretaries. Once he reproved Labby for absenting
himself from duty without leave, and received such a
shattering reply that the matter was referred to Bulwer.
Upon which Labby wrote to the Ambassador:

'It seems to me a singular dispensation that places
a Greek nobleman of Venetian extraction, who
profited by the advantages of a Pera education, in
authority over a body of English gentlemen.'

Labby was not a safe man to reprove at any time,
but indeed he was already tired of diplomacy and was
seeking for an opportunity to leave the service. This

was given him in the summer of 1864, while he was enjoying a holiday at Baden-Baden. He received a notice from the Foreign Secretary that he had been promoted second secretary at Buenos Ayres. He replied that if he could fulfil his duties in South America without leaving Baden-Baden he would be pleased to accept the appointment. The Foreign Secretary was not amused and Labby ceased to serve his Queen and country. About six years later he gave his considered opinion of his quondam associates:

'The diplomatists, who have been a little thrown in the background of late by wars and generals, must be delighted to find their old friend, the "Eastern Question" cropping up. The settlement of the Schleswig-Holstein question was a heavy blow to them; but for many a year they will have an opportunity to prose and protocol over Turkey. An Austrian wit – indeed the only wit that Austria ever produced – used to say that Englishmen could only talk about the weather, and that if by some dispensation of Providence there ever should be no such thing as weather, the whole English nation would be dumb. What the weather is to Englishmen, the "Eastern Question" is to diplomatists. For their sakes, let us hope that it never will be satisfactorily settled. Diplomatists, like many other apparently useless beings, must live.'

He did not hope in vain. The 'Eastern Question' is still unsettled.

# CHAPTER IV

### PLATFORM AND STAGE

A SHORT while before leaving the diplomatic service Labby paid a visit to his family. He had not seen them for many years and was naturally anxious to find out whether his father had softened towards him. He paused a little nervously before ringing the bell at No. 16 Portland Place; he entered his father's room with a feeling of awkwardness.

'How d'ye do?' said his father coolly, without rising from his chair, adding, before the prodigal could say how he did, 'How long do you propose to stay in London?'

Labby left the parental presence and spent the remainder of his holiday in the more congenial atmosphere of Evans's.

His father died in 1863 and his mother went to live near Dorking; all his relatives were religiously dull; so, on his return from Constantinople, he settled down to a comfortable bachelor's existence on the money that his father had left him and determined to enjoy London. Gambling still occupied a good deal of his time, but he was gradually toning down; and though he would occasionally spend evenings in disorderly houses and eat in cellars watched by the police and wander about Cremorne Gardens 'till the daylight, in lilac and purple, came out above the tall trees and put out the yellow glare of the gas', yet he was now rather a spectator than a participator of these delights. Already he was considering a political career, his experience of life and his own common sense having made a convinced radical of him. He had absolutely no illusions about his fellow-men and his convictions were the sole result of reason and observation. 'In sending me into the world,' he confessed, 'nature sent a person without prejudice or bias and consequently absolutely impartial. I form my conclusions upon facts and not either upon the dicta of other men or on foregone conclusions.'

As his wander-years were now behind him, we may pause here to fix a mental picture of him in our memories, to the better understanding of his more serious history. Most people act and speak under the stress of so many conflicting desires and hidden motives that their natures appear complex both to themselves and to the outside world. They cannot understand a man who acts and speaks as a result of pure logic and undivided purpose. This accounts for what was generally regarded as the enigma of Labby. He was in reality that very remarkable phenomenon, a perfectly plain and simple man, who spoke exactly what was in his mind, careless of the consequences, and who was completely free from conventional standards of thought, behaviour and speech. In any walk of life such a person was rare enough; in politics he was simply unique, and it was obvious from the start that he had to be treated as a joke, the only alternative being that the business of politics was a joke. People would not, dared not, take him seriously; nor were they able to do so, because their very natures rebelled against the notion that a humorist, a leg-puller, a cynic, a man who believed in expediences not principles, a man who was utterly unsentimental and laughed at mass-emotions, could be a serious, dependable and honest human being. Such a notion impeached themselves and the social world in which they lived. If he was right, then everyone and everything else was wrong.

Labby did not help the world to believe in him. He was too much amused by the spectacle of life to pass for a sympathetic critic. He had no reverence for anything and he could not be shocked. The weaknesses of human nature entertained him; and though, deep down, he chafed under the mystery of the world's misery, loathed injustice and pitied the wretched and oppressed, he was incapable of parading his feelings in a manner that could make people think of him as a brother. His physical appearance emphasised his mental singularity. The usual expression on his face was sceptical and sardonic, which made it clear that, while entirely disbelieving every word that was said to him, he realised that the speaker was fool enough to believe it. 'That is precisely what I should have expected you to say, ass that you are!' was the unspoken but obvious comment to be gleaned from his glance.

Any form of enthusiasm aroused his deep suspicion, any display of emotion, any burst of indignation; and he received such manifestations with a grim smile and a queer lift of the corners of his eyes. 'All sensible people smoke,' he once said, 'in order to preserve their equanimity.' And after listening to a passionate declamation by some social reformer he quietly observed: 'How much £ s. d. does he believe in what he says?' His enigmatic features seemed to look an interrogation, and there was an air of mockery about him which prevented people from showing off in his presence. His gentle, drawling, modulated voice, cultivated manner, and the slight suggestion of disdainful tolerance in his facial expression, put his acquaintances on their guard and sometimes had the effect of rousing them to a pitch of frenzy. It added greatly to their sense of injury that he was apparently invulnerable. Nothing could abash him, nothing shame him; he was supremely indifferent to what people thought of him, equally careless of what they might say and fearless of what they might do. For him the world was a joke, in many respects a tragic joke, but still a joke. Up to the point in his life at which we have arrived most people thought him either a knave or a fool, and this caused him considerable amusement; but from now onwards he was fairly generally regarded as a malicious jester, who was utterly unscrupulous in his love of mischief and who seemed to derive pleasure from making other people feel uncomfortable. Since he took as much trouble to be thought a trifler as other men take to be thought sincere, his associates can hardly be blamed for forming an entirely erroneous view of him; but his professed cynicism, his openly expressed belief that everyone's motives (his own included) were sordidly selfish, was the indispensable mask of an honest man in an age of hypocrisy and cant.

There was of course a great deal of the Gaul in his mental make-up, and it is a curious fact that Sydney Smith, the only other outstanding figure in public life whose humorously rational outlook at all resembled his, also had Huguenot blood in his veins. The mixture of Gallic wit and logic with British humour and humanity has certainly produced two of the greatest, most sensible, most amusing, most honest, most eccentric, and, to their contemporaries, most irritating characters in English history. But in several important respects the two men were quite unlike one another, a difference that was heightened by their physical dissimilarity: there was a richness and heartiness about the portly figure and cumbrous movements of the parson, there was a dryness and delicacy about the slight neat frame and quick graceful movements of the politician. Temperamentally they were as far apart as Dr. Johnson and Horace Walpole. Their natures fundamentally at variance: Sydney was ambitious, emotional, complex, an eddy in the stream of life; Labby was unambitious, unemotional, simple, a watcher on the bank; in fact he had little poetry in him and never knew that heart-ache for the unattainable which sometimes comes to men with the sound of church bells on spring mornings. Always misunderstood by the pushing, striving, quick-brained men of his own world, Labby eventually found among the hard-handed cobblers of Northampton a following which instinctively knew his scepticism for sincerity, his indiscretion for simplicity.

Convinced that the House of Commons would benefit considerably from contact with so sound a radical as himself, he became a candidate for New Windsor within a year of leaving the diplomatic service. His uncle, Lord Taunton, though far from sharing his political views, was delighted to hear that he was at last taking life seriously and offered to help him.

'Is there anything I can do?' asked his lordship.

'Really I think not, uncle,' was Labby's rejoinder. 'But I don't know,' he added reflectively, 'If you would put on your peer's robes and coronet and walk arm-in-arm with me down the main street of Windsor, it might help.'

He was elected to parliament in November, 1865, and promptly went about boasting to everyone who would listen that he had won by bribery and corruption. One tory voter, fond of fishing, had been taken out early in a punt and left all day in midstream without the means to get back; another timid tory had been kept at home by the simple expedient of having a hired cab driven furiously on to the pavement outside his house whenever he showed his nose at the door; such tales he related with gusto, and it was not surprising that the tories petitioned to have him and his fellow-member unseated for intimidation, undue influence, bribery and so forth. A committee sat to hear the case and among other things Labby was charged with presenting a silk gown to the wife of one of the electors. He frankly admitted that he had done so.

'The lady in question,' he explained, 'was extremely good-looking, and I have frequently noticed that a present of finery is a simple way to win the female heart. I regret that, in the particular case, I was unsuccessful; but good God! you do not, I hope, insinuate for a moment that I intended her husband to know anything about the affair?'

He was asked by counsel whether he had directly or indirectly paid money for corrupt purposes, and replied 'No.' But at the conclusion of the hearing, while the committee was consulting prior to passing judgment, he remarked to the counsel:

'You should have pushed your query as to expenditure.'

'Why?' asked the counsel.

'You asked if I had paid money for corrupt purposes. Being on my oath I was compelled to say that I had not.'

'Well?'

'I had however given bonds to be sold, but not being legal tender they are not money.'

Labby and his fellow-member were unseated on the ground that they had hired too many committee-rooms. Actually they had not done so, having inherited but not authorised a number from the previous candidate; but the petition of their opponents was granted and Labby, after six months in the House of Commons, went to Nice, where he learnt more about gambling by keeping the bank.

Returning to England he suddenly became extremely active. He took part in by-elections, possibly with the object of brushing up his oratory, and denounced the tories in good set terms. While helping one friend in a small borough he made the interesting discovery that the effect of a speech depends largely upon the amount of light in the room where it is delivered. The tory candidate was, in Labby's words,

'a most worthy and estimable squire, who resided

in the neighbourhood. It was, of course, my business to prove that he was a despicable knave and a drivelling idiot. This I was engaged in doing at a public meeting in the town-hall. The Philippics of Demosthenes were milk and water in comparison with my denunciation; when just at the critical moment, as I was carrying conviction into the breasts of the stolid Britons who were listening to me, the gas flickered and went out. Three candles were brought in. I recommenced my thunder, but it was of no use. The candles utterly destroyed its effect, and two days afterwards the squire became . . . a silent ornament of St. Stephen's.'

He was back in parliament as member for Middlesex in the spring of '67, this time unopposed, but it was not enough to keep him occupied and he looked about for more responsible employment, finding it at length as the proprietor and manager of a theatre. He had a childlike love of theatrical entertainments:

'Over the sufferings of heroines in melodramas I have shed abundant tears. Over the antics of low comedians I have laughed until I have cried. My blood has run cold when listening to the withering denunciations of tragedians, and I have derived much harmless pleasure from witnessing these same denunciations irreverently burlesqued.'

But his devotion to the stage was not his only reason for going into management. He wanted to test his capacity for worry and work:

'I was once crossing the Mont Cenis in the coupé of a diligence. By my side sat a man with a face furrowed with lines of care, and hair white as snow. We soon fell into conversation, and apropos of I forget what, he asked me how old I took him to be. "Sixty," I answered. "I am thirty-six," he replied, "but I have been the manager of a theatre for eight years."'

Yet another reason for his desire to own a theatre and produce plays was that he had fallen in love with an actress. This was Henrietta Hodson, a player of great charm and vivacity, who made a considerable reputation throughout the 'sixties and 'seventies in burlesque, especially in 'boy' parts. Her father was an Irish comedian who kept the Duke's Arms inn at Westminster. She was born in 1841, went on the stage in her 'teens, and while appearing at the Theatre Royal, Bath, met a Bristol solicitor named Pigeon, whom she married in 1863, retiring from the stage. But life as Mrs. Pigeon did not appeal to her. She ran away from her husband and returned to the stage, resuming her maiden name. While acting with the Bancrofts in '66 she got to know Labby, fell in love with him, and soon they were living together. Just before he became a theatrical manager they were on the Continent for a holiday. Arriving at a hotel in some Prussian town they found it full of guests. Labby sent for the landlord and said with an air of command 'I am an elector of Middlesex'. The landlord assumed that he was an Electoral prince and placed the best bedroom at their disposal. Although there was not an ounce of sentiment in Labby and scarcely more than an ounce in Henrietta, they were very fond of one another, understood each other perfectly, and when she was divorced from Mr. Pigeon they married. Meeting a friend not long after the ceremony, Labby asked:

'Do you see any difference in Henrietta?'

'No.'

'Oh, but there is a great difference! I took her to the registry office the other day, paid half a crown and made an honest woman of her.'

In partnership with Alfred Wigan, Labby opened the Queen's Theatre,[1] Long Acre, in 1867, and their

---

[1] Odhams Press now occupies the site of the Queen's Theatre; the front of the building remains much as it was when Labby, Irving and Ellen Terry still had their names to make.

management is notable in stage history for the first appearance together of Henry Irving and Ellen Terry on Boxing Day of that year in Garrick's version of *The Taming of the Shrew*. Other famous actors who appeared in their productions were J. L. Toole, Charles Wyndham, Lionel Brough and Samuel Phelps. It cannot be said that Labby's management was remarkable for the superior quality of its productions. True he dabbled in Shakespeare, but chiefly because it was a good advertisement to get people to vote for their favourite plays. Phelps appeared as Bottom in *A Midsummer Night's Dream*, which was a partial success because of Phelps, but less than five hundred people paid to see Ellen Terry and Henry Irving as Katharine and Petruchio, probably the two worst examples of miscasting in the history of poetic drama. Labby was always on the lookout for new pieces and asked several of his friends to write dramas full of exciting situations. One author, Herman Merivale, brought him a play called *Time and the Hour*.

'It's a splendid title,' said Labby.

'Delighted that you say so,' murmured the flattered author.

'It really is, you know,' continued Labby. More murmurs of gratification from the author. 'It would do for any play whatever that ever was written,' concluded Labby. The murmurs ceased.

A spectacular production of *The Last Days of Pompeii* was so full of unrehearsed effects that it was laughed and hissed off the stage, but it inspired an unknown playwright to send in a drama which opened with the following words:

'The broad Mississippi is seen rolling its turbid flood towards the ocean, and carrying with it the debris of a village. Steamers come and go on its surface. On a frail raft a man and a woman are crossing the river. Enter the negroes from a plantation monotonously singing.'

In that script Labby read no more, though in justice to the author's memory it should be said that something not unlike his description has been seen in recent years at Drury Lane Theatre.

The management produced a play by Charles Reade, who occupied a box with Labby on the first night.

'They seem to be hissing, Mr. Reade,' said Labby.

'What of that?' replied the furious author; 'if you want to please a public such as this, you should not come to me for a play.'

This gave the manager a distaste for highbrow authors and he fell back on scenic effects and sentiment. *Lancashire Lass* was his most successful production, its chief attraction being a steamboat full of passengers which crossed and recrossed the stage to loud applause; and next to that *Oliver Twist*, with Irving as Sikes, Toole as the Dodger and Henrietta Hodson as Oliver. Many years later, at a big banquet on the stage of the Lyceum Theatre, Irving made a speech recalling his early days, in the course of which he turned towards his old employer with the words:

'And to think, Labby, that I was once receiving five pounds a week from you.'

'Three pounds, Henry, my boy, only three,' interrupted Labby.

Finding it difficult to get authors to write the sort of play he wanted, Labby adapted one of Sardou's pieces, *La Patrie*, and put it on; but its plot was unconventional and it was a dismal failure. After that he lost interest in the drama and often, when wanted by his partner, could not be found, having gone abroad at a moment's notice in the hope of picking up at the tables what he was losing at the theatre. An aspect of theatrical management which thoroughly upset him was the distribution of free seats. When his tailor asked for a free seat he retaliated by asking the tailor for a free suit of clothes; but he could not revenge himself so easily on other applicants. He found that, not only did a large number of people expect to see his productions for nothing, but the actors expected to see the seats filled, whether paid for or not. When he resolutely refused to issue a single free ticket for one particular play, the theatre was practically empty, the actors complained, and for once his equanimity deserted him.

'Why don't you draw?' he said to them. 'Draw, confound it! Why don't you draw?'

He was regularly pestered by the parents of budding Garricks and Siddonses to give their children a chance. One girl was brought to see him by her mother, who suggested that he should engage her daughter to play the part of Lady Macbeth. Labby looked at the girl and said:

'Walk across the room and make me think of your mother.'

'Oh, I cannot! Mamma is older than I am, – and – and –'

'When you can, come again and talk to me about an engagement,' said Labby, civilly bowing them out.

He recommended this test to all mothers with stage-struck daughters, believing that a girl who could not do something to remind spectators of a person entirely unlike herself but with whom she lived on terms of intimacy would never make a good actress.

Tired of authors, would-be authors, actors, would-be actors, bad plays, poor houses, unappreciative audiences, deadheads, critics, and everything else to do with the theatre; tired above all of losing money in the cause of art, Labby at last got rid of his theatre. He was for a while oppressed with a feeling which he could not shake off that he was destined to be crushed by financial disaster and would end his days in a workhouse. The feeling disappeared when the theatre was off his hands. But already his interest in the drama had been diverted by a General Election in 1868. This time he was opposed by a liberal as well as a conservative, and as the liberal was a lord, and he did not like lords, there was considerable acrimony during the election, which resolved itself into a fierce fight between two men of the same party. As so often happens in such cases, the split vote put their political opponent at the head of the poll, and Labby was again without a seat in parliament.

The irregularity of his domestic arrangements had been made a feature of the Middlesex election, and he was frequently assailed with the cry "Ow's 'Enrietta?" In order to put a stop to this he had opened one meeting by walking to the front of the platform and making the following announcement: 'I wish to convey to you all the gratifying intelligence that Henrietta is quite well.'

His social carelessness in this respect was one of the reasons why Queen Victoria disapproved of him and caused something of a scandal in circles where matrimony was regarded as holy. At a dinner-party given by Lady St. Helier the guest of the evening was Lord Halsbury, then Lord Chancellor, who was accompanied by his wife. On the stroke of the dinner-hour, when the company seemed to be complete, the door opened and the butler announced Mr. and Mrs. Labouchere. Although their relationship had for some time past been placed on a respectable basis, this was one of their earliest appearances together in the social world. After a long and painful pause, the Lord Chancellor approached his hostess, whispered a word in her ear, and then, with Lady Halsbury on his arm, left the house dinnerless.

Except for an unsuccessful attempt at Nottingham in 1874, Labby did not try to re-enter parliament until 1880, when he became member for Northampton and represented that borough for the rest of his political career. He did, however, speak for the radicals on all sorts of occasions and shocked the rustic population with his views on landlords. After a stirring speech at Ramsey in Huntingdonshire he went with a party of local notabilities to inspect the church. With a sense of awe which gave emotion to his voice, the churchwarden informed them that the late squire could stand on the tower and not behold a yard of land in any direction which did not belong to him. 'Thank God he's under some of it,' said Labby.

His uncle, Lord Taunton, was greatly concerned over his heterodox opinions and made speeches in the House of Lords which reassured the listeners that there was sterling stuff in the family. As it was generally known that Labby would inherit Lord Taunton's fortune, some people mistook the peer for his father.

'I have just heard your father make an admirable speech in the House of Lords,' said one of them.

'The House of Lords?' queried Labby. 'Well, well, that is very satisfactory. Since his death the family have always been a little uneasy as to his whereabouts.'

The thought that his disreputable nephew would gamble away his money after his death disturbed Lord Taunton's later years. His father, Pierre-César, had made a will leaving his vast fortune to the oldest surviving male of the family, and though Lord Taunton had married twice and had produced two considerable families, there was not a male amongst them. It did not help matters when his nephew called to congratulate him on the appearance of each daughter of his second marriage: there was an unmistakable note of triumph in the fellow's: 'My dear uncle, this is *most* gratifying.' Taunton was furious, but forced himself to reply in a complacent manner, maintaining an air of mellow dignity in the presence of his callous heir.

The worthy nobleman died, probably from apoplexy, in 1869, and Labby inherited about a quarter of a million pounds, at the same time declining the succession to his uncle's peerage. The money was especially useful to him just then, for not only was he losing heavily at the Queen's Theatre but he had recently purchased a quarter-share in the *Daily News* for £14,000 and the paper was not doing well. Indeed, in its early career as a penny newspaper things were looking so black that its manager, John Robinson, wondered where the money was coming from to pay the costs of production in addition to his own salary. Labby advised him not to worry about trifles of that kind but to accept shares instead of ready-money. Robinson did so and in time the investment proved highly lucrative. Many years later he thanked Labby for having given him such excellent advice. 'My dear fellow, you are quite mistaken,' returned Labby, 'I never did anything of the kind.'

But neither of them could have guessed in 1869 that a year later the daily sales of the paper would suddenly jump from fifty thousand to three times that number, and that this would be largely due to certain literary contributions by Labby himself.

# CHAPTER V

*'Rouen, draw thy sword! Lille, take up thy musket! Bordeaux, take up thy gun! Marseilles, sing thy song and be terrible!'* (From Victor Hugo's Address to the French Nation in 1870.)

WHEN the Franco-Prussian war broke out Labby was staying in Paris. He left it for a while during the early stages of the campaign in order to show a party of American ladies the sights of Rouen, but returned just before the surrender of Sedan with the intention of spending a night there. His interest in the political situation being aroused, he prolonged the visit; and on the morning of September 4, 1870, a cloudless day of bright sunshine, he helped to found the French Republic in a manner that terrified his companion, Sir Charles Dilke.

The news of Sedan had convinced the populace that Napoleon III was an upstart, unworthy to rule a great nation, and the boulevards were crowded with people in a revolutionary frame of mind. At first the attitude of the mounted guards was a little uncertain and the people abstained from precipitate action while there was any danger of being sabred or shot down. During this trying period of inaction they received the sympathetic encouragement of Labby, who went from place to place delivering speeches. But what caused Dilke to perspire with fear was the fact that every time Labby made a speech he changed his character: sometimes he addressed the crowd as a Marseillais, sometimes as an Alsatian, sometimes as a fellow-republican from America, sometimes as an English sympathiser. It did not appear to strike him that, if anyone in the crowd had caught him playing two different parts, he would probably have been lynched as a Prussian spy. Dilke was greatly relieved when the mounted troops began to shout *Vive la Republique!* and the crowd marched on the Tuileries, because he felt sure that there would be no further opportunity for Labby to exercise his oratory. But when the crowd stopped at the Statue of Strasbourg, which was decorated with flowers and worshipped on account of the gallant defence of that city, Labby seized his last chance of celebrating the triumph of Liberty and harangued the multitude; which alarmed Dilke so much that he failed to notice whether the speaker's final appearance was in the character of a Polish patriot or a Swiss waiter.

The German armies drew nearer and nearer, but Labby could not tear himself away, and at last, anxious to be shut up in a place where no letters could reach him, he decided to see the siege out, in the belief that it would be over in a month. Had he thought for an instant that he was going to be locked in the city for five months, his love of personal freedom would have neutralised his interest in the proceedings; though it is certain that he would have acted in the same manner because Crawford, the Paris correspondent of the *Daily News*, was a poor man and had a wife and children dependent upon him. 'It would be an excellent thing for my heirs were I to stop a bullet or die of starvation,' he told Crawford, 'but were anything of the sort to befall you, it would be calamitous for your family.' He therefore appointed himself official Paris correspondent of the *Daily News*[1] and sent Crawford to Tours.

[1] Most of the quotations in this chapter are taken from the *Daily News*, Sept. 1870–Jan. 1871.

Making himself comfortable at the Grand Hotel, he inquired at the post office whether there was any chance of his letters reaching their destination.

'Put your letter in that box,' said an ancient clerk on a high stool.

'Will it ever be taken out?' asked Labby.

'Qui sait?' replied the clerk.

'Shall you send off a train to-morrow morning?'

'Qui sait?' from a chorus of clerks.

'What do you think of a man on horseback?' suggested Labby.

'Impossible!' was the unanimous answer.

'Why not?'

His query was received with a look of contempt which seemed to imply: 'Do you really imagine that a functionary – a postman – is going to forward your letters in an irregular manner?'

Having delivered his letter to an enterprising citizen of the new republic, who promised that it should be dispatched if possible, Labby left the post office, noticing as he passed through the courtyard that the postmen were seated on the boxes of their carts with no horses before them. It was their hour to transport the letters and they fulfilled their duty mechanically; and it occurred to him that though English government officials had been jeered at as men of routine, the most ancient clerk in Somerset House was a man of wild impulse and boundless expedient in comparison with the average Parisian functionary, great or small.

When Paris was completely cut off from the outside world letters were sent by pigeons or balloons. All Labby's correspondence was addressed to Henrietta Hodson and forwarded by her to the *Daily News*, for he was well aware that his comments would be heavily censored if sent to the newspaper direct. Sometimes the postal balloon was shot down by the Prussians, sometimes it collapsed without the aid of bullets. One evening he was busy finishing his account of the day's

events when a gentleman rushed into his bedroom
and exclaimed:

'Celestine has burst!'

Further inquiries elicited the fact that Celestine was
the private balloon to which Labby was about to
entrust his record.

'Ernestine remains to us,' added the gentleman on
perceiving the other's despair.

Much relieved, Labby confided his letter to Ernestine.

Napoleon III was of course the villain of the moment and the Parisian papers were constantly exposing
the unsavoury deeds of *ce coquin sinistre*, dealing with
their opponent King William of Prussia in lighter
vein; for when the latter, 'to recompense his soldiers
and reward their valour,' made his son and his nephew
Field Marshals, the Paris editors wanted to know
whether the valour of the Bavarians would be recognised by the permission granted to their King to
inflict the operas of his friend Wagner on the French
people. All the same King William was not popular
with the Parisians, who called him 'the mystic drunk-
ard', and they subscribed in thousands for a musket
of honour to be given to the man who shot him.
On the musket was to be engraved the word 'Peace-
maker'.

Labby had a poor opinion of the Parisian journalists,
whose articles of faith he summarised:

'France is the world, Paris is France. The boulevards, the theatres, some fifty writers on the Press,
and the *bourgeoisie* of the fashionable quarters of
the city, are Paris.'

Their ignorance of everything outside their restricted
circle was abysmal and he gave a sample:

'I read a very clever article this morning, pointing
out that, if we are not on our guard, our empire

in India will come to an-end by a Russian fleet attacking it from the Caspian Sea; and when one thinks how very easy it would have been for the author not to write about the Caspian Sea, one is at once surprised and grateful to him for having called our attention to the danger which menaces us in that quarter of the globe.'

Without exception the newspapers echoed the passions of the mob:

'Editors and writers whose dream it was a few months ago to obtain an invitation at the Tuileries or to the Palais Royal, or to merit by the basest of flatteries the Legion of Honour, now have become perfect Catos, and denounce courts and courtiers, Bonapartists and Orleanists. War they regard as the most wicked of crimes, and they appear entirely to have forgotten that they welcomed with shouts of ecstasy in July last the commencement of the triumphal march to Berlin.'

Their advice on military matters was not always based on reason, for one of them asserted that a sortie of troops from Paris would have been far more successful if it had taken place on the anniversary of the promulgation of the Immaculate Conception. As the siege continued their patriotic gestures became more and more absurd. Of the editor of the *Liberté* Labby asked:

'Why is this gentleman still alive? For the last three months he has been making pacts with death.'

The Military Governor of Paris, General Trochu, was quite incompetent. In the early days of the siege he announced that he had 'a plan', the success of which he guaranteed. Though refusing to disclose its details to anyone, he deposited it with his notary, so that it should not be lost to the world in the event of his death. Slow to form his plan, he was obstinate in his adherence to it. Unwilling to move until all its details were perfected, he was, in Labby's view,

> 'better fitted to defend Troy for ten years than Paris for a few months. . . . I was looking at him the other day, and I never saw calm, serene, self-complacency more clearly depicted upon the human countenance.'

His admirers defended his public character by saying that he had adopted his brother's children. But Labby felt that

> 'in the desperate strait to which Paris is reduced, something more than a man estimable for his private virtues and his literary attainments is required. Trochu, we are frequently told, gave up his brougham in order to adopt his nephews. Richard III killed his; but these are domestic questions, only interesting to nephews, and it by no means follows that Richard III would not have been a better defender of Paris than Trochu has proved himself to be.'

Towards the end of the siege he used frequently to address the soldiers: 'Courage, my children, the moment is coming.' This was pleasant, 'but to what moment he alludes no one is aware', remarked Labby. The elaborate instructions issued to divisional commanders when sorties took place displayed a great talent for detail, but as the Prussian General Moltke usually interfered with the prearranged sequence of events, and as Trochu would never alter his plans to suit a change of circumstances, the instructions were only valuable in a literary sense.

> 'That batteries should be opened upon his troops, and that reinforcements should be brought up against them, were trifles – probable as they might seem to most persons – which filled him with an indignant astonishment.'

By the close of the siege he had lost the confidence of his fellow-citizens:

> 'His enemies call him a traitor; his friends defend him from the charge by saying that he is only a vain fool.'

The politicians were worse than the warriors. They never stopped talking and they never stopped lying;

> 'A day never passes without one or more of our rulers putting his head out of some window or other, and what is called "delivering himself up to a fervid improvisation". . . .I will say for the Government of the day that in any attempt to beat its predecessor in mendacity it had a hard task, but it has worked with a will and completely succeeded.'

The people of Paris, especially the *bourgeois* class, were as ridiculous as their papers and politicians. Labby described them comprehensively as 'two million amiable, ignorant, bragging humbugs'. Like most people they believed only what they wished to believe. Their credulity amounted to a disease. In common with a neighbouring nation forty-four years later, they eagerly swallowed anything and everything that was told them against the Germans; for example, that the invaders were starving, ragged and demoralised, that their communications with Germany were cut off, that their leaders were at loggerheads, that a French army from the Loire would shortly demolish them, that the Germans had already ravished thousands of French maidens, that Moltke had been shot, that Bismarck wished to negotiate, that many of the enemy's regiments had deserted, that wounded Bavarians and Saxons were perpetually crying *Vive la France!*, that the Crown Prince was either killed, wounded or taken prisoner every morning, and that the French army had, in the words of our chronicler, 'already slain and taken prisoner a far greater number of Prussians than, on any fair calculation, there could have been in the besieging army at the commencement of the siege'.

The Parisians entertained an exalted opinion of themselves and their capital.

'All are comparatively happy in the thought that the eyes of Europe are on them, and that they have already thrown Leonidas and his Spartans into the shade. . . .The Parisian is under the impression that his city is a species of sacred Ark, which it is sacrilege to touch. To bombard London or Berlin would be an unfortunate necessity of war, but to fire a shot into Paris is desecration. For a French army to live at the expense of Germany is in the nature of things; for a German army to live at the expense of Frenchmen is a barbarity which the civilised world ought to resent.'

After a few weeks' isolation and long before a shortage of rations, the average Parisian thought it impossible that the heroism of the population had not aroused the admiration of the world.

'They hope against hope that what they call their "sublime attitude" will prevent the Prussians from attacking them, and that they may pass to history as heroes, without having done anything heroic.'

It was their considered opinion that Paris was 'the principal jewel of Europe and the eternal ornament of civilisation'. An article in *Figaro* reflected the popular sentiment:

'In order that Paris, in which there is a genius which has given her the empire of the world, should fall into the hands of the barbarians, there must cease to be a God in heaven. As God she exists, and as God she is immortal. Paris will never surrender.'

'I should like to read your English newspapers now,'
said a patriotic Frenchman; 'your *Tims* told us we
ought to cede Alsace and Lorraine, but its editor
must now acknowledge that Paris is invincible.'

Labby replied that he was convinced the editor did
so regularly every morning.

'No peace,' shouted a little tailor, who had been
prancing about on an imaginary steed, killing imaginary Prussians: 'we have made a pact with death; the
world knows now what are the consequences of attacking us.'

'I who speak to you, I owe myself to my country.
There is no sacrifice I would not make rather than
capitulate to those Huns,' declared a grocer, while
pocketing about ten times the value of some candles
he had just sold and scowling into futurity with stern
but vacuous resolution.

Labby was not impressed by these patriots, whose
axiom was 'bad news, false news', and he confessed:
'In a question of military strategy between the grocers
of Paris and the Prussian generals I should have
thought that the odds were considerably in favour of
the latter, but I am told that this is not so, and that
in laying siege to Paris they are committing a mistake
for which a schoolboy would be deservedly whipped.'
Though it took 'about three days for any information
which is not in accordance with the wishes of this
extraordinary population to obtain credit', the most
absurd statements which seemed in any way favourable to themselves were accepted without demur.
One day a troop of fifteen hundred oxen marched into
Paris, and as they were French oxen everyone believed
that their behaviour had been dictated by patriotic
motives. It was also observed that no fires had
broken out since the siege began, a fact which was
probably due to the failure of the gas supply (owing to
coal-shortage) and the substitution of petroleum
lamps, but which was ascribed by the papers to the

existence of a republican form of government. 'I recommend this curious phenomenon to insurance companies,' remarked Labby. Needless to say, the least successful sorties from the capital were hailed in the press as victories, and when the Prussians claimed that the French had been beaten the Paris press was furious: 'How singular is this rage, this necessity for lying!' screamed the *Figaro*, on which Labby commented: 'It is notorious that, having gained two glorious victories, we returned into Paris to repose on our laurels, and I must beg the Prussians not to be so mean as to contest the fact:'

The Parisians loved the pomp of war but had no relish for its dangers and discomforts. Although, as Labby said, times had altered since Jericho, there was a great deal of drum-beating and trumpet-blowing. The Frenchman loved to don a uniform, to strut about with a martial swagger and to listen to a distant cannonade. 'We are still engaged in our old occupation,' wrote Labby, 'willing to die for our country.' Poetry was recited in the theatres to prove that the Prussians must eventually be defeated. Everybody in the street addressed everybody else. Troops of soldiers daily crowned the statues of popular heroes with laurels and signed round-robins to die for their country; and so clamorously in favour of sorties was that section of the community which could not possibly take part in them, that the *Figaro* had to check their exuberance with: 'Remember that you have wives and children; do not be too venturesome.' Labby did not think the advice was needed. Already he had observed that popular demonstrations did not necessarily represent private feelings. Paying a number of calls one afternoon he 'found everyone engaged in measuring the distance from the Prussian batteries to his particular house. One friend I found seated in a cellar with a quantity of mattresses over it to make it bomb-proof. He emerged from his subterraneous Patmos to talk to me, ordered his servant to pile on a few more mattresses, and then retreated.' Further our correspondent noticed the sobering effect on the population of the sound of cannon at close quarters; he remarked on the fact that 'the only prisoners we see are French soldiers on their way to be shot for cowardice' or the more fortunate ones who had run away when attacked and were 'paraded through the streets with a placard on their breasts, requesting all good citizens to spit upon them'; and he could not help thinking that the sudden desire shown by young Parisians to serve under the Red Cross was not wholly due to an overwhelming passion for anatomical knowledge. 'The flag of the Cross of Geneva waves over several thousand houses,' he noted, 'and such is the desire of brave patriots to become members of an ambulance corps, that the services of neutrals are declined.' After some reflection he came to the conclusion that 'the Parisian is not a coward, but his individuality is so strongly developed that he objects to that individuality being destroyed by some stray shot'.

Immediately the siege began every citizen 'indiscriminately assumed the uniform of the National Guard'. It was a motley force and it kept well out of danger throughout the operations, though it succeeded in making everyone believe that it would rather die than surrender, announcing at regular intervals that it had made 'a pact with death'. Labby, who did not care for smart uniforms or resounding phrases, amused his English readers with several anecdotes of the National Guards:

'On Saturday night ... 300 National Guards were drawn up ... and 25 volunteers were demanded for a service of danger. After some time the 25 stepped forward, but having heard for what they were wanted, 18 declined to go.

'I saw to-day a company of mounted National Guards exercising. Their uniforms were exquisitely clean. . . . Their commander ordered them to charge, when every horse butted against the one next to him. I believe a heavy gale of wind would have disconnected all these warriors from their chargers.

'That General Trochu will be able to beat the Prussians no one supposes; but if he can manage to get even 5,000 of the heroes, who have for the last two months been professing a wish to die for the honour of their country, under fire, he will have accomplished a most difficult feat.

'A battalion of National Guards were drawn up . . . A chance shell took off the legs of one of these heroes, his comrades fled in dismay – they were rallied and brought back with difficulty. A little later they were engaged in cooking their food, when some tin pans fell against each other. Thinking it was a bomb, they again scattered, and the General was obliged to ride along the line shouting "Courage, courage; it is the soup, my children".

'Whilst the battle was going on . . . the marching battalions of the National Guard were drawn up almost out of shot. An order came to form them into line. Their commander, General Clément Thomas, replied that this would be impossible, as they would imagine that they were about to be taken into action.

'Since the siege commenced they have done nothing but swagger about in uniforms, and go in turns on the ramparts. They have learnt to knock a penny off a cork at a distance of ten yards, and they have carried on a very successful campaign against sparrows.

'As yet all they have done has been to make frequent "pacts with death", to perform unauthorised strategical movements to the rear whenever they have been sent to the front, to consume much liquor, to pillage houses, and – to put it poetically – toy with Amaryllis in the trench.

'As for the National Guard, one would suppose that every one of them had been in action, and that they were only prevented from carrying everything before them by the timidity of their generals. The wonderful feats which many of these heroes have told me they performed would lead one to suppose that Napoleon's Old Guard was but a flock of sheep in comparison with them. I cannot help thinking that by a certain indistinctness of recollection they attribute to themselves every exploit, not only that they saw, but that their fertile imaginations have ever dreamt to be possible.'

Nevertheless, since they represented the civilian population they were buttered up by press and politicians all through the siege, and Labby reported that a curious new industry had been started in Paris:

'Letters supposed to be found in the pockets of dead Germans are in great request. There are letters from mothers, from sisters, and from the Gretchens who are, in the popular mind, supposed to adore warriors. Unless every corpse has half a dozen mothers, and was loved when in the flesh by a dozen sweethearts, many of these letters must be fabricated. They vary in their style very little. The German mothers give little domestic details about the life at home, and express the greatest dread lest their sons should fall victims to the valour of the Parisians, which is filling the Fatherland with terror and admiration. The Gretchens are all sentimental; they talk of their inner feelings like the heroines of third-rate novels, send the object of their affections cigars and stockings knitted by their own fair hands, and implore them to be faithful, and not forget, in the toils of some French syren, poor Gretchen. But what is more strange is that in the pocket of each corpse a reply is found which he has forgotten to post. In this reply the warrior tells a fearful tale of his own sufferings, and says that victory is impossible, because the National Guards are such an invincible band.'

By the end of the four and a half months' campaign the National Guard had not lost five hundred men, and at the fall of Paris they decided that instead of dying for their country they would live for her. Naturally most of them had been decorated with the Legion of Honour, of which Labby reported:

'It has been so lavishly distributed that anyone who has not got it is almost obliged to explain why he is without it, in the way a person would excuse himself if he came into a drawing-room without a coat.'

Meanwhile the serious defence of Paris had been maintained by regular soldiers and sailors and by regiments of raw provincial peasants – the Mobiles. Labby formed a high opinion of the sailors and the Mobiles. The former fought so well that he wondered at the ease with which British tars had always beaten them. The Mobiles were brave and did their duty uncomplainingly:

'The families with whom they lodge speak with wonder of their sobriety, their decency, and their simple ways, and in their hearts almost despise them because they do not ravish their daughters or pillage their cellars; and neither swear every half-hour to die for their country, nor yell the "Marseill-aise".'

On one occasion Labby spent an hour or so with the Breton Mobiles:

'While I was talking to these Bretons one of them

blew his nose with his handkerchief. His companions apologised to me for this piece of affectation.
"He is from Finisterre," they said. In Finisterre,
it appears, luxury is enervating the population, and
they blow their noses with handkerchiefs.'

As with the soldiers, so with the civilians: it was the
poorest part of the population which behaved best.
'The individual working man is the only reality in
this population of corrupt and emasculated humbugs;
everyone else is a windbag and a sham,' and after
listening to the bombastic twaddle of the better
educated townsmen, Labby found it refreshing to talk
with the dwellers in slums. To give his readers some
notion of the unreal world in which the wealthier
classes lived, he described a visit to a mansion in the
Faubourg St. Germain:

'In this solemn abode of a fossil aristocracy I have
a relative – a countess. She is, I believe, my cousin
about sixteen times removed, but as she is the only
person of rank with whom my family can claim
the most distant relationship, we stick to the
cousinship and send her every year cheap presents,
which she reciprocates with still more meretricious
*bonbons*.'

Ushered into this lady's drawing-room, Labby found
her taking afternoon tea with two old gentlemen, a
mild young man and a priest. A 'Lady of the
Faubourg' with any pretensions to beauty nearly
always enjoyed the tea-time society of two or three
old gentlemen, a mild young man and a priest.
'Are you come to congratulate us?' asked the
countess as Labby bent over her hand. 'What, have
you not heard of the victory?'
Labby expressed surprise.
'Madame,' said one old gentleman, 'alludes to the
taking of Choisy le Roy.'

Labby had to confess that the news of this world-shaking event had not reached him.

'Surprising!' exclaimed the old gentleman: 'I saw General Vinoy myself yesterday.'

'It does not follow that he has taken Choisy to-day,' Labby objected.

'Monsieur, perhaps, is not aware that 60,000 men have broken through the Prussian lines and have gone to the relief of Bazaine,' said the second old gentleman scornfully.

'I have not the slightest doubt of the fact; it is precisely what I expected would occur,' lied Labby.

'As for the victory,' struck in the mild young man, 'I can vouch for it; I myself have seen the prisoners.'

'Surely,' said the countess, 'you must have heard the cannon. Ah! you English are all the same; you are all Prussians, your Queen, your *Tims*, and all of you.'

Labby took refuge in a cup of tea. One of the old gentlemen went and stood before him. He knew what was coming and braced himself to meet it like a Trojan.

'Well, what does England think of our attitude now?'

Labby was ready for that one:

'Sublime!' he chanted.

'We are sacrificing our lives,' declared the mild young man, adding, after a glance from Labby, 'that is to say, we are prepared to sacrifice them.'

'Monsieur is in the Garde Nationale?' asked Labby.

'Monsieur is the only son of a widow,' hastily interposed the countess.

'But I mean to go to the ramparts for all that,' added the orphan.

'You owe yourself to your mother,' said the priest warningly.

'And to your country,' Labby put in, but he was disregarded.

'It is a grand sight,' observed one of the old gentlemen, as he placed a third lump of sugar in his tea and another into his pocket, 'a glorious spectacle, to see a population that was supposed to be given up to luxury, subsisting cheerfully week after week upon the simplest necessaries of existence.'

'I have not tasted game once this year, and the beef is far from good,' sighed the other old gentleman; 'but we will continue to endure our hardships for months or for years if need be, rather than allow the Prussians to enter Paris.'

Labby reflected that one could manage to support life for a few months on beef, mutton, flour, preserved vegetables, wine, milk, eggs, and every kind of sauce that cook ever contrived; but he kept the reflection to himself.

This, however, was in the early weeks of the siege. Later the food problem became more acute. Meat prices soared and 'to force a butcher to sell you a cutlet at the tariff price, one has to go with a corporal's guard, which cannot always be procured'.

'We must learn to vanquish the prejudices of our stomachs,' said a thriving grocer; 'even those who do not like mutton must make the sacrifice of their taste to their country.'

Labby remembered the advice a few days later when he had to dine on sheep's trotters, pickled cauliflower and peaches. 'My stomach,' he wrote, 'is still engaged in "vanquishing its prejudice" to this repast.'

Beef became dearer every week; it also became more dangerous; for if a man was seen carrying a joint through the streets, he was instantly assailed by patriots who relieved him of it on the ground that anyone who could obtain such a thing for love or money must be an aristocrat. As the days went by the citizens of Paris began to look hungrily at the horses which were still ridden by the more prosperous members of the community, and Labby sorrowfully remarked on the crowded condition of the omnibuses: 'I fear greatly that their horses will be far from tender when we eat them.' Within a month of the investment of the city its inhabitants were doing their best to believe that horseflesh was beef and cat was rabbit. Labby liked both; the horseflesh was a little sweeter than beef but resembled it; the cat was

'something between rabbit and squirrel, with a flavour all its own. It is delicious. I recommend those who have cats with philoprogenitive proclivities, instead of drowning the kittens, to eat them. Either smothered in onions or in a ragout they are excellent. When I return to London I shall frequently treat myself to one of these domestic animals, and even feel grateful to Bismarck for having taught me that cat served up for dinner is the right animal in the right place.'

A fortnight later he was again thanking the enemy:

'I never shall see a donkey without gratefully thinking of a Prussian. If anyone happens to fall out with his jackass, let me recommend him, instead of beating it, to slay and eat it. Donkey is now all the fashion. When one is asked to dinner, as an inducement one is told that there will be donkey. The flesh of this obstinate but weakminded quadruped is delicious – in colour like mutton, firm and savoury. This siege will destroy many illusions, and amongst them the prejudice which has prevented many animals being used as food. I can most solemnly assert that I never wish to taste a better dinner than a joint of a donkey or a ragout of cat – *experto crede*.'

Apparently the Parisians agreed with him because by the middle of November the market-price of cats had gone up, a good fat one costing twenty francs, and it is easy to believe that the surviving members of the tribe were 'exceedingly wild'. His taste was catholic

C*

and with the scarcity of cats he made no complaint of their inevitable successors:

'This morning I had a salmi of rats – it was excellent – something between frog and rabbit. I breakfasted with the correspondents of two of your contemporaries. One of them, after a certain amount of hesitation, allowed me to help him to a leg of a rat; after eating it he was as anxious as a terrier for more. The other, however, scornfully refused to share in the repast. As he got through his portion of salted horse, which rejoiced in the name of beef, he regarded us with horror and disgust. I remember when I was in Egypt that my feelings towards the natives were of a somewhat similar nature when I saw them eating rat. The older one grows the more tolerant one becomes. If ever I am again in Africa I shall eat the national dish whenever I get a chance. During the siege of Londonderry rats sold for 7s. each, and if this siege goes on many weeks longer, the utmost which a person of moderate means will be able to allow himself will be an occasional mouse. I was curious to see whether the proprietor of the restaurant would boldly call rat "rat" in my bill. His heart failed him – it figures as a salmi of game.'

By the commencement of December he reported that

'all the animals in the Zoological Gardens have been killed except the monkeys; these are kept alive from a vague and Darwinian notion that they are our relatives, or at least the relatives of some of the members of the government, to whom in the matter of beauty nature has not been bountiful. In the cellar of the English Embassy there are three sheep. Never did the rich man lust more after the poor man's ewe lamb than I lust after these sheep. I go and look at them frequently. . . .They console me for the absence of my ambassador.'

Strange food began to make its appearance in Paris:

'Yesterday I dined with the correspondent of a London paper. He had managed to get a large piece of mufflon, an animal which is, I believe, only found in Corsica. I can only describe it by saying that it tasted of mufflon, and nothing else. Without being absolutely bad, I do not think that I shall take up my residence in Corsica in order habitually to feed upon it.'

But even Labby developed a tender conscience when plain (not spotted) dog made its appearance on the menu:

'I own for my part I have a guilty feeling when I eat dog, the friend of man. I had a slice of a spaniel the other day; it was by no means bad, something like lamb, but I felt like a cannibal. Epicures in dog flesh tell me that poodle is by far the best, and recommend me to avoid bull-dog, which is coarse and tasteless. I really think that dogs have some means of communicating with each other and have discovered that their old friends want to devour them. The humblest of street curs growls when anyone looks at him.'

Before the winter set in the chief sport of the citizens was gudgeon-fishing in the Seine. Each fisherman

'was always surrounded by a crowd deeply interested in the chase. Whenever a fish was hooked, there was as much excitement as when a whale is harpooned in more northern latitudes. The fisherman would play it for some five minutes, and then, in the midst of the solemn silence of the lookers-on, the precious capture would be landed. Once safe on the bank, the happy possessor would be patted on the back, and there would be cries of *Bravo!*'

But when the Seine was frozen over the disciples of Isaac Walton found solace in the sewers, and the *Paris Journal* gave them a few hints:

'Take a long, strong line, and a large hook, bait with tallow, and gently agitate the rod. In a few minutes a rat will come and smell the savoury morsel. It will be some time before he decides to swallow it, for his nature is cunning. When he does, leave him for five minutes to meditate over it; then pull strongly and steadily. He will make convulsive jumps, but be calm, and do not let his excitement gain on you, draw him up, *et voilà votre dîner.*'

It is worthy of note that whereas an ordinary household rat only sold for one franc, a fat sewer-rat fetched one franc, fifty centimes.

In the first week of the New Year Labby had a fresh experience to report:

'Yesterday I had a slice of Pollux for dinner. Pollux and his brother Castor are two elephants, which have been killed. It was tough, coarse and oily, and I do not recommend English families to eat elephant as long as they can get beef or mutton. Many of the restaurants are closed owing to want of fuel. They are recommended to use lamps; but although French cooks can do wonders with very poor materials, when they are called upon to cook an elephant with a spirit lamp the thing is almost beyond their ingenuity. Castor and Pollux's trunks sold for 45 francs a lb; the other parts of the interesting twins fetched about 10 francs a lb.'

Towards the end of the siege the bread was almost uneatable; if put in water, straw and bits of hay floated about; while the scarcity of normal food was such that Labby declared:

'A good leg of mutton would, I am sure, win the

heart of the proudest beauty, and by the gift of half a dozen potatoes you might make a friend for life.'

The greatest care was taken over the health and wellbeing of domestic pets. One housekeeper, an Englishman, allowed him to peep into a closet wherein sat a huge cat which was being fattened for a feast. Calling at the house a few weeks afterwards, he noticed that the sole dish was a cat surrounded, sausage-fashion, by mice.

'I tasted one of the latter, crunching the bones as if it had been a lark. I can recommend mice when nothing more substantial is to be obtained.'

Certainly he had an accommodating stomach and a palate that was not squeamish.

He could also consider the state of his clothes with detached appreciation:

'I am seedy, very seedy. When I call upon a friend the porter eyes me distrustfully. In the streets the beggars never ask me for alms; on the contrary, they eye me suspiciously when I approach them, as a possible competitor. The other day I had some newspapers in my hand; an old gentleman took one from me and paid me for it. I had read it, so I pocketed the halfpence. My wardrobe is scanty . . . I had been absent from Paris before the siege, and I returned with a small bag. It is difficult to find a tailor who will work, and even if he did I could not send him my one suit to mend, for what should I wear in the meantime? Decency forbids it. My pea jacket is torn and threadbare, my trousers are frayed at the bottom, and of many colours – like Joseph's coat. As for my linen, I will only say that the washerwomen have struck work, as they have no fuel. I believe my shirt was once white, but I am not sure. I invested a few weeks ago in a pair of cheap boots. They are my

torment. They have split in various places, and I
wear a pair of gaiters – purple, like those of a respectable ecclesiastic -- to cover the rents. I bought
them on the Boulevard, and at the same stall I
bought a bright blue handkerchief which was going
cheap: this I wear round my neck. My upper man
resembles that of a dog-stealer, my lower man that
of a bishop. My buttons are turning my hair grey.
When I had more than one change of raiment these
appendages remained in their places, now they drop
off as though I were a moulting fowl. I have to pin
myself together elaborately, and whenever I want
to get anything out of my pocket I have elaberately
to unpin myself, with the dread of falling to pieces
before my eyes.'

There was one condition he could not view with
detachment: he hated the cold weather.

'If wars really must be made, I do hope that we
shall fall back upon the old system of carrying on
military operations in summer. . . . I am by no
means certain that I should be a hero at the Equator,
but I am fully convinced that I should be an abject
coward at the North Pole. Three mornings ago
I stood for two hours by the Ambulances de la
Presse, and my teeth have not ceased to chatter ever
since. . . . Unless the next battle is fought on a
warm day I shall not witness it.'

A 'seasonable' Christmas was the very devil to the
poor:

'but then we all know that poor people never are
contented, and seldom understand the fitness of
things. . . . For my part I confess that I never have
seen a paterfamilias with his coat tails raised, basking
himself before his fire, and prating about the delights
of winter, and the healthy glow which is caused by
a sharp frost, without feeling an irresistible desire

to transplant him stark naked on the highest peak of Mont Blanc, in order to teach by experience what winter means to thousands of his fellow-creatures.'

After the poor had been shivering in their cellars and garrets for some weeks he reported that 'the government is cutting down trees as fast as possible, and by the time it thaws there will be an abundance of fuel'. His own state was not much better than that of the slum-dweller.

'I sleep on credit in a gorgeous bed, a pauper. The room is large. I wish it were smaller, for the firewood comes from trees just cut down, and it takes an hour to get the logs to light, and then they only smoulder, and emit no heat. The thermometer in my grand room, with its silken curtains, is usually at freezing point . . . and I have found to my bitter experience of late that the proverb that "there is no smoke without a fire" is untrue. The Tupper who made it never tried to burn green wood.'

However, he could not complain, for his landlord had to trust him until the siege was over:

'My landlord every week presents me with my bill. The ceremony seems to please him, and does me no harm.'

Labby found much to blame and much to praise during his period of incarceration. He thought the women of the poorer classes behaved splendidly; they suffered more and repined less than the men. But he was not enthusiastic about the recruitment of a corps of Amazons, noting:

'The pretty women keep aloof from the movement; the recruits who have already joined are so old and ugly that possibly they may act upon an enemy like the head of Medusa.'

It appears that Flag Days, popular features of the
1914–18 War, were going strong in the siege of Paris,
for he remarked: 'Another abuse which has been put
an end to is that of ladies going about begging for
money for the "wounded". They are no longer
allowed to do so unless they have an authorisation.'
The female population spent hours in the streets
watching the gunfire from the forts that protected
Paris. Their favourite fort, on Mont Valérien, they
loved as a sailor loves his ship. 'If I were near enough,
I would kiss it,' said a girl one day with great fervour.
'Let me carry your kiss to it,' replied a Mobile, and
the pair embraced amidst the cheers of the bystanders.
When this fort was not firing the Parisians became
uneasy and its commander was removed as a result of
protests against his inaction. Naturally his successor
banged away at every German in sight, and the public
were reassured.

As in all wars the spy mania broke out with great
intensity at regular intervals, when coveys of people
would be arrested because they were supposed, 'by
lighted candles and other mysterious devices,' to be
in communication with the enemy. Everyone who
did not frequently express hatred of the Germans was
suspected of being in the pay of Bismarck; and of
course there were spies at headquarters. 'General
Schmitz has a valet who has a wife, and this wife is a
German. What more clear than that General Schmitz
confides what passes at councils of war to his valet –
generals usually do; that the valet confides it to his
wife, who, in some mysterious manner, confides it to
Bismarck.' Labby himself experienced an awkward
moment. Without warning he was requested by two
National Guards to accompany them to the nearest
commissary. He asked why and was told that a
woman had heard him speak German.

'But I am English,' he complained.

'Zat ve sall soon zee,' said one of his captors ominously; 'I spek Anglish like an Anglishman; address to me the vord in Anglish.'

Labby replied that the other spoke English with so perfect an accent that he could only assume he was a fellow-countryman. The National Guard was quite disarmed by this tribute and told the crowd, which had collected in order to lynch the spy, that Labby was not only an Englishman but *un Cockné*; that is to say, he explained, an inhabitant of London. He then shook Labby by the hand; his friend shook Labby by the hand; several ladies and gentlemen shook Labby by the hand; and so they parted. Labby was saved a great deal of personal inconvenience by his knowledge of French character. Some Mobiles arrested him in the suburbs and he only evaded imprisonment as a spy by saying that his mother would be anxious about him if he did not return. 'If you want to inspire a Frenchman with a sort of sentimental respect, always talk of your mother; the same effect is produced on a German by an allusion to your bride.' Another evening there were groups on the boulevards discussing spies and traitors. A patriot observed to Labby that all foreigners in Paris ought, as a precautionary measure, to be extirpated:

'Parbleu!' replied Labby, rolling his eyes and shrugging his shoulders in true Gallic fashion.

Some of the English residents decided to quit Paris when the novelty of the siege began to wear off and arrived at one of the gates with a number of Americans and Russians who were also leaving. But as the list of the English wishing to go had not reached Bismarck in time, they were told that their departure would be delayed. So indignant were they that 'the guard had literally to be turned out to prevent them from endeavouring to force their way through the whole German army'. Labby conversed with an English butler who was of the party and who was clearly of opinion that the end of the world was at hand when a most respectable person was treated in this fashion.

'Pray, sir, may I ask whether Her Majesty is still on the throne of England?' he inquired with bitter scorn.

'I believe she is,' said Labby.

'Then has this Count Bismarck, as they call him, driven the British nobles out of the House of Lords? Nothing which this feller does would surprise me now.'

The American residents adopted a more philosophical attitude towards the siege. One of them, having considered the matter carefully from every angle, broke a long silence with: 'They will squat, sir; mark my words, they will squat.' Labby felt it his duty to report the utterance, though he was a little vague as to its meaning. He also reported a statement by an American lady who had been in a southern city of the States when it was under fire during the Civil War: 'I regard a bombardment as the finest and most interesting effort of pyrotechnical skill,' she said, 'and I want to see if you Europeans have developed this art as fully as we have, which I doubt.'

Labby kept in touch with the ultra-democratic section of the population by constantly attending the meetings of the workers' clubs in the poorer quarters. At one of these he heard an orator denounce crucifixes as 'impure nudities, which ought not to be suffered in public places, on account of our daughters'. At another he listened to a discussion concerning the existence of a deity, the question eventually being decided by a general scrimmage. At a third he learnt that Citizen Mottu, a communistic mayor, had solved the matrimonial problem by declining to celebrate marriages, because he considered such a bond an insult to those who wished to ignore it. 'As regards marriage, consequently,' wrote Labby, 'and that alone, his arrondissement resembles the kingdom of heaven.'

At the Club Rue d'Arras,

'which is presided over by the "venerable" Blanqui in person, and where the ultras of the Ultras congregate,' Labby found 'a place on a bench by the side of a lady with a baby, who was occupied, like most of the other babies, in taking its supper. Its food, however, apparently did not agree with it, for it commenced to squall lustily. "Silence," roared a hundred voices, but the baby only yelled the louder. "Sit upon it," observed some energetic citizens, looking at me, but not being a Herod I did not comply with their order. The mother became frightened lest a *coup d'état* should be made upon her offspring, and after turning it up and solemnly smacking it, took it away from the club.'

A different atmosphere prevailed at the Club Montmartre:

'Every time I have been there an old man – I am told an ex-professor in a girl's school – has got up and with great unction blessed the National Guards – the "heroic defenders of our homes". Sometimes he is encored several times; and were his audience to let him, I believe that he would continue blessing the "heroic defenders" until the next morning. The old gentleman has a most reverent air, and I should imagine in quiet times goes about as a blind man with a dog. He was turned out of the school in which he was a professor – a profane disbeliever in all virtue assures me – for being rather too affectionate towards some of the girls. "I like little girls – big ones, too," Artemus Ward used to say, and so it appears did this worthy man.'

Fraternal sentiments of a very strong order were expressed at another club where a lady sat on the platform.

'When anyone makes what she considers a good

speech she embraces him on both cheeks. She is by
no means ugly, and I had serious thoughts of making
a few observations myself in view of the reward.
That bashfulness, however, which has been my bane
through life prevented me. The lady occasionally
speaks herself, and is fond of giving her own experiences. "I was on my way to this club the other
evening," she said, "when I observed a man following me. *What dost thou want?* I asked, sternly eyeing
him. *I love you,* replied the vile aristocrat. *I am the
wife of a citizen,* I answered, *and the mother of the
Gracchi.* The wretch sneaked away, abashed, to
seek other prey. If he addresses himself to some
princess or duchess he will probably find a victim."
The loudest applause greeted this "experience", and
several very unclean-looking patriots rushed forward
to embrace the mother of the Gracchi, in order to
show her how highly they appreciated her noble
conduct.'

On October 31st there was a riot, when the Government was deposed, imprisoned, released, and again
resumed the direction of affairs. It was a day of great
excitement during which nearly every Frenchman of
note voted himself into a position of authority and was
outvoted by the selfishness of his compatriots. Even
the 'venerable' Blanqui had his moment of power,
after suffering a moment of ignominy when he had
been 'pushed up in a corner, where certain citizens
had kicked his venerable frame, and pulled his venerable white beard, before they had recognised who he
was'. On the whole, however, there was very little
opposition to the Government throughout the siege,
because the poorer classes were clothed and fed and
paid for doing nothing, and the death-roll from gunfire
was not large enough to cause alarm. 'I suppose about
ten people are hit every 24 hours,' Labby wrote in
January, '71: 'Now as above 50 people die every day

in Paris of bronchitis, there is far more danger from
the latter than from the batteries.'

Actually there was more of an outcry over the
damage done to buildings than over the casualties
among human beings; but this correspondent refused
to feel alarm on behalf of the architecture:

'I would rather that every statue and every plant
in the world were smashed to atoms by shells than
that I were. This, in an aesthetical point of view,
is selfish; but it is none the less true. *Chacun pour soi.*
The Panthéon was struck yesterday. What desecration! everyone cries; and I am very sorry for the
Panthéon, but very glad that it was the Panthéon,
and not me.'

He never went out of his way to look for danger:

'I confess I am not one of those persons who snuff
up the battle from afar and feel an irresistible desire
to rush into the middle of it. To be knocked on the
head by a shell merely to gratify one's curiosity
appears to me to be the utmost height of absurdity.'

Once he found himself in an awkward spot and for
about half an hour hid behind a tree,

'for whenever I moved a bullet came whizzing near
me. At last a thought, a happy thought, occurred
to me. I rolled myself into a ditch, which ran
alongside the road, and down this ditch I crept until
I got close to the barricade, over which I climbed
with more haste than dignity.'

As a rule, though, he took no more risks than were
absolutely necessary to the competent discharge of his
duties as a war correspondent, and the phrase, 'I reserved investigations for a more quiet moment', ade-
quately expressed his general demeanour when metal
was flying about.

It was not always easy to fill up his letters with

exciting events and sometimes he had to describe incidents of little news value. One day he was walking through a suburb with the correspondent of *The Times*. By the roadside they saw a man with his legs shattered, his head in the lap of a girl who was crying bitterly. The ambulance people had left him to die where he was, and though the two correspondents rendered what aid they could the man was soon beyond their care.

'Shall you give a description of what we have seen?' asked *The Times* correspondent as they made their way towards the firing.

'Probably,' replied Labby.

'Don't you think that it belongs to me? It was on my side of the road.'

'Well, no; we both saw it, and it belongs to both of us.'

'But if we both describe it, one of our letters may be published the day after the other, and the newspaper which publishes the last of our letters will be supposed to have stolen it from the other paper.'

'That's true. Let's toss for it.'

*The Times* correspondent agreed, and won the toss. Labby did not overestimate the dangers of warfare:

'I would at any time prefer to be 24 hours in the most exposed portion of a bombarded town than walk 24 times across Oxford Street in the middle of the day. A bomb is a joke in comparison with those great heavy wagons which are hurled at pedestrians by their drivers in the streets of London.'

But he had a very low opinion of war as a means of settling a dispute:

'There is nothing either noble or inspiriting in watching a quantity of unfortunate Breton peasants, who cannot even speak French, and an equal number of Berlin grocers, who probably ask for nothing better than to be back in their shops, destroying each other at a distance of two or three miles with balls of lead and iron, many of them filled with explosive materials. I confess that I pity the horses almost as much as the men. It seems a monstrous thing that in order that the Alsacians should be forced into becoming subjects of King William of Prussia, an omnibus horse, who has honestly done his work in the streets of Paris, should be taken outside the walls of the town to have his head blown off or to stump about on three legs until he dies of cold and hunger. Horses have a way when they are wounded of making desperate efforts to get up, and then letting their heads fall with a bang on the soil, which is very horrible to witness.'

As for the so-called glamour and glory of war, he decided that distance lent enchantment to the view:

'Had the charge of Balaclava taken place on Clapham Common, or had our gallant swordsmen replaced the donkeys on Hampstead Heath, even Tennyson would have been unable to poetise their exploits.'

The worst aspect of war was its ghastly tedium.

'Never did time hang so heavily on human beings as it hangs on us. Every day seems to have twice the usual number of hours. I have ceased to wind up my watch for many a week. I got tired of looking at it; and whether it is ten in the morning or two in the afternoon is much the same to me. Almost everyone has ceased to shave; they say that a razor so near their throats would be too great a temptation. . . . Here is my day. In the morning the boots comes to call me. He announces the number of deaths which have taken place in the hotel during the night. If there are many he is pleased, as he considers it creditable to the establishment. He then relieves his feelings by shaking his fist in the direction of Versailles, and exits growling, "Canaille de Bismarck." I get up. I have breakfast – horse, *café au lait* – the *lait* chalk and water, the portion of horse about two square inches of the noble quadruped; then I buy a dozen newspapers, and after having read them, discover that they contain nothing new. This brings me to about 11 o'clock. Friends drop in, or I drop in on friends. We discuss how long it is to last – if friends are French we agree that we are sublime. At 1 o'clock get into the circular railway and go to one or other of the city gates. After a discussion with the National Guards on duty, pass through. Potter about for a couple of hours at the outposts; try with glass to make out Prussians; look at bombs bursting; creep along the trenches; and wade knee-deep in mud through the fields. The Prussians, who have grown of late malevolent even towards civilians, occasionally send a ball far over one's head. They always fire too high. French soldiers are generally cooking food. They are anxious for news and know nothing about what is going on. As a rule they relate the episode of some *combat d'avantposte* which took place the day before. The episodes never vary. 5 p.m. – Get back home; talk to doctors about interesting surgical operations; then drop in upon some official to interview him about what is doing. Official usually first mysterious, then communicative, not to say loquacious, and abuses most people except himself. 7 p.m. – Dinner at a restaurant, conversation general; almost everyone in uniform. Still the old subjects – How long will it last? Why does not Gambetta write more clearly? How sublime we are; what a fool everyone else is. Food scanty, but peculiar. At Voisins to-day the bill of fare was ass, horse, and English wolf from the Zoological Gardens. A Scotchman informed me that this latter was a fox of his native land, and

patriotically gorged himself with it. I tried it, and
not being a Scotchman found it horrible, and fell
back upon the patient ass. After dinner, potter on
the Boulevards under the dispiriting gloom of
petroleum; go home and read a book. 12 p.m. –
Bed. They nail up the coffins in the room just over
mine every night, and the tap, tap, tap, as they drive
in the nails is the pleasing music which lulls me to
sleep.'

His London letters, one or two of which got through
to Paris, gave great offence to the patriots on the press,
and there was some talk of lynching him. He prud-
ently shifted his quarters at the end of '70 from the
Grand Hotel to a quiet out-of-the-way hostelry where
he was not known.

He never had the least doubt that Paris would fall
and Prussia would win the war, and he stressed the
necessity of a no-annexation policy for the future peace
of Europe.

'A treaty of territorial spoliation imposed by force
never has and never will bind a nation. If Prussia
took Alsace there would be another war, for if
France agreed to the cession her agreement would
only be binding on her until she was strong enough
to repudiate it.'

He was far ahead of his time, for politicians still believe
in territorial acquisition by force. He also strongly
advised England to keep her fingers out of the continental pie. He hoped we should have the common
sense not to guarantee the independence of any more
small nations: 'We have a whim about Belgium,' he
said; 'one day it will prove a costly one.'

Paris surrendered at the end of January, much to
everyone's amazement, because right up to the last
moment no one had dared to hint at such a possibility;
but then, as Labby said, 'a besieged town is never so

near surrendering as when it threatens to hang the
first man who speaks of surrender'. As soon as possible he left Paris for Versailles, where he plunged his
head into a pail of milk and was with difficulty weaned.
At Versailles he discovered that the Germans had been
making good use of their time:

'As soon as a German is quartered in a room he
sends for a box and some straw; then carefully and
methodically packs up the clock on the mantelpiece,
and all the stray ornaments which he can lay his
hands on; and then, with a tear glistening in his eye
for his absent family, directs them either to his
mother, his wife or his lady-love. . . . Pianos they
are very fond of. When they see one, they first sit
down and play a few sentimental ditties, then they
go away, requisition a cart, and minstrel and instrument disappear together. . . . They have got
now into such a habit of appropriating other people's
property that I confess I tremble when one of them
fixes his cold glassy eye upon me. I see that he is
meditating some new philosophical doctrine which,
some way or other, will transfer what is in my pocket
into his. His mind, however, fortunately works but
slowly, and I am far away from him before he has
elaborated to his own satisfaction a system of con-
fiscation applicable to my watch or purse.'

Returning to Paris in company with an American
general and a leg of mutton, Labby was stopped at the
gate of Versailles and told that no meat could be
allowed to leave the town. He protested; the American general protested; in vain. Mild, blue-eyed
Teutons with porcelain pipes in their mouths bore off
his mutton to the guard-house, where there was a
youthful officer who looked so pleasant that Labby
determined to appeal to the heart which beat beneath
the uniform.

'It is the fate of all to love,' lamented Labby.

The officer sighed and agreed that it was.

'My lady-love is in Paris,' pursued Labby. 'Long have I sighed in vain. I am taking her now a leg of mutton. On this leg hang all my hopes of bliss. If I present myself to her with this token of my affection, she may yield to my suit. Oh, full-of-feeling, loved-of-beauteous-women, German warrior, can you refuse me?'

Since it is doubtful whether the English version would have had the desired effect, it must be remembered that this speech was spoken in German to a German officer. At any rate, Labby and his leg of mutton were allowed to proceed. Had the speech been made in French to a French officer, the lady-love would have given place to an aged mother, and the appeal would have been equally successful. No one has yet discovered the surest way to an Englishman's heart; it would probably be a sporting bet of two to one.

Labby knew both Frenchmen and Prussians a great deal better than the average well-educated and widely-travelled Englishman has ever known them, and his summary of their characteristics has therefore a special interest:

'I really am sorry for these vain, silly, gulled humbugs among whom I am living,' he wrote from Paris. 'They have many amiable qualities, although, in trying to be Spartans, they have mistaken their vocation. They are, indeed, far too agreeable to be Spartans, who in private life must have been the most intolerable of bores. It is a sad confession of human weakness, but, as a rule, persons are not liked on account of their virtues. Excessively good people are – speaking socially – angular. Take, for instance, the Prussians; they are saints compared with the French. They have every sort of excellence: they are honest, sober, hard-working, well-instructed, brave, good sons, husbands and fathers; and yet all this is spoilt by one single fault – they are insupportable. Laugh at the French, abuse them as one may, it is impossible to help liking them. Admire, respect the Prussians as one may, it is impossible to help disliking them. I will venture to say that it would be impossible to find 100 Germans south of the Main who would declare, on their honour, that they prefer a Prussian to a Frenchman. . . . A Prussian lieutenant is the most offensive specimen of humanity that nature and pipeclay have ever produced. Apart from all political considerations, the supremacy of this nation in Europe will be a social calamity, unless France, like vanquished Greece, introduces the amenities of society among those pedants, squires and martinets.'

This was written on November 5, 1870. Had he been living to-day he would not have altered a syllable.

# CHAPTER VI

## GOD AND MAMMON

BEFORE the siege of Paris Labby struck one observer as a young man. After it was over he looked quite old. The addition of a beard, already streaked with grey, gave him a more reverend appearance. His letters to the *Daily News* had been read with such eagerness both in England and America that a publisher offered him 'a sum of money for them which I was not such a fool as to refuse', though in correcting the proofs he feared that the publisher's optimism was excessive:

'I feel, indeed . . . much like a person who has obtained money under false pretences, but whose remorse is not sufficiently strong to induce him to return it.'

He still believed in a republican form of government, but his recent experiences in France had convinced him that the French people were not ready for it; they had not sufficient common sense, and until they were better educated they would only be fit for a constitutional monarchy.

'A Republic would soon result in anarchy or despotism,' he wrote; 'and without any great love for kings of any kind, I prefer a Constitutional Monarch to either Anarchy or a Caesar. One must take a practical view of things in this world, and not sacrifice what is good by a vain attempt to attain at once what is better.'

This rational attitude towards men and things was
one of his outstanding mental qualities; the other was
a healthy scepticism concerning the judgment of
human beings in their acceptance of superstitions and
their interpretation of occurrences outside their sphere
of knowledge. When accused of believing a 'ghost'
story merely because he had published it, he thought it
a little hard that he of all people should be charged
with credulity: 'I who have doubts even about the
talking donkey that remonstrated with the prophet and
the flirting serpent of the Garden of Eden.' And he
went on to relate a 'ghost' story of his own which had
failed to convince him that ghosts were all they pretended to be.

In his bachelor days he had taken a house, No. 2
Bolton Street, where a man had recently cut his throat.
'I used this as a successful argument to obtain a re-
duction in the premium that was demanded.' The
house consisted of a basement and three floors. In
the basement were the kitchen and scullery, on the
ground-floor was a dining-room in which he used to
sit, on the first floor were two drawing-rooms (in one
of which the man had cut his throat); he slept on the
second floor and his valet and two maids occupied the
rooms on the top-floor. One night he came home late
and sat reading in the dining-room. The servants
had retired to bed long before and the house was quite
silent. Suddenly, at about 2 a.m., a terrific shindy
broke out in the kitchen beneath him. It sounded as
if all the plates and pots and pans were being thrown
about the room. At first he thought it must be one
of the servants on the rampage; then he wondered
whether it was a burglar who had broken in and got
drunk; or possibly a cat in one of its darker moods.
He dismissed the last on the ground that in no conceivable mood could a cat play football with the pots
and pans. As his curiosity was aroused and the noise
continued, he determined to go down and see what was

happening. Taking the precaution to heat the poker, he descended to the basement with a candle in one hand and a poker in the other. As he approached the kitchen the noise suddenly subsided and when he entered it there was not a sign of anything having been disturbed. He inspected the scullery with the same result and then went upstairs to bed.

This performance was repeated frequently, varied by another of a still more sinister nature. Sitting in the dining-room in the small and quiet hours, he would often hear what sounded exactly like a man ascending the stairs from the kitchen, crossing the hall and going on to the upper stories. He could hear each footstep distinctly and the creak of the stairs beneath it. The first time it happened he took no notice, thinking it might be the valet going to bed late; but the next time, the moment he heard the footsteps on the basement flight, he went into the hall and waited for the nocturnal walker. The moment he appeared in the hall the footsteps ceased. Seeing no one he returned to the dining-room and instantly the sound continued. Every time he opened the door there was silence; every time he shut it the man pursued his journey across the hall and up to the floors above.

This happened many times and, taken in conjunction with the fairly regular game of crockery-football in the kitchen, he thought he had better have the drains and pipes inspected. The plumber reporting that all was in order, he carried his investigations into the next-door house, with no more success: peace reigned throughout the night in the house of his neighbour, whose drains and water-pipes were also in excellent condition. For some time he did not mention the disturbance to his servants, who might have left in a panic, but one morning, after a particularly rowdy night in the basement, he asked the valet whether he had heard anything.

'I suppose that you have heard the footsteps,' said the valet.

'What do you mean?'

'We all hear the steps; they come up to our floor and then stop. The maids say that it is the man who cut his throat, but I don't believe in such nonsense.'

Nor did Labby believe in such nonsense. Though provided with enough phenomena to please the greediest bogy-believer, he would not fall back on a cheap and convenient solution. 'There must be some explanation for these noises,' he affirmed; 'but because I could not hit on it, I am not going to believe that the spirit of a man who cut his throat in the house came back to the premises after death to rattle the pots and pans and to take exercise by stalking up the stairs.'

He maintained an open mind on the questions of God and a future state, refusing to be bamboozled into belief by so-called spirit-manifestations. Like all honest unbelievers he had no fear of the future, a fear entertained, perhaps with reason, by most Christians. Once he called on a female friend and was asked to wait as she was taking part in a séance. He picked up a book and sat down. At length the door of the room in which the séance was being held opened and a number of people trooped out, Home, the notorious medium, amongst them. They all began talking of the wonderful things that had happened, assuring Labby that they had just seen a piano pass through the wall dividing their room from the one in which he had been sitting.

'That,' he declared, 'is quite impossible, as I have been here for the last twenty minutes and must have remarked a piano arriving in such a fashion.'

He was generally regarded as a sceptic whom no evidence could convince. But he felt there was a great deal beyond what were supposed to be the laws of nature that would one day become common knowledge and everyday fact.

Revisiting the United States not long after his internment in Paris, he met the president of a railway who was an enthusiastic spiritualist, always talking of the miracles performed by a medium named Forster. Labby was curious and wanted to see Forster, but nothing was done to bring about a meeting until the night before his departure from New York. He was giving a farewell-dinner to a few friends in a private room at Delmonico's, among them the railway magnate. Towards the end of the meal Labby remarked that, after all, he would be leaving the country without seeing Forster.

'Shall I send for him now?' asked the president of the railway.

'By all means.'

An invitation was promptly dispatched to Forster asking him to come and smoke a cigar with them.

Dessert was on the table when Forster appeared. He sat down, drank his wine, smoked his cigar, and joined in the general conversation. Labby liked the look of him: he was a pleasant, genial, well-bred person, the very reverse of what might have been expected. After a while the subject of spiritualism came up.

'What do you think of me?' Forster asked, turning to Labby.

'You are my guest, so I do not wish to offend you,' replied Labby; 'but if you really want to know, I regard you as a clever conjurer.'

'I have a certain power,' Forster admitted: 'whether it is derived from spirits acting through me, I do not know, but I am certain that I have this power.'

While he was speaking the chair on which he sat began to creak portentously as if it were about to collapse in pieces.

'Give me the chair,' said Labby, who then wriggled about on it, trying with all his might to produce a creak. But the chair was a remarkably solid piece of furniture and he failed to obtain the least sound from it.

D

However, Forster's efforts were not confined to the chair, for Labby suddenly became conscious of loud explosive sounds from all parts of the room.

'Is that conjuring?' asked Forster.

'Probably,' replied Labby.

'Can you do it?'

'No, I cannot.'

The ceiling now suffered from the prevailing agitation. Loud bangings issued from it as if someone were flinging heavy articles about the room above. Labby rang the bell and asked the waiter in French who was in the upstairs room. The waiter went to find out, returning with the information that the room was vacant.

'A confederate,' Labby observed, but Forster denied it.

The company were then asked to sit round a bare table. Forster produced a card with the alphabet in large letters upon it, telling them to touch the letters, pausing when they heard a tap. A Scotsman present asked where an uncle of his had died, giving the name of his uncle. An unpronounceable word was tapped out.

'That was the name of his country-house and he did die there,' said the Scot.

Labby then asked where an aunt of his had died.

'In the Isle of Wight,' was rapped out.

'Wonderful!' exclaimed Labby, as indeed it was, for the lady happened to have died in London.

Forster got up and proceeded to give what seemed to Labby like an exhibition of physical exercises behind the chair on which one of the guests was sitting. Seizing his arm, Forster gave him a message from his sister who had died some years before. The message did not appear to Labby to be one of much urgency.

'Go into the next room and she will speak to you,' said Forster.

The guest went and reappeared a little later, pale

and discomposed, with the assertion that his sister had spoken to him.

'Well, what did she say?' asked Labby, but his guest would not tell.

Then the company were asked to write messages on pieces of paper, which were rolled up into balls, and by means of the alphabet Forster read them without opening them.

'Are you convinced?' he asked.

'Not in the least,' said Labby, who then retired to a corner of the room, turned his back on Forster, wrote a word on a slip of paper, folded it up and rang the bell. The waiter came and was dispatched for an envelope. Labby placed the slip of paper in the envelope, closed it, held it before a candle to see that the light could not shine through it, handed it to Forster and asked him to read the word. Forster pressed the envelope to his forehead and read the word correctly.

'Does this convince you?' he asked.

'It convinces me that you have some curious magnetic power, or that you are a singularly clever conjurer,' replied Labby, 'but it certainly does not convince me of spiritualism. Show me a spirit, or a ghost, or a head, or a hand.'

'To see these,' Forster told him, 'you must sit with me for hours in the dark, evening after evening, and perhaps one of these manifestations may appear to you.'

'That is to say,' remarked Labby, 'if I get thrown into a morbid dreamy state, you will persuade me that I see something that has no real existence. Thank you,' and he handed Forster a cigar.

Whereupon Forster lapsed from a medium into a pleasant companion.

Although he thought it a little curious that the dead should confine their information to those who made money out of it, Labby was quite anxious to be convinced. 'There seems to me no particular reason why the dead should not communicate with the living, except that they do not,' he said, after attending innumerable séances. 'Nothing would give me more pleasure than to have a visit from an inhabitant of another world. . . . I extend the most cordial invitation to one and all of the dead.' Perhaps the invitation was of too general a nature; at any rate, none of the dead availed themselves of it.

He was, however, at all times more interested in the quick than in the dead, and in the early 'seventies his attention was largely devoted to those among the quick whose practice was sharp, transferring his gambling activities from the roulette tables of the Continent to the London Stock Exchange. 'The intelligent man,' he asserted, 'lives by swimming with the current and by diverting a portion of the stream into his own reservoirs.' With a little care and study, coupled with a shrewdness for which few people at that time gave him credit, he managed to increase his already considerable fortune, though he had to confess that in the money-mart he felt like a missionary among a tribe of cannibals and was always a little anxious about the safety of his brand-new top-hat.

In the course of his experiences among the worshippers of Mammon he picked up something of greater value to his fellow-citizens than a method of improving his own investments, and the most notable enterprise in British journalism was based on the knowledge he managed to acquire during these years in the city, when, among other things, he made the discovery that 'a financial enthusiast is a more dangerous person than a thief'.

In the spring of 1874 he received from Edmund Yates the prospectus of a new paper to be called *The World*, in which he read that Mr. Yates hoped to reform the world. At first the idea appealed to his sense of humour. On Cup Day at Ascot that year he was occupying the box of a coach when Yates hailed him and wanted to know whether he had received the prospectus.

'Oh, yes,' he replied, 'and I thought it very funny.'

'But will you help us in carrying it out – will you be one of us?'

'You don't mean to say that you actually mean to start a paper of the kind set forth?'

'Assuredly we do, and we want your assistance.'

Labby roared with laughter and said that he would let Yates know about it. A few days afterwards he offered to write a series of city articles. The offer was gratefully accepted and his first article, which appeared in the second number of *The World* on July 15, 1874, opened with these words:

'Some years ago, Mr. John F. Walker, having derived a considerable fortune from cheating at cards in Mississippi steamboats, determined to enjoy his well-earned gains in his native city of New York, and purchased an excellent house in that metropolis. In order to add to his income he advertised that he was a "reformed gambler", and for a consideration would instruct novices in all the tricks of his trade. Mr. Walker was universally esteemed by his fellow-citizens, and died last year, greatly regretted by a numerous body of friends and admirers. In casting about for the city editor for our journal, we have fallen upon a gentleman who, by promoting rotten companies, puffing worthless stock, and other disreputable, but strictly legal, devices, has earned a modest competence. He resides in a villa at Clapham, he attends church every Sunday with exemplary regularity, and is the centre of a most respectable circle of friends; many of his old associates still keep up their acquaintance with him, and therefore he is in a position to know all that passes in the city. This reformed speculator we have engaged to write our city article.'

Having thus made it clear to his readers that they were going to get a good run for their money, he settled down to a weekly exposure of company-promoters, newspaper puffers, money-lenders and other swindlers in a manner that was entirely fresh to journalism and extremely obnoxious to many fellow-journalists. His qualifications for the job were stated in an early number:

'Just as the two Israelites who went down to Jericho dwelt with the harlot Rahab in the interests of society, so we have made it our business to dwell in the tents of the City Philistines, and we flatter ourselves that we have now acquired so complete a knowledge of their manœuvres that we are able to anticipate all their tricks.'

The main objects of the city articles in *The World* were explained with equal candour: to expose the behaviour of share-manipulators, so that readers could have the satisfaction of losing their money with their eyes open; to show that the writers on finance in the daily papers were thoroughly corrupt; to uncover the process whereby 'some poor scamp who was seeking like his betters to abstract money from his neighbour's pocket was held up to odium' while wealthy scoundrels went scot free; and, generally speaking, to call attention to bloodsuckers and vampires. A comprehensive programme, which was carried out to the letter in what the bloodsuckers and vampires considered a thoroughly reprehensible way.

But Labby wished to be quite fair. The rogues were not wholly to blame and he told his readers why:

'In the practical details of finance, in their relation to investment, Englishmen are, without any exception, the greatest idiots in the habitable globe. To find their equals in simplicity one must go amongst tribes of savages.'

No one had taken the trouble to educate them in the principles of investment. This task he had assumed because 'the ignorance of the many is the stock-in-trade of the few'. The main supporters of the vampire-gang were the clergy:

'We do not happen to be a bishop, but if we were we should issue a pastoral letter to the clergy of our diocese advising them to invest their savings in Consols. . . . Next to the clergy the most gullible class consists of women: their greed is great and their caution is small.' The writer himself was not entirely free from fault: 'We happen, for our sins, to have taken some shares in a mine. We take out our dividend in abusing our directors at the annual meeting.' But he had shed most of his illusions: 'What's in a name? A very great deal. If ever we are blessed with sons, we shall christen one Rothschild and the other Baring, and we are convinced that, such is the innate stupidity of mankind, we shall be spared making any further provision for them.' He did not claim infallibility for his opinions on stocks and shares: 'Distrust all advice and make no exception in favour of ours.' Above all, no one should mistake a good man for a good counsellor, or vice versa: 'If Euclid had murdered his mother and robbed his grandmother, these domestic details would not have altered the correctness of his problems.'

At first *The World* did not do well, though Labby's exposure of Mr. Sampson, the city editor of *The Times*, caused a sensation. Sampson's prestige in financial circles was enormous and for twenty-eight years his readers had considered him an oracle. When, therefore, he was denounced for having puffed the shares of an amalgamated Cable Company, while concealing from his readers that the dividends were shortly to be reduced, the effect may be imagined.

For two or three weeks in succession he was accused of bolstering up rotten concerns, of defending pernicious monopolies, and of being 'in the habit of receiving indirectly from financial magnates in the city *douceurs* in some form or another, not probably so much for advocacy of their projects as for reticence concerning them'. Within a month of the commencement of these attacks Mr. Sampson retired into private life and the city editor of the *Pall Mall Gazette*, Mr. Crump, reigned in his stead. But very soon Mr. Crump was showing where his personal interests lay, and Labby felt it his duty to show them still more plainly:

'A few days ago that strange successor to Mr. Sampson, who amuses the public daily with a column of pernicious twaddle in *The Times*, advised those who hold Erie shares to retain them. . . . When Mr. Crump obtains the commission for having introduced the Paraguayan loan to a city firm for which he is now suing in Chancery, we take the liberty to doubt whether he will invest it in any of the securities of the Erie Railway. . . . Mr. Crump, a few months ago, published a book entitled *The Philosophy of Modern Humbug*. Does he imagine that as city editor of *The Times* it is intended that he should favour the world with additional chapters of this work?'

Lest his own estimate of the value of Erie Railway shares should be in doubt, he added:

'Holders, however, need not despair. We ourselves make them an offer. We have a small room in our humble abode which we should like to paper with Erie shares; we therefore offer to give 2d. per lb. for all that are sent to us.'

*The Times* was not the only paper to suffer from his notice. Referring to Mr. Harper, the city editor of the *Daily Telegraph*, he suggested that the proprietors of that paper should suppress the city article and 'place the "Inventor's Column", which is so freely advertised, under the supervision of Mr. Harper'. This was the first rumble of a storm which was to break with full force some years later and involve Labby in his most sensational lawsuit.

But what saved *The World* from an early death, sent up its circulation by leaps and bounds and established it permanently as a paper of note, was the public spectacle of one gentleman in a top-hat threatening to horsewhip another gentleman in a top-hat and the consequent appearance of both gentlemen before the Lord Mayor of London. A certain stockbroker named Abbott was engaged in operations on behalf of a speculator who was being exposed by Labby in his weekly articles. Mr. Abbott did not like the tone of these articles, had a foreboding that his own name might at any moment appear in one of them, and felt it would be as well to prevent such an occurrence by swifter methods than the law allowed. Meeting Labby in the street one day, he went straight to the heart of the matter:

'You know that you write in *The World*,' said he; 'and if anybody were to attack me in that way in any other newspaper, I would show you what I should do.'

'If you are attacked in a newspaper unfairly, I presume you would bring an action for libel,' replied Labby: 'and if it was unfair, you would get very heavy damages.'

'I should not go into courts,' said Abbott grimly. 'I know what newspapers want: they always want to go into courts; it is a free advertisement for them. I should horsewhip the man.'

'Well, under the circumstances the observation is a personal one,' retorted Labby, 'and I reply to you in the words of Dr. Johnson: "I shall not be deterred from unmasking a scoundrel by the menaces of a ruffian".'

D*

'I presume you mean that for me?'

'Well, it looks like it. You were just now talking about horsewhipping. Here I am. Horsewhip me.'

This was unexpected and for a moment Abbott stared at his opponent uncertain how to counter it.

'Well, why don't you begin?' inquired Labby.

Abbott was now in the awkward position of one who had put up a wellnigh coward-proof bluff, only to find it 'called' by a journalist. Feeling that he had better support it by some show of action, he went through all the motions with which nervous pugilists try to impress their antagonists: he rolled his body about, adopted a crouching posture, clenched his fists and sawed the air with them. Labby observed these tactics with interest and then, as they appeared to be an end in themselves, again asked:

'Why do you not begin?'

At this Abbott threw constraint to the winds and, stepping forward smartly, struck the other on the shoulder or the arm – Labby was not quite certain which because it felt like an indiarubber ball bounding lightly against him. Having a stick in his hand, he raised it and had a shot at his assailant's top-hat, hoping to knock it off. Abbott caught his arm; he caught Abbott's arm; and in this embrace they leaned against a wall, breathing hostilities. Wondering what to do next, Abbott glanced about him and noticed a small boy who was taking a keen interest in the proceedings and behind whom a crowd of spectators was gradually forming. Like most persons of that period who wished to chastise other persons, Abbott could only think in terms of one instrument and asked the small boy:

'Do you happen to have a horsewhip about you?'

Labby thought this a childish question and said:

'Hadn't you better take my stick?'

The crowd was now about thirty strong and Labby addressed it:

'Is there a policeman here?'

Where there is a crowd there is usually a policeman, and the cry went up, 'Here he comes.'

'I give this man in custody for an assault,' said Labby to the policeman, and they all marched off to the nearest station, where Abbott was duly charged.

The case was tried on October 12, 1874, and in the course of it Labby was asked by his counsel:

'Have you any fear of Mr. Abbott?'

'Well, no,' he replied. 'When I was in Spezzia I used to bathe a good deal in the Gulf, and there was a quantity of porpoises – '

He was not permitted to draw the parallel between Mr. Abbott and a porpoise, for the defendant's counsel sharply intervened with:

'This is really making a farce of a Court of Justice.'

Though the public showed their desire to hear about the porpoises by hissing this interruption, Labby's counsel repeated the question in a 'Yes or No' tone of voice:

'Have you any fear?'

'Not the least.'

During the evidence it came out that Labby had previously been assaulted by someone named Farini at Homburg, the defence trying to show that he was a provocative person whom every decent citizen was justified in assaulting; but Labby had no difficulty in proving that Farini was a notorious swindler, against whom he had warned certain American ladies. Farini had raised his stick, Labby had closed with him, and there had been a scuffle.

Abbott was bound over for £500 to keep the peace; and as he was 'hammered' on the Stock Exchange a little later, it is clear that the horsewhip was his surest means of defence.

Labby made countless enemies while writing his city articles, and attempts were made throughout his life-time to convict him of doing what he was exposing others for doing – using his influence as a writer on behalf of shady companies in which he might have been financially interested.   But no one was ever able to charge him with anything worse than advertising the concerns which he believed were sound, and when someone complained that he invested money in those concerns he said: 'What greater proof can I give of my belief in the shares I write up than buying them?   Or what stronger evidence can there be of my disbelief in a share than my selling it?'

He was, however, not above giving his poor friends a tip.   To George Augustus Sala he once wrote: 'Next week *The World* is going to announce that the Atlantic Cable will be bought by the Government.   Buy.' Not long after he wrote to Sala: '*The World* is going to announce next week that there is no foundation for the rumour that the Government will buy the Atlantic Cable.   Sell.'

As he was a director of the Atlantic Cable, he was able to place his inside knowledge at the service of a friend, and possibly to use his inside knowledge for a personal flutter.

# CHAPTER VII

## ASSAULT AND BATTERY

WHEN Sir Henry Lucy was asked to become the editor of a daily paper, Labby gave him a few tips. 'I have never understood why each London paper ignores the existence of other papers. I should be perpetually answering them and ridiculing them.' That was one tip. Another ran: 'I should start with revolutionary ideas, and especially study the American papers.' A third: 'An outcry of literary men is raised against sensationalism. It is the business of a newspaper to create a sensation.' Finally he described the difference between a good and a bad editor: 'The former looks at things subjectively, the latter objectively. The former forms an estimate of what the public likes by what he likes, and proceeds to endeavour to force it down their throats. The latter gives them what they like and cooked as they like it.'

Some time in 1876 Labby had an inspiration and acted upon it with the promptness that distinguished him. Not content with telling the truth about the city, he decided to tell the truth about politics, society, the drama, everything; which meant that he would have to found a journal and run it himself. He discovered a first-rate manager, Horace Voules, put up £1,000 as capital, and the first number of *Truth* appeared in the first week of 1877. When asked by a friend 'What is Truth?', he answered, 'Another and a better *World*.' He also said that people would buy it in order to see what new lie he could invent each

week, which suggested an alternative title, and he was
with difficulty persuaded not to call it *The Lyre*.
Later, when someone pretended to believe that he was
as big a liar as he pretended to be, he changed ground:
'When I was at Bishop Auckland . . . I found a Lying
Club existing and flourishing. There were different
grades of proficiency. If a man could not lie at all, he
was expelled. If he lied rather badly, he was given
another trial. I never knew anyone expelled. I was
blackballed.' As was to be expected, he advised the
manager of *Truth* to take a sporting chance, and Voules
was sensible enough to accept £600 a year, plus a
percentage of the profits. The paper was a success
from the beginning, and Voules, like Robinson of the
*Daily News*, lived to thank the man who had put him
on to such a good thing. The original capital was
never touched and the sale of the paper increased with
every number.

At the start Labby was like a child with a new toy.
For the first year or so he wrote as much of the paper
as he possibly could – dramatic criticism, city articles,
society news, political comments, personal reminiscences, pen portraits, and his hand is even discernible
in the fashion and cookery departments. He loved
writing, above all he loved the freedom to write
exactly as he wished; and as he was interested in
everyone and everything, and did not care what he
said about anyone or anything, the first hundred
numbers of *Truth* contained the strangest variety of
miscellaneous and irresponsible excursions in the history of journalism, from which one may construct the
most entertaining personality who ever occupied an
editorial chair. Of course he could not sustain this
output, and since it was his nature to be as quickly
tired as he had been fired, it is a wonder that he kept
it up so long. After the paper had been running for
about two years, Voules went for a holiday on the
Continent. One day he received a letter from Labby

saying that things were a bit dull and adding casually:
'I don't think I shall bring the paper out next week.'
Voules was thunderstruck; he knew that Labby was
quite capable of shutting up shop at a moment's notice,
and the prospect nearly drove him out of his mind.
He caught the first train home, arrived at the office in
a state bordering on collapse, and was told by Labby:
'You need not have worried yourself so about it;
probably I should have brought the paper out all
right.' This taught Voules a lesson; never again did
he leave Labby in charge of the paper; even his
holidays were spent within an hour of London; and
every week for the next fifteen years he saw *Truth* to
press himself. Labby was delighted; gradually he was
able to relinquish all control of the paper, and when
he re-entered parliament in 1880 he completely lost
interest in it, though he went on contributing political
articles, occasional reminiscences and the like.

Needless to say, *Truth* caused trouble from the outset. Labby had been chairman and director of the
Westminster Aquarium, and when the company was
getting into difficulties he criticised it in his columns:
'The affairs of this company,' he wrote, 'are under the
control of Mr. Wybrow Robertson, a manager already
dismissed for dishonesty.' Mr. Robertson felt that this
statement reflected on his character and took an early
opportunity of expressing his feelings. Early in
August '77 Labby attended the annual fair at Boulogne
with several friends: Mrs. Rousby, the actress,
Alexander Henderson and another lady. They
gambled away many sous and at length Mrs. Rousby's
perseverance was rewarded with a glass butter-dish
on a long glass pedestal. 'This result of one hour's
steady gambling was consigned to me,' said Labby,
who then, his hands occupied with the butter-dish and
Mrs. Rousby on one of his arms, began to leave the
booth. While threading their way slowly through the
crowd, he became conscious of the proximity of Mr.

Wybrow Robertson, who from his manner seemed to be tipsy.

'If your hands were empty, I would knock you down,' said Mr. Robertson.

Not wishing to give the French a poor opinion of English behaviour, Labby took no notice of this threat and continued to push his way towards the exit.

'I will insult you wherever I meet you,' pursued Mr. Robertson, showing no disposition to close the conversation.

'I shall be obliged to call a *sergent de ville* to you, my good man, if you disgrace yourself in this way,' said Labby, turning his back on Robertson and speaking to Mrs. Rousby.

Robertson now resolved that the moment was ripe for action and struck Labby on the face with his glove. Disliking brawls in any shape or form, especially in France where the loudest disagreement seldom ends in a fight, Labby would have wished to leave the issue in the sphere of polemics, but his nature rebelled against such treatment and before he realised what he was doing he hurled the butter-dish complete with pedestal ('the precious trophy of persistent enterprise') at Robertson's head, which it missed. Then he went for Robertson with his stick, dealing several shrewd blows before the arrival of reinforcements in the shape of Robertson's brother. Things were looking bad for Labby, but a moment later his friend Henderson appeared on the scene and the forces were equally matched.

'I know you and you know me,' snorted Robertson's brother, when he realised that the odds were no longer against Labby and that a retreat was indicated.

'Then you have the advantage of me,' returned Labby, who did not know him by sight.

The brother then withdrew, still snorting defiance, and Robertson, who had already withdrawn, was being urged by a female friend not to endanger himself further. The Robertson family, having gone into committee on the subject, at length abandoned the field, and Labby had the mortification of overhearing the remarks of the peasants who had viewed the scene with scientific curiosity:

'*Sont ils drôles, ces Anglais?*' said one.

'*Ils a'amusent toujours comme cela,*' said another.

'*C'est peut-être le criqué,*' said a third.

Mr. Robertson duly lodged an action for libel, and Labby pleaded that the charge of dishonesty was true. The case came on at the end of November '78 and was notable in legal history for the first forensic success of Charles Russell (afterwards Lord Russell of Killowen) who was briefed without a leader because Labby and George Lewis, the solicitor, had a high opinion of his ability. The jury decided that the charge of dishonesty was fully proved and found for the defendant.

Throughout the later 'seventies, the 'eighties and 'nineties, Labby was a famous and popular figure in the law-courts. It may be doubted whether anyone not directly concerned with the legal profession ever appeared so often in a witness-box or in the 'well' of a court, from which he frequently conducted his own cases. Blackmailers, impostors, baby-farmers, wife-beaters, bogus business-men, hypocrites, cheats and charlatans of every description were exposed by him; and, whenever they thought there was a chance of damages, the exposure was invariably followed by a legal action. That was the epoch of the individual swindler; the profits of industrialism were mounting up and the middle classes were getting more money to invest. It was the great boom period, when long rows of tall, red-brick, hideous houses were defiling the country about London, houses built for large families and several servants. The Victorian Age was gathering in its harvest from sweated labour; the Victorian shark was reaping from the rich what had

been sown by the poor; and Labby was playing for
the shark in the pages of *Truth*.

The libel actions in which he was the defendant were
usually so dramatic that people fought for places in
the court. The drama lay, not only in his conduct
of the case, but in the quaint quality of his personality.
His cross-examinations were conducted with an air
of bland and innocent inquiry and were usually of so
disarming a nature that witnesses were soon off their
guard. Having first of all put them at their ease by
his friendly manner and gentle drawling voice, he
next established complete confidence by a series of
simple questions which apparently had nothing to do
with the matter in hand. At last they became ex-
pansive, chatted away merrily and enjoyed his
homely banter as much as the gallery of listeners;
in fact they could not understand why the opposing
counsel kept raising objections to the harmless childlike queries this genial gentleman sometimes put, for
he was clearly at one with them; he was even helping
them to remember things they had forgotten, things
that favoured the side for which they were giving evidence. Suddenly the atmosphere of harmony seemed
to change. A tenseness crept over the court. The
genial gentleman was asking them, in as charming a
manner as ever, 'But I thought you said just now – ?'
Had they been led into a trap? Impossible, because
their questioner was smiling in a most engaging manner. They paused, remembered a previous admission,
suffered a moment of panic, tried to reconcile the
contradiction in their next answer, failed to make it
sound convincing. And now Labby (they recalled
with horror the warnings they had received before
entering the box) was not smiling; nor was he speaking
with that pleasant well-bred courtesy that had encouraged them to talk so indiscreetly; a hard, metallic,
displeasing voice was rapping out a series of condensed
phrases beginning with such words as: 'Did you or

did you not – ?", 'Never mind what you thought', 'Remember you are on your oath', 'Are you quite certain – ?', 'I put it to you again', 'You really ask the jury to believe – ?' All was over at last; they had gone from bluster to blunder; and their ignominy was sealed with a curt dismissal from the gentleman who was no longer genial.

As time went on Labby's popularity with the poorer classes became enormous; they regarded him as their one completely trustworthy champion both in parliament and the law-courts, for it was obvious that he had no personal ambition and no axe to grind. People came from all parts of the country to hear him speak on platforms or watch him conduct a case. Sometime in the 'eighties, while waiting for one of his cases to begin, he wandered towards the criminal court and was about to enter when a Yorkshireman accosted him: 'Say, mister, can you tell me t'coort where Labby is to be tried?' Realising that his reputation had become tarnished on its way north, and anxious not to disappoint a man who had come so far to see a favourite villain, he led the Yorkshireman into the criminal court, pointed to a red-haired ruffian who was on trial for an exceptionally shocking crime, whispered 'That's Labby,' and disappeared.

We cannot follow the founder of *Truth* through twenty-five years of litigation. A volume of Labby's cases may some day be compiled, but not by the present writer. It would make entertaining and refreshing reading, because it would show us, among other things, that if the Victorians were more respectable than we are, we have become more respectful than they were. Ours is a mealy-mouthed age in comparison with its predecessors. So sensitive is the modern conscience that if Labby were alive to-day, and publishing his opinions of people with the candour permissible in the nineteenth century, his time would be fairly evenly divided between law-courts and prisons and he would probably end up in a workhouse. The social fabric is nowadays in too shaky a condition to be exposed to such criticism as his.

Even in his own time however, one of his cases stood out above all the rest, and it must find a place here not merely on account of the sensation it created but chiefly because almost every aspect of Labby's character was revealed in the course of the quarrel which gave rise to it and in the conduct of the case itself. He has been described by various people as (1) a man entirely without malice and (2) the most malicious of men. It is a little difficult to reconcile these extremes, but we may come near the truth if we put it this way: he was a good hater on impersonal grounds. The truly malicious man is one with a personal grudge, one whose disposition to hurt others is caused by personal envy or resentment. Now Labby was incapable of envy because he despised all the things that most people covet and esteem: titles, decorations, popularity, authority, prestige, the trappings, ostentation and comforts of wealth. He was also incapable of nursing a grudge against anyone on account of personal pique, because, having no vanity, he could not feel offended; and, it may be added, having no conceit, he could not be personally offensive.

On the other hand, he was capable of extreme enmity towards those who harmed the causes he knew to be good, and in fighting for his political beliefs he was often extremely offensive in an impersonal way. This made his behaviour all the more unbearable, because it gave his enemies the impression that he was judging them from an Olympian viewpoint, as if he were the final court of appeal, as if he voiced the universal conscience of mankind. The absence of individual rancour in his attacks on them, his constantly expressed wish to remain on friendly terms with the people he was abusing and his amazement when they did not share his wish, increased instead of abat-

ing the anger he aroused; and most of his enemies, not
willing or able to draw these nice discriminations, felt
that he was the prey of some insane malevolence.
His occasional outbursts in print did not help them
to make the necessary distinction. 'I like a good
honest hater,' he said when hearing of a man who had
left his fortune to two nieces on condition that neither
of them married a clergyman or a soldier. And on
the same theme: 'I cannot say that I often heap
coals of fire on the heads of my enemies by any kindness towards them. I feel that they deserve every
evil that can befall them, for otherwise I should not
hate them. Being an excellent hater, I strongly
approve of those who stand by their friends.' Yet
it is clear from such statements that his antipathies
were caused by a general sense of evil, not a particular
feeling of venom. The malice which many men mistook for personal spite was simply the pertinacity with
which he pursued and attacked humbug or cruelty or
snobbery or treachery or anything else that he disliked
on social grounds.

It is necessary to grasp the essential impersonality
of his hatreds in order to understand what follows.
A naturally kind-hearted man who was not moved by
a conviction of right which transcended all private
feelings could never have carried on the war which
Labby waged with unremitting zeal against Mr. Levy-
Lawson. Besides in this case we happen to know that
Labby was the first to strike, so he cannot be accused
of merely returning evil for evil.

The real cause of it all was Mr. Gladstone. Labby's
reverence (and irreverence) for that remarkable figure
will be shown in the next chapter; at the moment
all that need be said is that he came as near to wor-
shipping Gladstone as his nature would allow him to
worship anybody. He believed that Gladstone was
the only man in parliament who could and would
carry through the reforms of the Radical Party; he

believed that Gladstone was the one absolutely sincere
and incorruptible man in politics, the chief champion
of progress, the sole hope of the poor and oppressed;
and this man, this high-minded, selfless, upright
Englishman, was being unmercifully assailed by a Jew
who was editor and part-owner of the *Daily Telegraph*.
Labby had no objection to Jews as a race. On the
contrary he felt that 'their numerous excellent qualities'
were not sufficiently appreciated and praised them so
frequently that some American writer assumed he was
one himself. He was not a Jew, but he certainly
would not have minded if he had been, and this was
another reason for his annoyance with Mr. Edward
Levy-Lawson, who had done his best to cover up his
Hebraic origin by adding 'Lawson' to 'Levy'. But
we must go back a little.

In the 'fifties of last century a gentleman named
Colonel Sleigh brought out the first London daily
penny paper. It consisted of one sheet and was called
the *Daily Telegraph*. The printer, Joseph Moses Levy,
was in a very small way of business. The paper did
not go as well as the colonel had hoped it would and
when he came to the end of his money Levy took it
over for the sum that was due to him for printing it.
But Levy was not a rich man and he appealed to
his brother to raise the necessary capital with which
to run it. This brother, who had changed his name
from Lionel Levy to Lionel Lawson, had done fairly
well for himself. He was born with a silver spoon in
his mouth; everything he touched turned to gold;
no sooner did he take over a losing business than it
began to flourish; if he bought the most depreciated
securities they were bound to rise; if he purchased
real estate it soon became more valuable. In the
'fifties he was running a prosperous ink manufactory
in Paris and was called by his friends, in the playful
manner of the age, 'Inkerman Lawson'. After his
return to London he purchased a large share in the

Star and Garter Hotel at Richmond and bought the Gaiety Theatre, where his stout figure in a private box reserved for himself became one of the features of the place. He answered his brother's appeal by raising £1,500, in return for which he was to receive half the profits of the undertaking. Still the paper did not go well enough; a further sum was raised by selling a share to a publican named Moss, who owned a pot-house close to the printing-office; and the reserve of money was nearly exhausted when the paper duty was removed. The sales increased at once and before long it was a thriving concern. Lionel Lawson had nothing whatever to do with the running of the news-paper, contenting himself with the profits which he invested in houses and securities, and leaving the direction in the hands of his brother and nephew. For some years it was edited by Joseph Moses Levy, who then concentrated on the management, giving his son Edward the post of editor.

Throughout the 'sixties and 'seventies the *Daily Telegraph* was a Liberal paper, strongly supporting Gladstone, who was described by Edward Levy as 'The People's William'. But when in 1878 Gladstone's Eastern Policy became anti-Turkish the *Telegraph* trans-ferred its allegiance to Beaconsfield and began to attack the private character and public policy of Gladstone with extreme virulence. Up to this point Labby's dealings with the Levy family had only been slight. He was friendly with Lionel Lawson, who was a real 'character' and whose pride in being a self-made man appealed to him. He had made fun in *The World* of Joseph Moses Levy for demanding a free box at theatrical first-nights for himself as editor of the *Daily Telegraph*. He had, as we have seen, ex-pressed a poor opinion of that organ as an authority on investments. And because Edward Levy when a liberal had twitted Lord Beaconsfield with being a Jew in the columns of his paper, Labby had not

concealed his opinion of Edward Levy for attempting to
obliterate his own racial tracks by adding 'Lawson'
to his name. In order to provide an excuse for this
change of name, Levy had begged his uncle for a
small and valueless plot of land; and when the uncle
told this to Labby, the already-cool relationship between himself and Edward Levy was strained to
breaking-point by his humorous comments on the
subject.

But when the *Daily Telegraph* deserted Gladstone
for the tories over the Turkish question, Labby let
fly in *Truth*. Several things about the changed policy
of his contemporary annoyed him. First, he believed
that Edward Levy-Lawson was merely feathering his
own nest, because when the liberals were in power
he was a liberal and when the tories were in power
he became a tory. Next, Labby hated the convention that enabled a man to hide his personal ambitions and work off his private feelings and express
his idiosyncratic and irresponsible views under the
first person plural of an editor. In those days people
read the newspaper editorials with care, believing
them to express the considered opinions of large
sections of the community, and it was repugnant to
Labby's sense of fitness that the public should mistake
personal greed or pique for national policy. Then,
too, Labby was aware that Lionel Lawson had invested
largely in Turkish Bonds, and as most of his fortune
would probably be inherited by his nephew Edward,
it was impossible not to connect the sudden pro-
Turkish policy of the *Daily Telegraph* with a pro-Levy
financial policy. Finally, and of paramount importance to Labby, there was the attack on Gladstone
both as a statesman and as a man. To throw over
and insult the only person who was able to benefit
the English people, merely because he considered the
Turks to be barbarians; to betray the poorer classes of
Great Britain merely because some of the Levy family

securities might become a little insecure, was unfor-
givable.  At least that was how Labby saw the situation, though naturally Mr. Levy-Lawson viewed it
from a different angle.

'Let us unveil the men who are sitting in judgment
on Mr. Gladstone,' was the burden of Labby's attacks
on the *Daily Telegraph*; 'let us look at the people who
claim to speak for the English nation.'  In number
after number of *Truth* he carried out this duty of
unveiling and looking with a relish which showed that
he was going on to the sweet or bitter end.  Needless
to say Edward Levy-Lawson writhed under the constant exposure, but his feelings were hampered by the
editorial 'we'.  At last something happened to bring
matters to a head, in two senses of the phrase.  Lionel
Lawson died in September 1879 and Labby wrote an
obituary notice of him in *Truth*.  After giving a brief
outline of his life and mentioning that in order to
raise the capital for the *Daily Telegraph* he had obtained
£500 from a fund of which he was trustee, Labby went
on to say:

'Although not a genius, he was a shrewd and clever
man and he was a very pleasant companion.  I
used to know him very well and although I never
concealed from him my low opinion of the *Daily Telegraph* as an organ of public opinion we were always
the best of friends.  He cannot be said to have been
sordidly stingy, for he never denied himself the best
of everything, and I really believe that had I told
him that £5 would have saved my life he would
have given me this sum.  But his mania was to die
an exceedingly rich man.  I remember that he
once came to me to propose that a combination
should be entered into between the London papers
to force the First Lord of the Admiralty [1] to take

[1] W. H. Smith, the famous newspaper agent, whose appointment
as First Lord was ridiculed by Gilbert in *Pinafore*.

them *out-and-out* and not *on sale or return.* "But surely
my good friend," I said, "you make more money
already than you know how to spend." "That," he
replied, "is not the question. There are people who
say that if only I live long enough, I shall die the
richest commoner in England, but if Smith does not
accept the fair risks of trade, he will die richer than
me." I looked at him to see if he were joking, but
not at all. He had almost tears in his eyes at the
thought of this possibility. Of death he had always
the greatest dread, not from any abstract thought
of what would occur to him in another world, but
because the grave would bring accumulation to an
end. I used sometimes to look at him sadly. Seeing my eyes fixed on him he would become nervous
and would ask me what was the matter. "You
are not looking well," I would say. The blood
would at once rush to his face. "Look at yourself
in the glass," I would continue, "you are flushed."
When he perceived that this was true, his anxiety
would become great, and he would hurry home to
put himself into the hands of a physician. He
lived over a shop in Brook Street, where he had
caused, at considerable expense, a fire-escape to
be constructed, down which he could flee in case
of danger. . . . A year or two ago he made such
extensive purchases in Turkish Bonds that they were
transported to his broker in three cabs, which they
filled. Had he only lived his proverbial luck would
have rendered this rubbish valuable, but with his
death the last hope of Turkey ever extricating herself from her financial difficulties is extinguished.
To say that Lawson was either a philanthropist or
an exceptionally useful citizen would be exaggera-
tion, but there were many good points about him;
I and others who knew him well liked him and we
shall miss his portly presence and his cynically clever
small talk. If only my poor friend could read the

amount of probate to which his personal estate is sworn, it would be a great comfort to him, but this, alas, is denied to him.'[1]

Now there can be no doubt that Labby wrote this excellent summary of a man's character with no ill-intent. But obituary notices are usually written in such a fulsome and mawkish manner that this particular specimen, so frank and good-natured that it might henceforth be regarded as a model for that class of composition, did not provide Lawson's relations with the spiritual consolation of which they stood in need. Its artistic merits were entirely lost on them; they were so much concerned for the honour of Lionel that they were shocked by the honesty of Labby; and certainly the statement that a deceased relative had used Trust Funds for bolstering up a groggy business is not the kind of thing that mourners like to meditate upon at the grave-side of the dear departed. Indeed the style of the whole memoir seems to have jarred on Mr. Edward Levy-Lawson and his uncle's corpse was scarcely cold in its grave before his temperature was at boiling-point.

Between 11 and 12 o'clock on Monday night, September 29, 1879, Labby left the Beefsteak Club in King William Street, Strand, and was standing in the middle of the road to hail a passing hansom cab when without the least warning he received a violent blow from behind on the head, which temporarily dazed him. Partially recovering, he turned round and saw a stout gentleman flourishing a stick, executing a sort of war-dance and hurling insults at him. As it was too dark to make out the features of his assailant, he supposed him to be an escaped lunatic, and, not wishing to have his skull cracked by another blow, he closed with the fellow. A period of ineffectual buffeting and pummelling followed, varied by several

[1] *Truth*, September 25, 1879.

clumsy passes of stick and umbrella, and at length
they were pulled apart by certain members of the
crowd that had gathered to witness the demonstration.
Not till then did Labby realise that he had been
'engaged in single combat with the editor of the *Daily
Telegraph*'.

'You insult me, you insult my family, you insult
my uncle!' raved Mr. Levy-Lawson.

Most of the crowd were anxious for the fight to
continue; it was not often that they were treated to a
gladiatorial show provided free by the respectable
classes; but others regarded the exhibition as disreputable and stood between the gladiators. One lady
held on to them in turns, crying out:

'My dears, don't go a-fighting like this, or you'll
hurt yourselves.'

On which a male bystander, who was sucking at a
pipe, removed it and observed:

'*They* hurt themselves! They don't know how
to!'

At last Mr. Levy-Lawson uttered a final threat,
turned away and walked towards the Beefsteak Club.
Labby followed him.

'Don't, sir, follow me!' said Levy-Lawson.

'I have as much right to the street as you,' answered
Labby.

They went into the club separately. When Labby
entered the main room, several members were present
and Levy-Lawson was standing by the fireplace.

'Do not insult me here,' barked Levy-Lawson.

'You seem to forget we are in a club,' returned Labby
softly.

Levy-Lawson then went to the far end of the room,
made a final remark to Labby, 'I thrashed you at the
door of the Club,' and disappeared. Labby afterwards
learnt that his own movements in the club prior to the
assault had been watched and reported to Lawson by
two of the latter's friends, who had then witnessed

the fight in the street; and that therefore the club had been used for an ambuscade.

The same night one of Lawson's friends suggested a duel in Belgium and a proposal to that effect reached Labby, who was quite agreeable and sent to Lawson for the address of a friend who would act for him. All the next day Lawson was talking wildly about what he would do to the dog who, etc., and it was generally understood that a duel would take place. 'For one whole day,' wrote Labby in *Truth*, 'Bobadil vapoured like a very Hector. Then his courage, like that of Bob Acres, oozed out.' In other words, the outraged representative of the Levy family was transformed by degrees into the cautious proprietor of the *Daily Telegraph*, and at 6 p.m. his 'second' had to make the desolating confession: 'My man won't fight.' Instead, Lawson wrote to tell Labby that he despised him too much to risk his own life in a duel, that he had thrashed him once and would thrash him again, and that Labby had better apply for protection to a police magistrate. 'I should as soon think of applying to a police magistrate to protect me from an irate jelly-fish,' was Labby's comment in his paper. But he also dealt very fully with his antagonist by letter, which he printed in *Truth* in case Lawson mislaid his copy. Explaining why he was not able to put up a better defence when attacked from behind in the dark, he said: 'I had not probably had your experience as a child in gutter warfare.' He called Lawson a 'sneaking dastard' and accused him of cowardice for first assaulting him, then proposing a duel and then backing out of it. To the charge that he had insulted Lawson's family, he replied that Lawson himself had insulted it: 'The man who for no cause, except that he despises his father's honest name, abjures it, commits to my mind a very despicable act.' The real reason for all the trouble was, however, made manifest by Labby in the following passage:

'As regards yourself, I consider you a disgrace to
journalism. I respect alike Conservatives and Liberals. But you are a base servile wretch who, when
Mr. Gladstone was in power, sneaked up the
Liberal backstairs and hung about in the lobbies
of the House of Commons to pick up crumbs of
quasi-official information that might be pecuniarily
useful to you. In the hopes of currying favour, you
bespattered Mr. Gladstone with slavish adulation.
No sooner, however, was he out of office than you
commenced to attack him in a vein of scurrilous
and mendacious vilification which excited the disgust not only of those who, like me, regard that
eminent man with feelings of deep respect, but of
those most bitterly hostile to his political views,
whilst at the same time you denounced as traitors
many eminent statesmen because they declined to
rat opportunely with you. So long as you publish
articles in which you speak of yourself as "the nation"
and as "the nation" vilify and malign those before
whom you formerly cringed, so long shall I continue
to inform the public who the person is that arro-
gates to himself the right to speak with grandiose
impersonality as the representative of the entire
country. In doing so I am convinced that I am
engaged in a most useful task.'[1]

Such comments could have but one result, as
Labby knew, and a week later he published this:

'I believe the man to be an exceptional coward.
He has now selected his course. On last Saturday
I received a summons to appear at the Guildhall to
answer the charge of having libelled him.'

He duly appeared before Sir Robert Carden, who
expressed the wish that *pendente lite* they should ignore
one another in print and person. To make sure of
having his case presented in as favourable a light as

[1] *Truth,* October 9, 1879.

possible, Mr. Levy-Lawson retained the Attorney-General, the Solicitor-General, the Senior Counsel to the Treasury, the Junior Counsel to the Treasury, Serjeant Ballantine (the most famous cross-examining counsel of the age) and three or four of the minor legal fry. To make certain of having his case presented in the only possible light, Labby retained 'Labby'.

Unfortunately Mr. Levy-Lawson did not keep to the spirit of Sir Robert Carden's advice and an article appeared in the *Daily Telegraph* which, while ostensibly dealing with the Langtry libel case, reflected throughout on *Truth*. A month later Labby was defending one of his numerous actions, a lengthy account of which appeared in the *Telegraph*. 'I really cannot too fervently express my thanks to Mr. Levy-Lawson for the kind interest he takes in the most trifling affair in which my name appears,' wrote Labby, who now proceeded to take his gloves off; and throughout the eighteen months that elapsed between his appearance at the Guildhall and the commencement of the case before the Court of Queen's Bench he frequently referred to both Lawson and the *Telegraph*, calling the latter 'The Daily Levy'. Here are a few characteristic passages:

'That eminent political sage, Mr. Levy-Lawson.'

'Even in regard to dogs "The Daily Levy" cannot write without making absurd mistakes.'

'As "The Daily Levy" has not published an article on the 70th birthday of Gladstone, I supply the omission by republishing its article upon the 60th birthday of that eminent man.' (Which he did. The article was of course highly laudatory and expressed the wish of the entire nation that Mr. Gladstone should have many years of public life before him.)

'*Tout arrive*, says Talleyrand. Levy-Lawson has managed to pick up one or two invitations to official *omnium gatherums* by donning the livery of successive ministries, but it would now appear that he aspires to effect an entrance into Buckingham Palace, for of late this abject waiter upon Providence has never lost an opportunity to grovel at the foot of the throne.'

'For arrant gushing twaddle commend me to an article in "The Daily Levy" of to-day upon the feelings of the wife of one of the men who was saved from the Penycraig mining accident. . . . Is nothing to be held sacred by these ghouls on the search for some incident on which to hang the sensational trash that they publish for the benefit of housemaids?'

Labby also attacked 'The Daily Levy' for publishing 'foul advertisements at a fancy price'; but as the attempt of the Levy family to dictate to the country, coupled with their abuse of Mr. Gladstone, was one of the causes that had rallied the Liberal Party and brought it back to power in 1880, he felt that they deserved some reward:

'Public morality renders it impossible to confer any dignity either upon Joseph Moses Levy or "my son Ted" after the exposure of nasty advertisements being charged exceptionally high prices in "The Daily Levy" – otherwise I should have suggested that a knighthood or a trifle of that sort be bestowed either on the father or the son on account of their services to the Liberal Party.'

In short, Labby's general policy during the period that preceded the hearing of the case was contained in the phrase with which he closed one of his attacks: 'My eye is on you, Levy.'

Meanwhile he had been engaged in controversy with the Beefsteak Club. He wrote to the committee complaining that Lawson and another member had used the club for the purpose of carrying out the assault and that Lawson had announced in the club that he had thrashed Labby. The committee replied that a special meeting would be called to consider the complaint and that in the meantime he must promise not to attack any member of the club in print. At the special meeting it was resolved that both Labby and Lawson should be called upon to resign. Both at first refused, though Lawson eventually did so. Labby wrote:

> 'I am not aware that I have done "anything injurious to the welfare and interest of the Club". I must therefore decline to act upon this resolution.'

He called attention to the differences between himself and Lawson, stated the facts respecting the assault, denied that the committee had any right to take notice of what happened in the public journals, and concluded:

> 'I feel that, were I to resign, I should be sacrificing the rights of any independent member of the Club, and the rights of the Club itself; that I should be establishing a precedent by which a Press censorship is established; that I should be admitting that the misconduct of one member may so react upon another that such misconduct can be used as a means for forcing the innocent as well as the guilty member to resign. I must therefore respectfully decline to deprive myself of the pleasure of occasions to meet the many agreeable gentlemen both on and not on the committee, who collectively form the Beefsteak Club.'

Sterner measures had to be taken to meet the challenge of this recalcitrant member. A general meeting of the club was called, presided over by the Earl of Wharncliffe, and by a majority of one the members voted in favour of Labby's expulsion. But they did not know their Labby, who instantly appealed to the

E

law and entered a motion 'for an injunction to restrain the defendants, the committee of the Beefsteak Club, from interfering with the enjoyment by the plaintiff as a member of the club of the use and benefit of the club, and the buildings and property thereof'. The case was argued on November 28, 1879, before Sir George Jessel, Master of the Rolls, who, in giving judgment, indulged in one of those lengthy rigmaroles so dear to the judicial heart, but which, boiled down, came to this: that the committee had acted without making sufficient inquiry into the pros and cons of the case and that Mr. Henry Labouchere should be reinstated as a member of the club.

Such episodes were, however, of trifling significance compared with the arraignment of Labby on a criminal charge, when the case of 'The Queen v. Labouchere and Wyman' came before the Lord Chief Justice (Coleridge) and a special jury on Friday, March 18, 1881. For the Prosecution: Sir Hardinge Giffard, Q.C., Sir John Holker, Q.C., Serjeant Ballantine, Mr. Holl, Q.C. and Mr. Poland. For the Defence: Charles Russell on behalf of Wyman, the printer of *Truth*; while Labby conducted his own case.

Sir Hardinge Giffard opened the case for the Prosecution and said that Levy-Lawson had been on good terms with Labouchere until the latter wrote some articles in *The World* wherein the Levy family was held up to scorn. After that Levy-Lawson dissociated himself from Labouchere, but when the obituary notice of Lionel Lawson appeared in *Truth* it was more than his nephew could stand and he assaulted the writer of it. The case for Lawson was argued with considerable ability by Sir Hardinge, but by placing Edmund Yates in the witness-box Labby had no difficulty in disposing of the assertion that he had defamed the Levy family in *The World*. However his chief object, as we know, was a political one; he wished to discredit Levy-Lawson as a representative spokesman of the English people, and this is how he commenced the cross-examination:

'Now, may I understand that your name was Levy?'

'It was.'

'You bore that name until when?'

'Five years ago, I think.'

'You were married under that name?'

'I was.'

'You are, I think, of the Hebrew persuasion, are you not?'

'I am.'

'You have always been?'

'Always.'

'Were you married as a Hebrew?'

(*After some hesitation.*) 'I was married in church.'

'A Christian church?'

'Yes.'

'Then your father, I believe, is a member of the Hebrew persuasion?'

'Yes.'

'And your uncle?'

'He was.'

'Your whole family are, I believe?'

'Yes.'

'When did you take the name of Lawson?'

'I think in 1875.'

'Was it a name borne by any other member of your family except your uncle?'

'It was a name which he took years ago, as I have always understood, from a friend who left him property, but I have no information distinctly on the subject.'

'Do you swear to the best of your belief that a friend had left him property?'

'I have always heard so.'

'Did you ever hear who he was?'

'No.'

'Did your uncle never speak of this friend?'

'No.'

'Did you never out of curiosity ask your uncle why he had taken this name?'

'No.'

'Or who this friend was?'

'No.'

'Did you ever ask your father?'

'No.'

'Is it in your knowledge that your father knows?'

'No.'

'You had not the slightest curiosity?'

'Not the least.'

'Then from whom had you understood that he had taken it from a friend who had left him money?'

'I had generally heard it stated.'

'But how generally? The statements didn't float about in the air, did they?' (*Laughter.*)

'I have always taken it as my general impression. I did not inquire.'

'Well, who stated it to you?'

'I cannot call to mind the particular people's names, but I know that it was generally believed round about me.'

'Round about you! I don't quite know what you mean by round about you. Was it the general belief of any particular member of your family?'

'I cannot answer that.'

'But whose general belief was it?'

'In my family.'

'Well, give me the name of some member of your family who stated to you at any time that he entertained that impression.'

'My father stated it to me.'

'But you swore that he did not.'

'No. I beg your pardon, I did not say that. I have a general impression that he did so.'

'Well, you are not prepared to swear that he did?'

'Not explicitly.'

'Then I may take it that the origin of this floating idea was an impression on your mind that there was an impression on your father's mind – ' (*Much laughter.*)

'I have made you the only answer I can.'

'Then you accept the conclusion I have drawn from your answers?'

Levy-Lawson did not make an audible reply but presumably gave a sign of assent, for Labby said, 'You do.' The cross-examination proceeded:

'Was there that impression upon the mind of anyone else of your family?'

'I don't know.'

'Then what did you mean by the expression floating about or round about you?'

No answer.

'Then in point of fact, I may take it that you have not the remotest idea of why your uncle took the name of Lawson?'

'Not distinctly.'

'Then you have no idea. Was no allusion made to that person by Mr. Lionel Lawson?'

'Not to me or to anyone that I know of.'

'Then I may take it that, so far as the family knew, this was a fancy alias taken by your uncle?'

'I have no doubt whatever that he complied with the law in everything that he did in reference to changing his name, and that therefore your term "fancy alias" would not apply.'

The Lord Chief Justice: 'The law requires no particular agency for changing names.'

'Then,' continued Labby, 'your uncle complied with the law because the law required him to do nothing' (*laughter*) 'and one day he suddenly appeared in the midst of his family and said, "Call me Lawson instead of Levy"?'

'No such incident is within my recollection.'

The cross-examination continued for some time,

Labby trying to make Levy-Lawson remember how old he was when his uncle changed his name. At last the Lord Chief Justice interrupted with:

'If you have done with the uncle, Mr. Labouchere, we will adjourn.'

'We have not quite done with the uncle, my lord, but I do not think we should object to some refreshments,' answered Labby.

After lunch Labby continued with the family history and wishing to discover why the nephew had taken his uncle's name he eventually obtained a statement from Levy-Lawson that he had 'a general impression' his uncle would leave him money in his will.

'These general impressions seem peculiar to your family, if you will excuse me saying so,' said Labby amidst laughter. 'Did you obtain that impression from him?'

'I did.'

'But how did you obtain it from him if he never told you so? Was it from his looks?' (*Laughter.*)

'It was from general conversation.'

Labby then wanted to know how much Lionel Lawson had left: 'Did he leave two millions sterling all told?'

'Let me see, what was it?' said Levy-Lawson reflectively.

'What! Don't you remember even that?' asked Labby. 'Can't you give it me within a million?' (*Great laughter.*) 'What was the general impression of your family about it?'

Later in the trial, in order to prove to the jury that he had taken his uncle's name for a very good reason Levy-Lawson got his counsel to ask him a question.

'I am reluctant to ask you this question,' said Sir John Holker, 'but was your uncle a bachelor?'

'He was,' replied Levy-Lawson.

'And you were made trustee for his son?'

'I was.'

Very delicately conveyed, but Labby did not fail to remark in his final speech that Levy-Lawson's position as sole legitimate representative of the family could have been authenticated in a manner still more delicate.

At one point in the cross-examination Levy-Lawson contradicted himself and Labby appealed to the judge for confirmation of this.

'I must not let you cross-examine me, Mr. Labouchere,' replied Lord Coleridge, 'for I am no match for you.'

Having got the family question firmly fixed in the jury's minds, and as he hoped in the minds of the British public, Labby dealt with the assault:

'When I came out of the club, where were you?'

'On the pavement. You walked down the street and I followed you and called you by name.'

'And then what happened?'

'I said "Henry Labouchere", and you turned round and we stood face to face. I then told you that you were a liar and a coward, purposely keeping my hands down.'

'Why?'

'Because I wanted you to have a fair chance to do anything to me for making that remark.'

'But you came there to assault me?'

'But not in a cowardly manner. I kept my hands down sufficiently long for you to have knocked me down three times over, but you did nothing.'

'Did you expect me to knock you down?'

'I expected you to try.'

'You think that if you wish to assault anyone, you ought to walk up to him, put your hands down, and leave him time to knock you down three times?' remarked Labby, while the court showed its appreciation of the picture with a burst of laughter.

The hearing was resumed on Monday, March 21, and Labby's cross-examination of Levy-Lawson was

continued. This time he took the witness phrase by
phrase through the obituary notice which had inspired the assault, and Levy-Lawson objected to it
phrase by phrase. He would not even pass the harmless suggestion that Lionel Lawson was not a man to
fling money about:

'I object to the observation that he would have given
you £5 if he really thought it would have saved your
life.'

'Do you complain of that on the ground that it was
too much?' inquired Labby, to the great amusement
of the court.

Labby next went into the question of the objectionable advertisements of quacks, baby-farmers, etc.,
which had appeared in the *Daily Telegraph*; but in
spite of the fact that Levy-Lawson's attention had
been drawn to them by W. T. Stead in the *Pall Mall
Gazette* and Labby's own remarks in *Truth*, the witness refused to admit that he knew anything about
them. The business side of the paper, he said, was
entirely in the hands of his father. Labby's comment
on this in his speech was received with roars of merri-
ment:

'You remember how Abraham was going to sacrifice
his son Isaac,' said he, 'but here Isaac is sacrificing
Abraham.'

On the third day of the trial Labby dealt with what
was to him the gist of the whole business. He read
extracts from the *Daily Telegraph* in which Beaconsfield was first vilified and then eulogised and in which
Gladstone was first eulogised and then vilified.

'You did not obtain from the Conservative Government any prior information?' he asked.

'I do not know what you mean by prior information,'
Levy-Lawson answered.

'Then you are the only man on the press who does
not,' was Labby's dry remark.

However he could not get Levy-Lawson to admit

that he had benefited by changing his party, and indeed Labby hardly expected to obtain such an admission. But having exposed the origin of the man who pretended, on behalf of the English public, to judge Gladstone, he now wished to expose the ignorance of the man who dared to judge Gladstone's Eastern Policy.

'Where is Epirus?' he asked.

'In Greece,' Levy-Lawson answered.

'In the kingdom of Greece?'

But Levy-Lawson quickly noted from Labby's manner that he had made a wrong shot, decided not to be led further into error, and made no reply.

'Is it in the kingdom of Greece?' Labby persisted.

'My lord, I decline to answer,' said Levy-Lawson, appealing to the judge: 'it is an attempt to create laughter and I decline to answer.'

The Lord Chief Justice ruled that Mr. Labouchere had a right to ask.

'Well,' continued Labby good-naturedly, 'Epirus shall be taken to be in Greece. Where is Thessaly?'

A pause.

'I decline to go on with this,' said Levy-Lawson.

'My lord, I must go on with these questions,' insisted Labby.

'He declines to answer,' objected the judge.

'Then I may take it that he don't know,' said Labby. 'How far is the Bosphorus from the Dardanelles?'

'I decline to answer.'

'I'll ask you a very simple question: how far is Constantinople from Egypt?'

'I decline to answer.'

'How far is Constantinople from Odessa?'

'I decline to answer.'

'Is the Black Sea north or south of the Caspian Sea?'

'I decline to answer.'

'Do you know where the Aegean Sea is?'

E*

'I decline to answer.'

'What were the terms of the Treaty of Paris after the Crimean War with regard to the Black Sea?'

'I decline to answer.'

'Where is Merv – in what part of Turkey?'

'I decline to answer.'

'Do you mean to tell me that you do not know in what part of Turkey Merv is?'

'I decline to answer.'

'Do you know where Herat is?'

'I decline to answer.'

'Do you know where Cabul is?'

'I decline to answer.'

'How many passes are there, are there two or four, leading from British India into Afghanistan?'

'I don't know. I decline to answer.'

The Lord Chief Justice interposed: 'There may be a great many things which you know and others which you do not know. Why do you not say so?'

'If I were more skilled as a witness I might make the reply you suggest,' replied Levy-Lawson, 'but when these things are put for the purpose of laughter I decline to answer.'

'I am putting these questions to Mr. Lawson relatively to the assertion that he differed from Mr. Gladstone on the Eastern Question,' explained Labby.

'You have a right to ask the questions,' agreed the Lord Chief Justice.

'And if he will not answer, I must take it that he does not know.' (To witness): 'Do you know to whom I referred in a paragraph of the libel when I spoke of Dr. Franklin?'

'I do not recollect it.'

'Does the name of Dr. Franklin recall to you an eminent man?'

'I do not recollect that it does.'

'Do you know of any eminent man of the name of Dr. Franklin?'

'I do not recollect.'

'Does the name recall to your mind any eminent man?'

'No, I do not recollect.'

Labby had now, so far as he cared, achieved his object. It would not be his fault if the people of England continued to be impressed by editorials inspired by Mr. Levy-Lawson. But he continued to cross-examine the other witnesses with care. One of them, G. O. Phillips, who had married Levy-Lawson's sister, had connived at the assault and witnessed it:

'Would you like to know the reason why he stated he intended to thrash you?' he demanded of Labby.

'We don't want to lengthen this case unnecessarily,' was Labby's pleasant retort.

For more than a week the case went on and every day the court was packed to the doors. One day the spectators experienced the thrill of seeing Mr. Gladstone in the witness-box, giving evidence in support of Labby's assertion that the *Daily Telegraph* had put an entirely false construction on a letter written by the Prime Minister. The assaults on Labby by Abbott, Farini and Wybrow Robertson were all dragged up by the prosecution in order to make him seem like a glorified 'rough' whose mere appearance was sufficient to justify extreme measures; but the worst that could be proved against him was that in a light-hearted seasonable spirit he had ridiculed the Levy family in the Christmas number of *Truth*, and he was quite astonished to hear that they resented such harmless fun. He, on the other hand, had every reason to complain of the nauseating sentimental stuff about love, mangers, self-sacrifice and crosses that was turned out by the *Daily Telegraph* at Christmas and Easter; for it was all part of the policy of a man who was ashamed of his race.

Labby's speech in his own defence was a masterly summary of his behaviour, which had been dictated entirely by Levy-Lawson's denunciations of Gladstone.

He was able to show that the attacks on the characters
of John Bright and Gladstone which had appeared in
the *Telegraph* were quite as exceptionable as his attack
on Levy-Lawson; and it was, he said, 'a very undesirable thing that a newspaper that had been so anxious
in the interests of Turkey should have as its proprietors
the persons who would most have profited if their views
about English aid to Turkey had been carried out'.
When he sat down there was an attempt at applause,
sternly checked by the Lord Chief Justice.

The jury disagreed and Labby was released on his
own recognisances, apparently remaining in that condition for the rest of his life.  As he passed through
Westminster Hall after the trial he was loudly cheered.

'I am perfectly satisfied with the result of the trial
in which I have unwillingly been forced to play a
part during the past week,' he wrote in the next
number of *Truth*, 'and I hope that Mr. Levy-Lawson
is equally satisfied.  The issue raised by the plea
was whether the aforesaid Levy-Lawson was a
coward and a disgrace to journalism. . . .  The Lord
Chief Justice stated that the jury "were as nearly
as possible equally divided" and therefore dis-
charged it.  Six men, therefore, it would appear,
out of twelve, taken by hazard from the inhabitants
of the county of Middlesex, held that the plea had
been proved. . . .  My mission is now fulfilled.  The
WE of the *Daily Telegraph* had acquired a fictitious
influence by impudent bombast and by pretentious
assertion.  I weakened this influence by the very
simple expedient of showing who this WE really
was who aspired to be the Autocrat of our breakfast-
tables. . . .  The circulation of the *Daily Telegraph*
has gone down since I took its editor and its proprietor in hand about 50,000, according to Mr.
Lawson's own evidence. . . .  The *Daily Levi* as a
political organ has lived.  R.I.P.'

For more than a year after the conclusion of the case Levy-Lawson received sharp reminders that Labby's eye was still on him, but by the end of 1882 all references to the *Daily Telegraph* ceased, for Labby was by that time absorbed in political business. The future career of Levy-Lawson has been described as 'one of the romances of modern journalism'. He went from strength to strength. Becoming High Sheriff of Buckinghamshire in 1886, he was created a baronet in 1892, and for the last twelve years of his life was a Justice of the Peace and Deputy Lieutenant of the county. He purchased Edmund Waller's old home, Hall Barn, near Beaconsfield, where King Edward VII visited him yearly. As the founder of the *Daily Telegraph* Shilling Funds, on behalf of national and charitable causes, he secured the esteem of many. His friends spoke of him as a genial, kind-hearted man, 'a rattling good fellow', and Lord Northcliffe described him as 'the best journalist of us all'. He was raised to the peerage as Baron Burnham in 1903, and died in 1916.

But we must close the story of Labby's dealings with the future Lord Burnham on a domestic note. Shortly after the trial Labby met a friend, who congratulated him on the result.

'Thank you. But how remarkable is the instinct of animals!' was the unexpected reply.

'Animals? What on earth have they to do with it?'

'You know my dog?' said Labby.

'Yes.'

'Then you may remember that every morning he goes to the station to fetch my newspapers. Well, you will hardly credit it, but ever since the trial started he has refused to bring home the *Daily Telegraph*.'

# CHAPTER VIII

## THE CHRISTIAN MEMBER

'I THINK future generations will care uncommonly little about what we are saying at the present time. Future generations will not care to look back at our debates, and I think that even if they do we ought not to minister to their folly.'

These words were spoken in the House of Commons by Henry Labouchere during a discussion on the cost of printing parliamentary debates, and he would certainly have agreed with many modern readers that there are few things so tedious as the politics of the past. The business of politics is simply the business of housekeeping on a large scale, though politicians would like us to believe that theirs is a 'calling', a skilled profession, requiring some very special aptitude and ability in the practitioner. Labby knew better than that. Feeling that politics ought to be at least a serious and honest occupation, he found that when it degenerated into party-politics it became a dishonest if amusing game, in which a number of men whose brains should have been better employed were engaged in the silly business of obtaining distinctions or the shady business of getting money. Being a realist he made the best of the situation, working steadily for the reforms he knew to be necessary and finding much entertainment in watching the grown-up children who were playing the game.

'Who is the ordinary minister after all?' he once asked the House. 'He is a very common third-rate sort of person, who may fill a place in the city, but could hardly be called a statesman. He is perhaps a good administrator; he does not get into mischief in this House, and performs his duty, which may be somewhat subordinate, requiring no vast amount of intelligence, to the satisfaction of the House.' He also asserted that the position of Leader of the House could be filled by a postman who received 16s. a week, with a possible rise to 25s. Things have changed since his time. Nowadays many politicians qualify in the House for 'a place in the city'.

Although most of his later life was spent in politics, it is impossible to think of Labby primarily as a politician. His was much too various a character to be confined to such a profession. Indeed it may be said that no great man, no remarkable character, is ever associated in the public mind with his profession, except of course the great artist who reflects and enriches life; the point being that every profession apart from the artist's is a restrictive influence on life, and, in so far as it operates on personality, debars its followers from self-expression. This is proved by the fact that when a critic wishes to belittle a great man he adopts the subtle strategy of praising him for skill in his profession, as when Mr. Hilaire Belloc harps on the brilliance of Cromwell as a cavalry leader. But no genius can be caged in a profession and when a man is chiefly remembered for his achievements as a politician, a soldier, a clergyman, and so on, it is usually safe to assume that he was not a genius.

Labby, in his curious and rather negative way, was a genius; at least he was something very much more remarkable than a politician; and so there is no need for us to follow him through the political intrigues of his time. Besides, this is a biography, not a history, and the biographer who writes a 'Life and Times' is mistaking his function; he should leave the 'Times' to the historian. Certain aspects of Labby were, however, more clearly seen in the House of Commons than elsewhere and to throw light on them it will occasionally be necessary to speak of his political background; remembering always that, for this book, his character is more important than the destinies of England.

I

Firstly, since strongly-held opinions reflect something of a man's nature, we must briefly survey Labby's radicalism.    Perhaps he never expressed his outlook better than in the phrase: 'My idea of a government is that it should interfere as little as possible with human liberty.'    And with regard to Great Britain: 'Political liberty we have but we make up for it by abrogating all social liberty.'    As a firm believer in individual freedom, he frequently shocked the House of Commons by telling it that revolutions were occasionally necessary: 'I have always been in favour of revolution when people have not got their rights and are unable to obtain them by constitutional means.' He described the taking of the Bastille as one of the noblest deeds in history, 'a deed which was for the benefit of the whole human race'.    On general principles he favoured rebellion: 'Who would now be called the greatest man in the United States?    Why, Washington.    And who is known as the greatest man in England?    Hampden.'    Law and order were no doubt admirable things in their way, but they should not be bracketed together, because the worst disorders that ever occurred in the world were due to laws — unjust laws:

'The Emperor of Russia had transported half the people of Poland on the plea of maintaining law and order there.    The Emperor Napoleon was never tired of saying that he wished to maintain law and order whenever he wanted to transport French people to Cayenne. Charles I wanted to maintain law and order, and the people, most properly, cut his head off. James II wanted to maintain law and order and he was turned out of the country.'

He was not in any sense of the word an idealist; he did not believe in the perfectibility of man. Although he regarded a republic as the best form of government, he did not, as Joseph Chamberlain once did, openly advocate a republic for England. Until the people were worthy of a republic they did not deserve one: a republic for republicans was his motto. For the same reason he was against socialism:

'Socialists are very well-meaning sort of people. . . . Their plan, however, is only suited to a state of things where every man would do his duty. . . . If I am alive when the millennium comes, and we have all become angelic, I am by no means sure that I shall not become a socialist. As it is, I am not one, for I am perfectly certain that the theory would break down in practice.'

In the matter of government he wished to see the local questions of each parish and each county dealt with by local assemblies, so that parliament could devote itself to legislation and the supervision of expenditure. He thought it irrational that a democracy should be governed by a 'class'; the people should have control of everything: that is to say, the heads of all the parish and county assemblies should displace the territorial aristocracy as magistrates, large holdings of land should be prohibited, the number of small freeholders should be enormously increased and given fixity of tenure, the game laws should be abolished, the Church of England should be disestablished and disendowed, the House of Lords should be done away with, and all men should be 'so far equal that neither political nor social pre-eminence will be given to any class'. He was one of the first to advocate payment of M.P.s, his reason being that until poor men could afford to enter parliament the poor would never be represented. He wished to destroy privilege of class and creed, then as now rampant throughout the country, though since his day the privilege of aristocracy has given place to that of plutocracy

'I would make the future of the people dependent on the goodwill of no man, whether peer or commoner. To attain their due and to maintain that due when attained, they should trust alone to themselves.'

It was the primary duty of the state to see that its citizens were well paid and to provide for the unemployed. He was the first, and so far the only, politician to realise that the so-called problem of unemployment could not be solved; he saw that it would become more and more acute with the improvement of machinery:

'It seems to me that in a community which aspires to the title of a civilised one some organised provision should be made for those who must always be deprived of their livelihood when machinery takes the place of human labour. . . . It is a disgrace to us that the humblest and weakest members of the community should suffer for every step that is made in the progress of industrial development.'

There is even a foretaste of the Douglas Credit Scheme in his remark that the state ought to establish stores where articles of primary necessity should be sold at cost price, and

'a minimum wage ought to be laid down by the state – but a man is worth more than this minimum wage and if he chooses to work overtime I see no reason why he should not do so'.

Knowing that his perfectly reasonable views were regarded as utopian, he attacked the ranks of privilege and bigotry on minor issues whenever he got the chance. Old Age Pensions, he urged, should be given to everyone at the age of sixty. When the Attorney-General got up in the House and said it would be cruel to make a man sell a famous old family picture in order to pay the death duty on the sum for which it was assessed, Labby remarked:

'The man would be a perfect fool not to sell it. I have always regarded Charles Surface as a most sensible man because he sold his ancestors. Unfortunately I have no ancestors to sell, but if I had I should sell them at once.'

On the subject of rent he also told the tories an unpleasant truth:

'The landlord has not an absolute right to rent from his land. The only right he possesses is either to cultivate it himself or to see that it is cultivated by others, and this right should lapse after a certain time if the land is not cultivated. Some hon. gentlemen opposite seem to think that they have a divine right to rent; but rent is only the margin that is left after payment of the taxes due to the state and after the cultivator has been enabled to live and thrive on the land.'

He further declared that to talk of the natural proprietary rights in land was

'as absurd as it would be to talk of a man having a natural property in the air that we breathe'.

On another occasion he held out a threat which impressed his opponents because it would have interfered with the shooting season:

'I shall be ready to sit until October or November

in order that the Education Bill may be passed and the great radical principle of free education be granted to the country.'

The Established Church was a constant object of his scorn. Most of its members were tories first and christians next. It owned vast properties which by rights should have belonged to the nation. 'Let each sect sit like a hen on its own eggs and hatch them, and not use the state as a sort of incubator to hatch its own sectional eggs.' That was his view, and as the Church of England wallowed in profits at the expense of believers and unbelievers alike he was always urging disestablishment and disendowment. On points of doctrine he did not distinguish between the various beliefs. 'I respect all religions equally,' he said, which was his way of saying that he respected none. 'I have no objection to any man in the world believing in anything he pleases,' he further declared, with no doubt the mental addition, 'if he wishes to be such an ass as to believe in anything'. And when the question of the burial of nonconformists in Anglican church-yards was discussed, he declared: 'I am in favour of religious equality not only above but below the sod,' which for some recondite reason the House of Commons received with cries of 'Oh! Oh!'

When speaking against alien immigration on the ground that, by taking less wages and living like pigs, aliens lowered the standard of livelihood among English workers, he objected to the prejudice against 'Jewish aliens'. It was a trade question, not a religious one. 'I do not care whether these aliens arrive with the Koran, the Talmud or the 39 Articles of the Church of England in their pockets,' he announced. In a debate on Woman's Suffrage a member was speaking in favour of giving the vote to women and said that the most stupid argument urged against it was that women were so easily subjected to improper influences. 'Now I should very much like to know what these influences are,' said the speaker in tones of irony.

'The Church,' interjected Labby.

He was, by the way, quaintly old-fashioned in his attitude to female enfranchisement, which inspired his least Labbylike pronouncements. Even Queen Victoria must have felt she had misjudged him when she read such opinions as these:

'We place women on a social pedestal and I object to bringing them down into the sordid arena of politics. We should thereby destroy all the amenities of existence . . . I am one of the advocates of the domestic angel doctrine in regard to women. It would be destructive of all the charms of domesticity if women were given votes. . . . For 6,000 to 7,000 years every intelligent man has held the views which I entertain. . . . I shall oppose all attempts to break down the barrier which nature has placed between men and women. I believe I am supported by the vast majority of women in this country.'

The barrier has since been broken down, but as the marriage-rate has gone up one can only assume that domesticity has not lost its charms.

Labby did not confine his criticisms to the Established Church. One of his bugbears was the Nonconformist Conscience. In those days people paid a lot of attention to the raving pastors of the Free Churches, for whom Christianity was merely another name for misery and whose highest conception of happiness was a chat about Jesus over a cup of tea. Their main spiritual stand-by was a Sunday of such soul-subduing dismalness that for want of better entertainment the people flocked to hear them denounce the devil and all his works, including man. They were in unusual good spirits when some public man had 'sinned', because then their congregations could gloat with them in vicarious enjoyment of the 'sin', and on such occasions they indulged in orgasms of indignation. When Lord Rosebery became Prime Minister and maintained his interest in the Turf, one of these preachers, Hugh Price Hughes, thundered forth, 'The nonconformist conscience will no longer tolerate a racing Premier,' and for the best part of an hour his listeners were able to enjoy the Derby, as they had so often enjoyed adultery, without leaving their seats. Labby administered a gentle reprimand: 'No public man should be required to do more than so to shape his private life that he does not offend against the generally accepted moral standard of his country-men. This accepted standard does not condemn a man for owning race-horses.' And when W. T. Stead went on the moral warpath, his victim being a prom-inent radical M.P., Labby alone in the press of his time exposed the hypocrisy of the age.

Sir Charles Dilke was supposed to have seduced the young wife of his friend Crawford, a Scottish M.P., who brought an action for divorce and named Dilke as co-respondent. At that time Charles Dilke and Joseph Chamberlain were the two outstanding radicals in parliament and on the resignation of Gladstone one or other of them was almost certain to become leader of the Liberal Party. But in Victorian England a man who was even suspected of familiarity with another man's wife was not considered a fit person to sit on a committee, and although Dilke's guilt was never conclusively proved there was quite enough salacious material in the case to provide the puritans with food for thought. The outcry was great when at the General Election in 1886 Dilke again stood for parliament: he was denounced from pulpits, and W. T. Stead started a press campaign against his candi-dature in the *Pall Mall Gazette*. Labby advised the electors of Chelsea to take no notice of the outcry and to remember that the question before them was not home-breaking in England but Home Rule for Ireland. Thereupon Stead publicly rebuked him for 'cynical immorality' and he hit back in *Truth*. 'I would sooner be cynically immoral than pruriently pure,' he said. Remarking upon the stuff with which Stead filled the columns of his paper – spicy details from the Divorce Court, reports of unnatural crimes, descriptions of assaults on women and so forth – Labby explained:

'It is very difficult to touch Purity without being defiled. . . . Too much Purity has made him mad. . . . His object seems to be to show the world what a very tasty thing Purity is when properly devilled. Poor Sir Charles Dilke has been a perfect godsend to him. Whenever he could find nothing else to "draw" he has trotted out this unfortunate statesman and mixed up an adultery never yet proved with every public question under the sun.'

A few months later the public were savouring another famous scandal and Labby wrote:

'I am of course most anxious not to anticipate in any way the verdict of the jury in the Colin Campbell divorce case . . . but besides the immediate parties to the suit there is the great chaste public of this metropolis and (in view of Mr. Stead's preoccupation with Irish affairs) I feel it incumbent on me to raise my voice and cry aloud that, until Captain Shaw of the Fire Brigade[1] has cleared his character from the "damning charges" (I believe I have the correct expression) only less heinous than an accusation of wilful murder now hanging over him, he shall not be permitted to put out any fires occasioned by the children, servants or paraffin lamps of the pure. Captain Shaw may or may not be guilty; as

[1] Captain Shaw, Chief of the Metropolitan Fire Brigade, who was introduced by Gilbert into *Iolanthe*.

to this I pronounce no opinion. But at present he lies under a cloud and fires are occurring nightly. Not all the water of all the companies' mains will wash out our guilt if we allow the brazen helmet of a man who (guilty or innocent) is at any rate a co-respondent to flaunt itself at a London conflagration. If remonstrance has no effect on Captain Shaw, the Home Secretary must be appealed to. If Mr. Matthews (a Roman Catholic, alas!) declines to act, then the virtuous (or, what is the same thing, the unfound-out) men and women of London must assemble in their thousands in Trafalgar Square and present a monster petition to Her Majesty – in her character of virtuous wife and mother – praying that this scandal be abated. Scarcely a fire takes place that is not attended by large numbers of pickpockets, mostly young lads between 14 and 18, an age peculiarly liable to be led astray by temptations similar to those to which Captain Shaw is alleged to have yielded. For these poor boys we are nationally and individually responsible, and for my part I do not envy the feelings of the man or woman whose pocket-handkerchief or perhaps watch has been stolen by a boy who is not pure. *Maxima reverentia pueris* is a motto never to be forgotten.'[1]

By taste and temperament Labby was spartan. He hated all forms of over-indulgence and described with disgust any exhibitions of 'gormandising and swilling' that he happened to witness. As a boy at Eton he had sampled punch and after the first sip had poured the remainder into a cupboard, much enjoying the look of admiration with which the astonished waiter noted the empty bowl and the still-sober schoolboy. This had given him a lifelong distaste for any form of alcohol and his usual drink was water, varied in the hot weather by skimmed milk.

[1] *Truth*, November 4, ·1886.

When he had to drink alcohol on special occasions, or on the Continent where the water was unsafe and he took diluted wine, he made a wry face. In the matter of temperance, therefore, he found himself in the uncomfortable company of nonconformist fanatics and favoured the system called Local Option, whereby the inhabitants of each locality could decide as to whether the public-houses should be opened on Sundays. Believing in freedom he did not, of course, join a temperance society, because he hated the idea of forcing his own opinions down the throats of those who disagreed with him, but he was a constant advocate of temperance and detested the gin-palaces that were a feature of those days. People were encouraged to get drunk, he said, in order that the trade might flourish. 'What, another Bung got a Beerage?' he remarked when the news that a certain brewer had received a title filtered through to the smoking-room of the Commons.

'I have now a sad confession to make,' he told the House. 'Before I found temperance salvation I was myself a liquor trafficker. I had fallen so low as to occupy the degraded position of a director of a large London brewery. An hon. friend behind me shakes his head. He evidently thinks this impossible in me; but I got some advantage out of it, for I learned the tricks of the trade.'

Yet so strong was his hatred of bigotry that he emphasised the absurdity of being unable to get a drink on Sunday unless one were a bona fide traveller, frequently urged the advisability of encouraging people to drink German lager beer instead of the stuff to which they were accustomed, and never ceased to compare the harmless gaiety of the continental Sunday, its crowded theatres, cafés, and beer-gardens, with the social horror of a British Sabbath, its shut picture-galleries and museums, its empty streets, deserted restaurants and long faces. He had, by the way, a genius for maintaining friendly relations with men whose views he attacked or ridiculed, and so it is not surprising to learn that in spite of his anti-sectarian sentiments he sometimes stayed with Bishop Mandell Creighton, and liked him, sometimes called on Cardinal Manning, and admired him.

With the help of a speech by Labby we may make the transition from his opinion of beer-making to his views on peer-making:

'What sort of people are created peers? I will take a recent instance, that of Sir Henry Allsopp. This gentleman brewed beer and by so doing acquired a fortune. No one could say that he had distinguished himself very much as a politician. No doubt he voted very often for his party in the House of Commons and very likely he subscribed to the Carlton Club. As a consequence he was made a baronet. No one objected to Sir Henry Allsopp or anybody else being made a baronet. It would be almost cruelty to animals to refuse a baronetcy to anyone who asked for it. A baronetcy pleased the gentleman himself and was a matter of perfect indifference to everyone else, except perhaps his wife. I should as soon think of refusing a thistle to a hungry and pleading donkey. But Sir Henry Allsopp was not satisfied with his baronetcy and he was considered worthy of the dignity of a peerage. This affords good cause of complaint, for it gives him and his descendants the hereditary right of legislating for the country. It is often said that the House of Lords is retrograde. This is scarcely surprising. What was the first step Sir Henry Allsopp took when he became a peer? He wrote to *The Times* complaining that he had been described as a brewer and saying that he had ceased brewing; and at a bucolic festival which occurred in the country shortly afterwards, when his tenants congratulated him on being made a peer, some gentleman present suggested that Lord Hindlip (*né* Allsopp) was descended from one of the Plantagenet kings. I have taken this gentleman as an example and do not know whether he has a son. An hon. member near me says that he has a son in this House. Very well. Now will the future Lord Hindlip prove a useful member of the Upper House in connection with commerce? Will he allude to the paternal butt? In all probability he will think a great deal of his Plantagenet ancestors, and the respected vendor of intoxicating liquor to whom he owes his title will be entirely forgotten.'

Labby spent a good deal of his time in proposing resolutions for the abolition of the Upper House, the peculiar mission of which was 'to obstruct and mar and mutilate' every good bill that had been passed by the House of Commons. He suggested that, if it could not be abolished constitutionally, it could be swamped by the creation of radical peers: 'I really believe that, such is the patriotism on the benches behind me, I could easily find three hundred gentlemen who would be willing to ascend the political altar of their country and make the necessary sacrifice.' Indeed, so willing were some of them to make the sacrifice, that when Labby was asked whether he was likely to get a large vote for one of his resolutions against the House of Lords, he replied: 'I think not; you see, most of the radicals want to be peers.'

In those days a large number of tory M.P.s belonged to the aristocracy. One of them, Lord Cranborne, in a speech supporting the hereditary principle, said: 'That a man is the son of his father is the basis of modern society.' The annunciation of this great truth gave some force to Labby's notion of settling the question on a non-party basis: 'All you have to do

is to take five hundred sweeps from the streets of
London and make them into peers.' Another M.P.,
Lord George Hamilton, was defending his brother,
who was in the House of Lords, when Labby rose and
protested: 'Fraternal affection is all very well, but
there are so many gentlemen connected with the
peerage on the Treasury Bench that our debates will
never come to an end if all of them get up and defend
their relations.'

Under ideal conditions, no doubt, a House of Peers
might be useful:

> 'If the functions of an Upper Chamber were to be
> properly fulfilled by those who soared above party
> and class interest, we must not look for its members
> in this world; we must bring down angels from
> heaven. But as that would be difficult there is
> another alternative.'

In a democracy hereditary legislators were an anach-
ronism, an insult, an absurdity and an abomination.
Painters and poets were not hereditary, so why peers?
he asked.

> 'The best cure for those who admire the House of
> Lords is to go and look at it when sitting. On great
> occasions they flock together from all parts of the
> country and sit on their benches like sheep and vote
> like sheep; but on ordinary occasions a visitor will
> find some peer droning forth a speech to half a
> dozen others until, at the approach of the dinner-
> hour, all of them vanish like ghosts.'

To expect to make statesmen out of such material was
as silly as if 'one were to take a lady's lap-dog and breed
it up in a drawing-room in the belief that it would turn
out a good sheep-dog'. As for their much-vaunted
disinterestedness, 'a more self-seeking body of men
does not exist. Since 1855 each duke has had fifty-
six relatives living upon the public exchequer,' and

the peers were always being bribed with offices and distinctions.

'We are told that they save the country from precipitate legislation. It is absurd to talk about the House of Commons being precipitate. Precipitate! Why, it is the longest-winded assembly in the world.'

He did not think the English peers were worse than other aristocracies or other men:

'I have no doubt that if any other class were given such honour it would legislate for itself. I even believe that the best and purest of men – I am alluding to journalists – would do the same. . . . What could be more absurd than to suppose that any single class, when in power, would legislate for anyone but themselves? One might as well, in an assembly of cats and mice, imagine that the cats would legislate in the interests of the mice.'

The subject that brought forth all Labby's powers of invective, mockery and scorn, was war. It was the only subject on which he spoke with strong feeling and bitterness. To him warfare was nothing better than legalised murder and sanctified butchery. Its stupidity was not even funny; which would have been the most damning thing he could have said about anything. Throughout his parliamentary career England was rapidly extending her colonial possessions and spheres of influence, and he must have divided the House about a hundred times on military and naval expenditure. In his view we had no right to spend any more money on armaments than was absolutely necessary for self-defence.

'During the last 150 years,' he informed the House, 'we have been at war with Austria, Russia, Italy, Spain, Portugal, Denmark, Holland and France –

with France four times – but in no one instance had
we gone to war because England was directly or
indirectly attacked. In most cases we went to war
for that mirage, the European equilibrium, and we
have wasted hundreds of millions in these wars.'

And again:

'In every war during the last three centuries we
meddled in matters that did not concern us except
the Spanish Armada, and that was an attack upon
us because of our depredations upon Spanish
commerce.'

In a speech punctuated with ironical laughter, he
explained exactly why wars were made:

'I perfectly understand what all this vast expenditure on armament means. It means that you want
to stem the advance of Liberalism in this country.
(*Laughter.*) The right hon. gentleman laughs.
Surely he has to a certain extent read history. The
game has been played again and again in the world.
Whenever there has been any attempt to advance,
the ruling powers have distracted the attention of
the country by going into a foreign war. I regard
these jingos as utter cowards. They go about the
world swaggering and bragging and then get so
afraid of what will be the consequence that they rush
away and urge the country to spend its money in
further defence.'

So that people should be convinced of the brutality
and stupidity of war, he wanted it to be made as
terrible and as injurious as possible to every human
being of the countries engaged in it. Until everyone
suffered from it in body and pocket, people would
continue to think it noble, wonderful, glorious, etc.,
instead of the despicable, silly thing it really was.
War and foreign politics were not party questions with
him. He was opposed to jingoism, whether of the

liberal or the conservative variety, and in 1898 he supported Lord Salisbury's conciliatory policy in the Far East, just as in 1889 he attacked the liberal policy of interference in the Turkish and Armenian troubles:

'What earthly business is it of ours? I protest against the doctrine that we are to roam all over the world redressing grievances and establishing good government. I am not willing that a farthing of English money be spent or a drop of English blood shed for the purpose of establishing the best of governments for Armenians.'

The business of colouring the map red, which was the main occupation of every leading English politician except Gladstone between 1880 and 1900, found in him a relentless opponent.

'The only thing that would give us a right to annex a country would be the desire of the inhabitants of that country that we should do so,' he told the House when the future of Burma was being debated in '86.

And a year later, when Zululand was being subjected to imperial treatment, he said:

'We are without exception the greatest robbers and marauders that ever existed on the face of the globe. We are worse than other countries because we are hypocrites also, for we plunder and always pretend we do so for other people's good.'

He had little difficulty in smashing the case put forward by annexationists that we were suppressing the Slave Trade in Africa, and he provided evidence that English merchants hired and employed slaves.

'I respect and honour such missionaries as Livingstone who have gone out fearlessly as missionaries only and have not asked this country for Maxim guns, who have killed no one and never called upon the British taxpayer to assist them by railways to get to the place they desire to reach with as little fatigue as possible. . . . It is a dispensation of Providence that Europeans should be unable to live in some parts of Africa. If it were otherwise, so greedy are they that they would either destroy or reduce to servitude the whole African continent and establish themselves there as the masters. . . . I really believe, if the North Pole were discovered, we should have hon. gentlemen opposite insisting on its annexation. People who do not agree with them are traitors or have petty and parochial minds. . . . I have always objected to all these Protectorates and annexations and I mean to do so as long as I am in the House. I know it is said I am a false and base Englishman. . . . We have want and misery here and if we have money to spend it is taken from the mass of the people: let it be spent on the well-being of the mass of the people.'

He complained frequently and indignantly of the barbarity with which we waged our wars of conquest in Africa. Not content with killing the wounded and burning villages in the Egyptian campaign of '98, we even disinterred the body of our former enemy, the Mahdi, and flung it into the Nile. When questioned in the House on the subject, the spokesman for the Government implied that the ritual had been carried out in a dignified manner. On which Labby made this comment:

'The First Lord has said that the head of the Mahdi was not decapitated. Very likely the head was not cut off; I understand it was simply taken from a quantity of bones, and that the rest of the bones were thrown into the Nile. The right hon. gentleman says that was done decorously. But I cannot understand how you can take up a lot of bones decorously and throw them into the river.'

Occasionally he was forced to remind his country-men of their religion:

'I see that some persons are proposing that prayers should be offered up regularly on behalf of our troops in Afghanistan. Seeing that our troops are armed with Martini-Henries and our generals are able to win "decisive victories" at the cost of one or two wounded but with "great slaughter" among the enemy, would it not be Christian-like and magnanimous if someone were to propose that prayers be also offered up for the unfortunate Afghans?'

It is almost certain that if his advice had been taken, when speaking on the Anglo-German Agreement Bill in 1890, there would have been no European War twenty-four years later:

'I am glad that Germany has interposed to prevent the connecting links being made between our north-ern and southern territory in Africa. . . . I am only sorry Germany has not got more (*cries of "Oh!"*) . . . it would be a judicious step to take because it would tend to the security of peace. The more Germany has to look after, the less likely is she to go to war. She seems to want colonies. We have enough. Let Germany have what she wants of these territories and undertake the work of civilisa-tion which that possession will necessitate. We shall have a guarantee that Germany will not attack us because if she does we shall then be enabled to lay hold of the whole of the continent which the Germans may have assisted in civilising at enormous cost. We laid hold of India and took it from the French. We did the same thing as regards America and we have done something like it in most places throughout the world. In fact we are the most thorough-going buccaneers and land-grabbers that

F

ever existed . . . I assert that Africa belongs to the
Africans . . . and we have no more right to the interior
of Africa than has any other country on the globe.'

Nearly half a century has elapsed since that warning
was given, and though several millions of lives have
been lost because it was ignored, we might save
several millions more by heeding it now.  But if, for
the sake of peace in Europe, Labby was anxious to
see Germany take her share of 'the white man's
burden', he did not really believe in the so-called
blessings of civilisation.  Until we could put our own
house in order, until there was freedom and plenty
for every individual in Great Britain, we had no right
to tell other people how to manage their affairs; and
in any case he felt that water closets and Christianity
were poor substitutes for personal liberty and national
independence.

Hating the butchery inseparable from Empire-
building, he was naturally opposed to the huge grants
that were voted in parliament to the leading butchers;
all the more so because the grant was usually made
to support a newly-created title, and he did not see
why the descendants of a man who happened to have
won a battle should be paid handsomely for helping
to misgovern the country.  In opposing the grant of
an annuity to Lord Alcester in '83, he remarked:

'It is not the kindness the Admiral has done the
country that is in question; it is the kindness the
country has done the Admiral in giving him
command of the Fleet.'

In the same year Lord Wolseley was voted £30,000,
and Labby asked:

'Why is a soldier to receive a pension and a statesman not?  Literary men for instance receive nothing
from the country.  If a literary man spent years
and years in works of benefit to his country, and

his wife and family were without means, they were lucky to get £100 per annum doled out as a charity.'

Military grants produced a military spirit, he said, which simply resulted in the violation of a foreign country and the destruction of the homes and happiness of harmless people:

'The artisan and labourer who gallantly fought against want and penury and vanquished them did a far nobler thing than these military people. We have far greater heroes at home.'

He knew why governments were so anxious to make these grants, and when a large sum was voted to Lord Kitchener after the slaughter of Omdurman he hit the nail on the head:

'I have always observed that when some deed of arms has been done the Government which is in power at the time invariably takes an exaggerated view of it, because they consider that, if the deed of arms is creditable, it reflects some special honour on themselves.'

Speaking on the grant to Lord Roberts in 1901, he made an alternative suggestion:

'I have no objection to large sums being voted for the soldiers themselves and for the widows and orphans of those who have fallen. In my opinion it is more desirable that we should distribute money among those unfortunate people who are without the comforts and even the necessaries of life than that we should heap huge sums upon particular individuals.'

As for Lord Roberts, the Government might give him shares in some of the rotten South African mines.

Quite apart from his sense of justice and rational humanitarianism, his natural frugality would have made a radical of Labby. There was a streak of the French peasant in him; he believed in thrift; and so the great radical cry of 'Retrenchment' found in him a doughty champion. Possibly too the blood of French bankers in his veins had more to do with his economical outlook than he would have been disposed to admit. We must not forget that he lived in an age when money was thought to have intrinsic value, when a piece of gold was not looked upon as a credit-counter but was believed, by some mysterious law of nature or economics, to be the embodiment of real wealth. In fact Labby believed in the sovereign power of gold just as his forefathers had believed in the sovereign power of God. It is true that in momentary flashes he saw through the superstition in which he put so much faith; but he would not have understood what one of his own disciples, Reginald McKenna, was talking about when he addressed these words to the share-holders of the Midland Bank: 'I am afraid the ordinary citizen will not like to be told that the banks can, and do, create money.'

Thus Labby advocated economy in the belief that there was a certain rigid and restricted amount of money in the world which, if spent on one thing, could not be spent on another. This belief was shared by all his contemporaries and is held by the vast majority of people to-day, many of whom pride themselves on having shed their illusions. Most of his onslaught on public expenditure concerned the sums voted to the Royal Family, but as these affected Queen Victoria's feelings towards him they will be dealt with in a later chapter. The salaries paid to ministers of the Crown also received his scrutiny and criticism and Gladstone complimented him on being 'a very vigilant guardian of the public purse'. He gave an example of minis-terial affluence:

'The Lord Chancellor receives £6,000 a year as

a judge and £4,000 a year for presiding over the House of Lords; in the first capacity he does nothing, in the second he does very little and the little he does is pernicious.'

But the salaries of all the ministers were too large, according to Labby. How dared they niggle over pence to postmen, he asked, and yet pay themselves such huge sums? Reduce salaries all round, was his advice, and good sound men would soon be at the head of affairs. No state official should receive more than £2000 a year, be he judge, general, admiral or minister, though perhaps the Prime Minister and Foreign Secretary might have an additional £1000 apiece. It was said that ministers had positions to keep up, that they had to give parties. On this point Labby diverted his opponents and irritated his partisans with a story.

He had gone into the lobby to vote with the Government in favour of Bradlaugh taking his seat in the Commons:

'I was standing in the lobby when a gentleman, a well-known radical, came up to me and said "I am sorry to say that my conscience will not allow me to vote in favour of Mr. Bradlaugh." "Well," I said, "the division is to be in five minutes and I have no time to discuss you and your conscience – what do you want? We want votes very badly now, and I do not know why you should not be a knight as well as other people. Do you want a knighthood?" He replied, "You are entirely mistaken in the person you are speaking to." Upon that I rejoined "Do you go to parties? Were you at So-and-so's ministerial party the other day?" "No," said he, "I myself and my family have been very much surprised that we have been left out." I answered at once, "Why did you not tell me? Of course you ought to have gone; you shall go in future; you shall go to all the parties." About five minutes afterwards I took him with me, family, conscience, bag and baggage, into the lobby to vote for my hon. colleague. These people, you know, are anxious to see their names in the *Morning Post* as attending these ministerial entertainments. They like to ask each other "Do you know Lord So-and-so?" and to be able to reply "Oh, no; I do not know him very well; but I have met him in society in such-and-such a place." I must say I object entirely to voting money in order to enable ministers to give those most corrupting parties.'

Though the power of the House of Lords has been curtailed and salaries have been granted to members of parliament, it cannot be said that Labby's influence on the history of reform has been remarkable. But one national benefit must definitely be placed to his credit: after sixty years of persistent agitation, the cabs of the middle classes may now be seen in Hyde Park.

## II

From 1880 to the end of his political career Labby represented Northampton in the House of Commons. Knowing that his constituents were mostly republican-minded cobblers, he tried to help them over the stumbling-block of his name by calling himself 'Citizen Le-Boucher'; but their fraternal feelings were stronger than his; before long they had perceived the man behind the manner and were all calling him 'Labby'. His fellow-member for ten years was Charles Bradlaugh, the famous atheist, who had dared God (if there were a God) to strike him dead inside five minutes at a political meeting. Either there was no God or the Almighty did not favour direct action; at any rate, after a period of suspense, it was agreed that Bradlaugh had scored a point and no one pressed him to extend the time-limit. Like all devout atheists, Bradlaugh was profoundly religious; that is to say, he had a strong sense of duty, took life very seriously, carried on his crusade against religion with fanatical fervour, and denounced the Prophets with sibylline zeal. The idealism of his moral code would have made most professing christians feel thoroughly uncomfortable, and the humility, honesty and benevolence of his every-day behaviour would have shaken their belief in the parochial clergy. The contrast between this bull-necked pugnacious giant with his flashing eyes and fiery tongue and the slight, languid, placid smooth-voiced Labby was so striking that when someone in the House referred to the latter as 'the member for Northampton' a howl of laughter greeted Labby's correction 'the *Christian* member'.

In spite of a statement by the leading clergyman of Northampton that Jesus Christ would have supported the conservative candidates, the two radicals headed the poll, and as a consequence Great Britain was rent by a war of conscience for the next five or six years. Bradlaugh did not wish to take the oath, which was vitiated for him by theological expressions, and asked to be allowed to make an affirmation. A cry of horror went up from the conservatives, not one of whom had previously regarded the oath as anything more than a formality. The matter was referred to a committee, which voted against Bradlaugh's claim to affirm. 'Very well, then,' said Bradlaugh in effect, 'I will take the oath.' Another cry of horror went up from the conservatives, who said that it would be blasphemy for a man to swear by a God in whom he did not believe. There followed an expulsion, a law-suit, a new election, the return of Bradlaugh, and a free fight on the floor of the House, during which the parliament-ary pagans were converted to Christianity in a manner wholly suited to the English temperament, their revelation taking the form of a football scrum with Bradlaugh as centre-forward on the side of Satan.

The atheist's clothes were torn off his back and if he had not been carried from the field in a dead faint he would almost certainly have been debagged.

Meanwhile the country was in an uproar and monster petitions against the 'bellowing blasphemer' were signed by the godly portions of the community. Labby gave valuable support to his fellow-member, his first important speech on re-entering parliament being a plea that Bradlaugh should be permitted to affirm. For the first and last time in his political career he was very nervous and his face was flushed. To a continuous accompaniment of mocking laughter, he delivered such phrases as this:

'It is contrary to and is repugnant to the feelings of all men of tolerant minds that any gentleman should be hindered from performing civil functions in this world on account of speculative opinions regarding another world.'

When Bradlaugh was unseated by a legal verdict Labby went down to Northampton to help him win another election, and from the spirit in which the Christian member assisted his atheistic comrade we may infer his ironic attitude towards the whole affair. At a public meeting he spoke of Mr. Gladstone in a phrase that has become historic:

'Men of Northampton, I come to you with a message from the Grand Old Man (*cheers*). I went to see him before I left London. I told him of our errand here and he laid his hand on my shoulder, saying in his most solemn tone "Bring him back with you, Henry, bring him back." '

The intimate nature of the interview was perhaps a trifle over-emphasised, but Gladstone was thenceforth to be known as 'the G.O.M.', sometimes even as 'Gommy', and the expression has since been debased by application to numerous decrepit celebrities.

He arrived at another meeting without having prepared a speech, but his difficulties vanished when he perceived that Bradlaugh had written out the headings of his own oration in large letters on a foolscap sheet which he had placed on the table before him. Labby was the first to speak and proceeded to deal with each of the subjects for which Bradlaugh had so thoughtfully provided the headings, though he was careful not to arouse suspicion by taking them in their written order. As he disposed of each topic Bradlaugh leant forward and crossed out its heading, and when he sat down there was nothing left on the paper. Bradlaugh's speech did not fulfil expectations.

Labby had often observed that the most successful political speeches were those which were least intelligible and that few perorations aroused so much enthusiasm as those closing with a classical quotation which no one understood. One of his speeches on behalf of Bradlaugh dealt with the right of a democracy to choose its own representatives, and he finished as follows: 'Gentlemen, what we want is government for the masses by the masses, or in the words of the old Greek classic *Zoe mou sas agapo*' (*loud cheers*). He did not think it necessary to add that the words, in the original English, formed the last line of *The Maid of Athens*, 'O life of me, I love thee!'

Although Labby had no profound convictions, he had strong attractions; and although he did not believe in the nobility of man or the moral standards of society, he preferred one class of men to another and one kind of behaviour to another. He entered politics with the object of fighting for his preferences; but it was also a superb field for the exercise of his only hobby, the observation and dissection of human nature, in which he found endless entertainment. It would be absurd to say that, because he got a lot of fun out of the game, he did not play to win. Only a fool confuses a sense of humour with insincerity. But unfortunately, as

Carlyle pointed out, the world is largely populated
with fools, and most human beings take themselves so
seriously that they cannot stand what they call
'laughter in the wrong place'. Labby was always
laughing in the wrong place and consequently a large
number of politicians, even on his own side, came to
look upon him as a buffoon. It may help us to understand their exasperation if at this point we read what
Labby had to say on the subject:

> 'I regard a sense of humour as one of the most
> precious gifts that can be vouchsafed to a human
> being. He is not necessarily a better man for having
> it, but he is a happier one. It renders him indifferent
> to good or bad fortune. It enables him to enjoy
> his own discomfiture. Blessed with this sense he
> is never unduly elated or cast down. No one can
> ruffle his temper. No abuse disturbs his equanimity.
> Bores do not bore him. Humbugs do not humbug
> him. Solemn airs do not impose on him. Senti-
> mental gush does not influence him. The follies of
> the moment have no hold on him. Titles and
> decorations are but childish baubles in his eyes.
> Prejudice does not warp his judgment. He is never
> in conceit or out of conceit with himself. He abhors
> all dogmatism. The world is a stage on which
> actors strut and fret for his edification and amuse-
> ment, and he pursues the even current of his way,
> invulnerable, doing what is right and proper
> according to his lights, but utterly indifferent
> whether what he does finds approval or disapproval
> from others. If Hamlet had had any sense of
> humour, he would not have been a nuisance to
> himself and to all surrounding him.'[1]

Labby was lucky to start his proper career as a
politician in partnership with so curious a specimen
of the human fauna as Bradlaugh, whom he studied

[1] *Truth*, June 9, 1898.

as a phenomenon and liked as a human being. The idea of a man taking religion (or irreligion) so much to heart that he was willing to suffer moral obloquy and physical violence for the sake of a formula, struck Labby as ludicrously funny. But Bradlaugh's simplicity and honesty appealed to him, and he admired the man while laughing at the mission.

In defending the antichristian member for Northampton Labby had gained the reluctant ear of the House. In attacking the memory of a famous conservative statesman a year later he created something of a sensation. Lord Beaconsfield died early in 1881 and a proposition to erect a monument in his honour was discussed in parliament. One might have thought that, of all the public men of his time, Dizzy would have attracted Labby. But here the Huguenot streak in him took charge; he did not think Dizzy a good man and he wrote in *Truth*: 'As a statesman he was beneath contempt, as a party-leader he was unrivalled. To use power for the good of his fellow-men never occurred to him.' It was Labby's opinion that 'a good and great statesman is not the man who makes no mistakes but the man who makes the fewest mistakes'. The broader a man's outlook the more liable is he to error, and Dizzy made no mistakes because his outlook was restricted to self and party. But the unusual thing about Labby was that he could not keep his opinions to himself. What he thought he wrote or spoke. Custom, convention and creed were unimportant to him in comparison with human liberty and the right to free speech. *De mortuis* was all moonshine. Death did not turn a scoundrel into a saint. And so the mood of the House of Commons changed rapidly from one of reverence to one of wrath as Labby's even words shattered the atmosphere of decorous ritual:

'Lord Beaconsfield possessed rare and splendid gifts (*murmurs of approval*) but rare and splendid gifts in themselves are a danger rather than an advantage to the state when the possessor of them does not use them for what is considered by the majority of his fellow-countrymen to be to the public advantage. (*A shocked silence.*) A statue is granted by a national vote to a politician because his country is grateful to him (*hostile muttering*). I do not consider that the country has reason to be grateful for anything that Lord Beaconsfield did. (*Loud murmurs of disapproval.*) It is impossible in my mind to separate the man from the minister, the statesman from the statesmanship.' (*Angry protestations from all sides of the House.*)

As these remarks were made within three weeks of Beaconsfield's death, it was not surprising that little groups of M.P.s stood about the lobbies, corridors and smoking-rooms of the House that evening giving vent to their feelings in such phrases as: 'Shocking!' 'Scandalous!' 'Beastly bad taste, what?' 'Not fit for decent society!' 'Of course he's a Froggie!' 'Rotten I call it!' 'Utter outsider!' '*De mortuis*, dash it all!' etc.

Towards the close of 1882 Labby commenced the series of attacks on imperialistic and jingo policy which gave him the leadership of the extreme Radical Party and provoked so much hostility in parliament and the country that twenty years later he found himself practically in a minority of one. His attitude first crystallised over the British occupation of Egypt, and in order to appreciate it we must briefly survey the political situation there.

For many years Egypt had been groaning under Turkish despotism and misrule. Khedive Ismail, appointed by the Sultan, had ruined the country by his extravagence. Having got through about £400,000,000, and unable to raise more money from a people already impoverished by taxation, he turned his attention to Europe. Disraeli, with Rothschild's help, obtained Ismail's shares in the Suez Canal for £4,000,000, and Egyptian Government bonds were eagerly bought the moment it was known that Great Britain had the control of Suez. A load of debt had already descended upon the natives and crowds of European revenue-collectors now descended upon Egypt. Ismail got into further difficulties and it was whispered abroad that he intended to repudiate the debt. Rothschild instantly brought pressure to bear on the Sultan of Turkey and Ismail was removed from office, but not before he had paid a flying-visit to the Bank, another to the Treasury, and cleared the till at both establishments. At this point Gladstone became Prime Minister and Egypt appeared to have settled down quietly under the nominal government of the new Khedive, under the actual government of the French and English ministers. But all this while a nationalist movement had been growing against the Turkish oppressors and when the Egyptians saw an endless vista of taxes payable to Europeans opening up before them the movement became formidable. Its leader, Arabi Pasha, naturally added the fuel of revenge to the flame of patriotism, and in 1882 matters came to a head. The town of Alexandria was patriotic-ally looted and partially destroyed, other towns were plundered and many Europeans were massacred. A force under Wolseley was sent out from England, the battle of Tel-el-Kebir was a walkover for the side with machine-guns, Egyptian nationalism was stamped out, and for all practical purposes Great Britain ruled on the Nile.

Up to the defeat of Arabi Pasha, Labby's attitude had been orthodox. He hated the Turkish misrule of Egypt; he realised that control of the Suez Canal was vital to a nation holding India; he knew that if England did not maintain her influence in Egypt, France would step in; he believed that Arabi, 'like most patriots, was "on the make" '; he hated the spectacle of pillage and murder masquerading as patriotism; and he was himself a bondholder. He was therefore backing his beliefs as well as his bonds when in July '82 he told Sir Charles Dilke, the Under-secretary for Foreign Affairs, that if the British Government did not establish itself permanently in Egypt it ought to be turned out of office. 'Success is everything,' he advised. 'This is the "moral law" as understood by the English nation. Bombard any place, but show a *quid pro quo*.' Which was simply Labby's method of taking the non-sense out of politics, a method called cynical by people who disliked facing the truth.

Dilke was disturbed by such irresponsible realism. He was a man of a curious cast of mind, rare enough then, unknown now. His knowledge of foreign affairs was encyclopædic and he could talk for hours on end, and indeed did talk for hours on end, about diplomatic entanglements, political undercurrents, the adjustments and readjustments of major, minor and medium-sized states, about pacts, protocols, treaties and what-not, until the heads of his listeners whirled and they were reduced to dumbness by boredom or amaze-ment. He could not believe that others did not want to share in the stores of knowledge at his command, and whenever someone interjected a comment during one of his immense monologues, he would pause, glance with incredulous surprise at the interrupter, and then continue the deluge of information from the precise point at which he had left off. To sum up his main characteristic in a phrase: he read blue-books on his death-bed.

Naturally, Labby's curtness, his indifference to the intricacies and solemnities of negotiation and his impatience with the mystical rites of diplomacy, annoyed Dilke, who once wrote to his friend Joseph Chamberlain when the latter was causing a split in Gladstone's cabinet: 'I should not negotiate through

Labouchere, but through a member of the Cabinet of high character who agrees in your view. . . . Labouchere is very able and very pleasant, but still a little too fond of fun, which often, in delicate matters, means mischief.' Such was the propriety, orderliness and gravity of Dilke's mind that it may be doubted whether he ever regarded Labby as a serious citizen, though Labby alone stuck to the radical colours to the end of his days, and, almost alone, welcomed Dilke heartily back to the House after the divorce scandal that had driven him from politics.

Labby's sudden turnabout in the Egyptian business must have seriously upset Dilke, whose mind moved slowly along well-considered lines and who was not subject to revelations. To Dilke the British occupation was simply the inevitable outcome of certain political conditions, and until certain other political conditions necessitated a withdrawal, the British would have to remain in occupation. To Labby the British had gone there to displace the corrupt Turkish government, to put down the wasteful and bloody rebellion of Arabi, to warn off the other powers, to take military control of the Suez Canal, and to establish a government of Egypt by the Egyptians with adequate security for the European bondholders. But he quickly realised, after Wolseley's victory over Arabi, that Great Britain was going to administer Egypt 'mainly for the good of the bondholders'. In short the future of the native population was to be dependent on the goodwill of European financiers, and the British taxpayer would have to maintain an army of occupation in order to assure the financiers of their dividends. The moment of realisation was the moment of action. He sold his Egyptian bonds; or, as Wilfred Scawen Blunt put it, 'they fell off his back like Christian's burden in *Pilgrim's Progress* and Labby became an honest politician'. He then wrote a letter to Dilke, which, coming only three months after his

advice to 'bombard any place but show a *quid pro quo*',
drove the Under-secretary to take counsel with Joseph
Chamberlain. They were both a little bewildered.
Was the man serious? Hand the country over to its
own inhabitants? Impossible! The man was not
serious.

But they soon found that he was extremely serious,
in his own funny way, for he began to ask awkward
questions in parliament, questions with which no loyal
supporter of the Government in power ought to have
embarrassed its ministers. 'Egypt for the Egyptians'
was his cry and he made it quite clear that a Liberal
Administration had no business to interfere with the
growth of nationalism. 'Clear out before it is too late!'
He harped on the evil that would come of our continued occupation. But his advice was not heeded and
the evil came from an unexpected quarter. A wild-
eyed fanatic who called himself the Mahdi swept across
the Soudan, a trail of blood and desolation in his wake.
It became necessary to withdraw the Egyptian troops
from threatened posts up the Nile and Gordon was
sent to Khartoum. Labby's questions became more
and more insistent. He realised at once the danger
of Gordon's mission, prophesied with uncanny fore-
sight the eventual outcome of the enterprise, told
Gladstone he was playing with fire, and did his utmost in and out of parliament to establish friendly
relations with the Mahdi. His tactics were not of a
kind to soothe Gladstone, because he insisted that in
dividing the House against the Government he was
merely 'strengthening the good intentions of the Prime
Minister'. Naturally Gladstone did not like the
implication that he was 'hedging' and gravely rebuked
Labby for levity. The sequel belongs to history, and
it need only be said here that if the Government had
listened to Labby there would have been no tragedy
for the British people at Khartoum. 'Christian heroes'
made no appeal to him and not the least ironic aspect

of Gordon's fate is that he might have been saved by
the only man who was completely indifferent to his
merits and who opposed the erection of a statue to his
memory.

Labby's main effort as a constructive politician was
the sustained and complicated series of intrigues
whereby he hoped to win the Irish vote and establish
a Radical Government in England. To understand
the part he played a brief record of events in Ireland
may be helpful.

In 1864, owing to the failure of the potato crop,
there had been a terrible famine in Ireland, and as
Great Britain had adopted Free Trade the Americans
had soon captured the English corn-market from the
Irish. Thus many of the Irish peasants were starving
and could not pay their rents. But the landlords had
also felt the pinch and began to rid themselves of
their defaulting tenants. Thousands emigrated to
Canada and the United States; the remainder made
war on the landlords by murder, arson, cattle-maiming
and other forms of destruction. In 1879 the Land
League was formed, with Charles Stewart Parnell as
president, and from that moment the cause of the
evicted peasants was run on organised, non-violent
and thoroughly effective lines. By the simple process
known as boycotting, so-called from the first landlord's
agent who had been victimised, Captain Boycott, the
Land League made the letting of farms from which
holders had been expelled extremely difficult. But
the Land League could not curb the actions of men
made desperate by want and injustice, and acts of
violence still took place, with the result that in 1880
Gladstone was urged by the Irish Viceroy and the
Chief Secretary, W. E. Forster, to repeal the Habeas
Corpus Act and resort to force. Gladstone at first
refused but agreed that legal action should be taken
against the leaders of the Land League. Forster
pressed his case and at length managed to get a

Coercion Act through parliament. An immediate result was the arrest and imprisonment of Parnell and other leaders. Another result was the formation of secret societies and a further outbreak of crime and violence. Forster then proposed more stringent measures, but Gladstone put his foot down and opened negotiations with Parnell, who let it be understood that he would be able to curb the atavistic tendencies of his countrymen if he were set at liberty. Parnell was freed, Forster and the Viceroy promptly resigned, and two days later the new Chief Secretary, Lord Frederick Cavendish, and the permanent Under-secretary, Burke, were assassinated in Phoenix Park, Dublin. Parnell was dismayed, England was horrified, Forster said 'What did I tell you?', and Gladstone agreed to a Crimes Bill which instituted the reign of force in Ireland.

Labby was entirely opposed to all coercive measures and espoused the cause of Ireland from the start. He instantly perceived that the future of radicalism in England depended upon a pacific solution by the Liberal Party of affairs in Ireland, and constituted himself unofficial ambassador between the Irish leaders in parliament and the chief radical in the British cabinet, Joseph Chamberlain. His efforts were rewarded by the whittling down of some of the harsher clauses in the Bill and by the trust which was thereafter reposed in him by Gladstone and Parnell when the subject of Home Rule for Ireland became dominant in English politics.

In 1885 Gladstone was defeated by the Irish vote because the tories had promised Parnell that, if in power, they would drop the Coercion Act. There was a General Election, during which Parnell issued his famous Home Rule manifesto and Gladstone, after anxious heart-searchings based on a desire for office, declared himself in favour of a parliament for Ireland. Following the Election a Tory Administration under Lord Salisbury was able to take office with Parnell's support, and a period of intrigue commenced, each party doing its best to buy the Irish vote without selling itself. On the liberal side the chief go-between was Labby, who wanted above all things to smash the whigs and the tories in order to establish a progressive government in England, and therefore spent his time trying to patch up an agreement on the Home Rule question between Parnell, Gladstone and Chamberlain.

Lord Salisbury's Government was defeated early in '86, Gladstone again became Prime Minister, the stage was set for the great Home Rule drama, and Labby's efforts to establish the reign of radicalism in England by uniting Gladstone, Parnell and Chamberlain on the Irish question were intensified.

Never did a politician set himself a more difficult task. The leading characters in the drama were politically in accord but personally at variance, each with the others, and the resultant clash provides one more proof that freaks of individual temperament have more influence on the fate of nations than ideals, policies and beliefs held in common.

Labby's admiration of the Liberal Prime Minister is sufficient to disprove the modern belief that Gladstone was a hypocrite, for no one could impose for a moment on the Christian member for Northampton. But with Labby irreverence went hand-in-hand with admiration and his statement that Gladstone was not a genius also disposes of the belief, still held by a few, that he was. The qualities that the clear-eyed radical so much admired in the fiery-eyed liberal were the tenacity of purpose and fertility of resource which he displayed in passing some great measure; the astonishing patience with which he listened to bores in the House, when often enough he would be the only man present who was not asleep or talking to his neighbour; a sense of duty which always got the better of inclination and forced him to give practical effect to the inarticulate aspirations of those for whom he fought; an absolute indifference to and independence of newspaper criticism; and finally that combination of moral integrity and mental capacity which established a trust in the man and a confidence in the leader such as no other Prime Minister in English history has been able to inspire in his party. When eventually he left politics and entered on that period of probation which, according to Labby, 'he requires before meeting his Maker', progress lost its champion and politics its interest.

The truth is that Gladstone possessed two virtues rarely seen together and possessed each in an extreme degree: he was an absolutely sincere man and a superlatively fine actor. His love of office cannot be urged against his sincerity, for he had an apostolic view of his function in politics. 'I don't object to Gladstone, always having the ace of trumps up his sleeve,' remarked Labby, 'but merely to his belief that God Almighty put it there.' That was the situation in a nutshell. Gladstone believed that he was the instrument of God and considered even his craftiest manœuvres to have the nature of divine strategy. Except at the instant of conflict his inspirations were the result of long premeditation. Having convinced himself that the course he had decided upon was right, the actor took charge and his oratorical exhibitions inspired Disraeli's famous statement that he was 'inebriated with the exuberance of his own verbosity'. Labby's comment was truer: 'When once an idea gets hold of his mind, it ferments.'

Gladstone's histrionic gifts, which gave him such ascendancy both in parliament and on the platform, were lost on Labby. After one of those spellbinding orations, which closed with a tremendous passage on the divine right of justice, the liberals streamed into the lobby muttering exclamations of wonder and admiration:

'The finest thing he ever did!'

'Splendid!'

'The old man on the top of his form!'

'He'll never beat that!'

'What a peroration!'

'Yes,' drawled Labby, 'but damned copy-booky.'

Again, after listening to a speech by W. H. Smith, Labby remarked thoughtfully to a circle of fellow-members in the smoking-room: 'It's sad to see how that good old man has learnt to lie; he'll soon be running our Grand Old Man hard.' And once, when some enthusiastic disciple burst out that Gladstone's mission was to bring light, Labby was heard to murmur 'Lucifer!'

It may seem strange that such an aloof and earnest prophet as Gladstone should have entrusted such a familiar and apparently cynical person as Labby with the secret and delicate negotiations which he carried on with Chamberlain, Parnell and others; but it merely goes to show that Gladstone recognised beneath the flippant exterior of Labby an honest and fundamentally sincere human being. Labby explained his value as an intermediary, to anyone who seemed interested, in such terms as these:

'I see you are a little astonished that Gladstone should make me his emissary. It does seem odd, doesn't it? But then I have my peculiar advantages, don't you see? And I got him to see them. . . . Another man would expect a baronetcy or a privy-counsellorship or a place in the cabinet or a peerage, whereas all I want is a good laugh now and then. Besides, I talk to everybody, and so nothing is inferred from my talking to anybody. Then I am not a serious politician; everybody says so, and what everybody says must be true. Therefore, of course, nobody would believe that so tremendously serious a politician as Gladstone would dream of taking me into his confidence. Then, if I were to let out the secrets, nobody would give them a moment's attention, seeing it's *me*, don't you know? Then again, if the worst came to the worst, I could be disavowed so easily. Oh, it's only Labby's absurd talk; nobody minds *him*, and the thing is at an end, don't you see?'

Certainly his diplomatic exchanges were made in a refreshingly unorthodox style, and it was difficult to resist a man who, calling unexpectedly on a cabinet minister, opened fire in this manner:

'Gladstone will be having a fit if he don't get into negotiations, or communication, or something, with somebody; so I thought I'd come, don't you know?'

At one point in the Home Rule struggle Gladstone decided that it was not a party question. 'The issue should be transferred to the forum of conscience,' he declared. 'An excellent tribunal when one's law is shady,' said Labby, who then advised Gladstone to get the measure through by promising titles to his wavering supporters: 'The Union was carried by corruption; it must be unmade by corruption.' Gladstone, shocked by such Gallic cynicism, asked Labby to sound one or two leading conservatives on the subject. It is doubtful whether Labby's method of sounding them would have appealed to his chief:

'The G.O.M. is taken with a sudden burst of public spirit, a rush of patriotism to the head, and all that sort of thing. He wants to give you tories the chance of helping him in his grand scheme – making it a national scheme, he says, not the scheme of a party. All rot, of course, but that's his humour. . . . Now as he's in this heroic and public-spirited mood, and wants to give you lot a chance of showing how heroic and public-spirited you can be, do you think there's any hope of an agreement on this one issue?

Of course I wouldn't give you a chance if I were Gladstone, but then I'm not Gladstone, and I'm not public-spirited, and there it is.'

Sometimes Gladstone entrusted Labby with matters of extreme delicacy. When Dilke was being threatened with political ruin Gladstone wanted to know whether anything could be done to save him and Labby promised to make certain proposals to Crawford with a view to keeping Dilke's name out of the divorce proceedings. A few days later the matter was again raised.

'Have you managed to make a settlement?' asked Gladstone.

'No, sir, but I have tried,' replied Labby. 'Crawford's price is too high.'

'What is his price?'

'He actually wants a judgeship.'

'A Scottish judgeship, I presume?'

'Oh, no! He demands to be made an English judge, which of course I told him was impossible.'

'Why impossible? Can any good reason be brought forward against his being made an English judge?'

As a matter of fact Crawford's reception of him had been grim enough to discourage Labby from offering a bribe, and the 'English judgeship' was a momentary inspiration to put Gladstone off. Filled with admiration for his leader's burst of compassion for Dilke, he again promised to see Crawford; but after an abortive interview he frankly confessed to Gladstone that Crawford had refused to consider the matter from the start.

Another aspect of the G.O.M. appealed to Labby's sense of humour. In debate Gladstone was sometimes as cunning as a fox. In the course of a discussion on the Crown revenues the First Lord of the Treasury made an incautious admission. Gladstone's eyes blazed with anger. Labby noticed this and greatly embarrassed the First Lord by repeating the admission with affected incredulity. 'I never said anything of the kind!' blurted out the First Lord in self-defence. Gladstone looked as shocked and amazed as only Gladstone could and Labby pursued: 'The First Lord denies in vain. I appeal to my right hon. friend the member for Midlothian to corroborate my statement that the words were spoken.' Instantly Gladstone's leonine visage fell; his body seemed to crumple up; and putting an open hand to his ear he asked feebly: 'What did my hon. friend say?' Labby repeated the First Lord's admission and again asked for confirmation. Gladstone, simulating advanced senility, quavered forth: 'If my hon. friend desires corroboration for any supposed remark by the First Lord, I would invite him to appeal to someone whose sense of audition is more acute than mine.'

Although Labby gave his leader many anxious moments Gladstone could always depend on his loyalty and often did things for him that he would have done for no one else. He made his single appearance in the strangers' smoking-room of the House at Labby's request, there to witness the performance of a thought-reader, and he was probably the only leading politician of the age to take quite seriously the wish of the extreme radicals that, after his own resignation or death, Labby should lead the Liberal Party.

His obvious successor was, of course, Joseph Chamberlain, and for many years no one was so anxious as Labby to see Chamberlain at the head of a Radical Administration. There was good reason for his anxiety. Chamberlain, who started his public life as a republican and ended it as an imperialist, came like a breath of fresh air into the stale atmosphere of decayed whiggism that enveloped politics in the 'seventies of last century. He was a man of enormous push and vitality, who had already turned Birmingham into one of the leading cities in the country, and his clear, incisive, masterful utterances in the House of Commons quickly marked him out as the man of the future. Labby felt at once that here at last was not only an Elisha who could worthily wear the mantle of Elijah-Gladstone, but one who had the power and personality to sweep the country with an advanced radical programme such as Labby himself had outlined. There is no doubt that for about a decade he was completely 'taken in' by Chamberlain, though some instinctive forewarning of the coming crash made him tell an Irish M.P. in 1883 that 'Joe is a good deal more likely than you to carry a nitro-glycerine cartridge up his sleeve, but it is only intended to be exploded under the coat-tails of his friends'.

It was unfortunate for Labby's schemes that he had to deal with three such humourless egotists as Gladstone, Parnell and Chamberlain, the first a man who saw himself as a messiah, the second a man who felt he had a mission, the third a man whose self-obsession sometimes amounted to mania. Chamberlain never really understood his fellow-men. All his mistakes were due to that one fact, and that one fact was due to his absorption in himself. He acted on what he would have called inspiration, without any reference to the human element in the situation, and by sheer driving-force he went far; but he would have gone a great deal further if he had possessed one-fifth of Disraeli's steady judgment of personal factors or of Gladstone's ready sympathy with the feelings of other men. The result was that he had no confidence in any idea that did not emanate from himself and he treated his followers like pawns, to be moved here and there at his discretion. Since many men are born pawns he never lacked disciples, but when he came up against his equals in will-power he could not stoop to conquer and the least disagreement provoked a crisis.

His brain was perpetually seething with ideas and schemes; his self-confidence was enormous; and those

who were not with him were against him, for his
gospel, whatever it happened to be at the moment,
had to be swallowed whole. After the Home Rule
split Labby told him a few home truths: 'My right
hon. friend always reminds me of Moses coming down
from Mount Sinai, when he broke the Tables of Stone.
He is just as amazed at anyone not accepting his inspired plan as Moses would have been if an Israelite
had suggested an amendment in the Ten Commandments.' He had been spoilt by the adulation of his
adopted city, said Labby on a different occasion, but
outside Birmingham he was regarded 'much as the
Apostles would have regarded Judas if he had come
swaggering in to supper with an orchid in his buttonhole and said that the Christian religion would not go
on if his "flower" were not adopted and himself recognised as its chief exponent.'

But all that lay in the years ahead and in the early
'eighties Labby was busy flattering him in the pious
belief that the more he was flattered the harder he
would fight for the radical programme; as indeed he
might have done had he possessed the patience and
understanding necessary to deal gently with a messiah
and a missionary. So keen was Labby to assure
Chamberlain that no one but he could step into
Gladstone's shoes that the Christian member poked
fun at the revered figure of their leader. 'You have
to get up a cheer for the G.O.M. by dwelling on his
noble heart and that sort of trash,' he wrote during the
General Election of '85, adding that the mere mention
of Chamberlain's name was enough to bring the
audience to its feet. 'To get into power I really
believe that the G.O.M. would not only give up
Ireland but Mrs. Gladstone and Herbert,' was another
of his caustic phrases, and he even went so far as to
describe Gladstone as 'a lunatic at large'. The
Liberal Party did well in the rural constituencies at
that Election because the radical programme included

the promise of 'three acres and a cow' to small holders of land, the number of whom was to be largely increased. This party cry was originated by Jesse Collings, parliamentary secretary to Chamberlain, who brought about the fall of Salisbury's ministry the following year with a Small Holdings amendment to the Queen's Address. 'Is not the cow doing wonders for us?' wrote Labby to Chamberlain. 'Next year we must have an urban cow.'

Just when everything seemed to promise so well for the future of radicalism, Chamberlain suddenly jibbed over the Home Rule Bill. Though in favour of Local Government for Ireland, he wished to retain the Irish members at Westminster, so that Ireland should have a say on imperial matters. Parnell objected. Gladstone objected. Labby was in a fever. What the devil did it matter one way or t'other? 'For my part I would coerce the Irish, grant them Home Rule, or do anything with them, in order to make the Radical programme possible. Ireland is but a pawn in the game.' Then came the tug of war, with Gladstone at one end of the rope, Chamberlain at the other, Parnell watching with disdainful interest, and Labby skipping about excitedly from side to side, now begging Chamberlain to give way, now urging Gladstone to make concessions, now asking Parnell to lend a hand. It was like the third act of a melodrama, in which three 'star' actors were fighting for the centre of the stage and a baffled but hopeful stage-manager was trying to persuade each of them in turn that, if only he measured the distances carefully, he would discover that his position was the central one. They all wanted Home Rule for Ireland, but Parnell was only concerned with Ireland, Gladstone was chiefly concerned with Liberalism, Chamberlain was beginning to be concerned with the Empire, and Labby's only thought was for England.

Though he intrigued and wheedled and appealed

and cajoled as he had never done before, though he
wire-pulled and argued and threatened and flattered
as he was never to do again, Labby thoroughly enjoyed himself. He was fighting for a new world, for
the very life (as he believed) of the British poorer
classes, but the fight was great fun because the prota-
gonists were so well-contrasted and so amusing: Gladstone growling like a lion, Chamberlain snapping like a
terrier, Parnell roaring like a bull. He wrote letters
by the score, sent off sheaves of telegrams, rushed from
place to place in hansom-cabs, buttonholed M.P.s in
the lobby or smoking-room, and talked mysteriously
with them in remote corners. Under an appearance
of great cunning he was by nature as simple as a child,
could not keep a secret for five minutes, and blabbed
out first to one man and then to another the most
sacred confidences. The whole business was conducted in such an openly secret fashion that the whigs,
whom he was out 'to dish', took alarm, guessing rightly
that if Gladstone, Chamberlain and Parnell came to an
agreement the country would soon be at the mercy of
radical legislation. 'Beware of Labby,' wrote one of
them, Sir William Harcourt, to Chamberlain; 'he
talks to everybody, writes to everybody and betrays
everybody.' Chamberlain replied that he received
Labby's advice with interest and amusement but did
not always take it. As a matter of fact Chamberlain
himself was over the ears in intrigue all through the
early part of '86, pulling this wire and that, sounding
this man and that, friendly with the whigs, toying
with the radicals and even flirting with the tories.
Labby's love of intrigue was due to his interest in
humanity; Chamberlain loved it for its own sake: 'If
he were alone on a desert island, he would intrigue
against himself,' was Labby's later summary.

But though we may well believe that Labby's
manner was not that of a born diplomat ('As well that
you should know what the little game of our revered

G.O.M. has been,' was how he once began a confidence to Chamberlain), yet there is not the least doubt that the final split was due to the personal antagonisms of the leading actors. Gladstone had been a party autocrat long enough to feel angry when one of his lieutenants challenged his judgment. Besides the challenge was of the 'take-it-or-leave-it' variety, for Chamberlain would not budge an inch on the question of Irish representation at Westminster, and the G.O.M. disliked both the method and the man, who had been a thorn in his side for several years. A public recantation of an important point in his policy, at the bidding of a radical rival, would have been a personal humiliation. Chamberlain, for his part, was tired of his leader's procrastination, longed for freedom from the thrall of this mighty figure of a past age, under whose shadow the forces of progress seemed to cower, and could no longer endure to be treated like a child in the art of government. He was intensely ambitious and quite honestly believed himself capable of running the country better than anyone else. Besides, Parnell got on his nerves, partly because the Irish leader was always demanding more than the Liberal Party could give, partly because the Irish vote was becoming the dominant force in British politics, and partly because Parnell had never made the least attempt to conciliate Chamberlain. As for Parnell himself, he was playing a lone hand and he did not play it according to the rules of the parliamentary game; he continually shifted his ground, making bargains, breaking them, demanding now one thing, now another, and careless of whether he aroused hatred or admiration in the breasts of men he despised and distrusted.

It is curious that Labby should have taken 'a really too Arcadian view of human nature', as he once said about someone else, in the early stages of the Home Rule crisis.

'I bet *this* Bill never passes its Second Reading,' said a liberal member after hearing Gladstone introduce it in the Commons.

'Done with you,' said Labby, who was walking just behind him: 'Shall we say a hundred?'

'I am no betting man,' said the liberal, who was also a lawyer, 'so let's make it a guinea.'

A fortnight later Labby made an offer to double the bet, which was accepted, and the loss of that sum was the least of his worries.

Right up to the last moment he believed that Gladstone would give way and all would be well, for the Prime Minister had practically promised to meet Chamberlain's demand that the Irish members should still vote in the British parliament, but when Gladstone rambled on without mentioning the subject and then sat down, Labby realised at last that the cause of radicalism was doomed, and turning to a fellow-member said:

'Isn't the old man a thimble-rigger?'

Chamberlain, with a number of followers who were henceforth to be known as the Liberal-Unionist Party, voted against the Second Reading, Gladstone resigned, and a General Election brought the tories back to power under Salisbury.

It was the greatest disappointment of Labby's life. He had worked to smash the forces of reaction; the Radical Party had lost its leader, its programme was stone dead; and all his hopes for the future disappeared for ever in an instant. Henceforth his political zeal cooled. He became primarily a critic of tory measures, and his resentment against the man who had betrayed the cause was lasting. 'What children these statesmen are!' he exclaimed; 'they won't agree because they don't like each other.' And: 'Such a lot of babies as Gladstone, Morley, Joe and Bright, I never came across!' But Chamberlain remained the object of his deepest scorn, because he had been the object

of his most fervent hopes; and though he once remarked, 'I blame no one who plays his cards to his
own best advantage,' he never ceased to blame 'Joe',
criticising him on every possible occasion, from the
floor of the House, in the smoking-rooms of the
Commons and the Reform Club, and in the pages of
*Truth*, from which we may extract a characteristic
passage:

> 'My sincere conviction is that sooner or later Mr.
> Chamberlain will end in an asylum with straws in
> his hair like Ophelia, with a paper crown on his
> head, with a broomstick in his hand as a sceptre,
> and with honest silly Jesse kissing the toe of this
> lunatic monarch.'

After which it will not surprise us to read a passage
in the diary of Sir Charles Dilke, February 4, 1887:
'Chamberlain again came to see me . . . he was very
sore against Labouchere.' And another, December
2, 1889: 'Saw Chamberlain . . . Labouchere sets him
against the Liberals and Balfour attracts him to the
Tories.'

The next six years of Labby's political life were
spent, with the Liberal Party, in opposition, and the
main political features of that period were the bullying
of Ireland and the blackening of Parnell. *The Times*
came to the aid of the tories with a series of articles
on 'Parnellism and Crime', which included a letter
alleged to have been written by Parnell condoning
murder on patriotic grounds. These articles paved
the way for a Coercion Bill, which practically treated
the Irish as a nation of criminals. It was passed
through the House by the new Chief Secretary, Lord
Salisbury's nephew, whose nickname of 'Pretty Fanny'
was soon dropped by the Irish members in favour of
'base, bloody and brutal Balfour'. The most extraordinary stories of callous outrage were told in the
House to excuse the Bill, and Labby referred to these

in one of his many hostile speeches: 'There is nothing more objectionable than for a minister of the Crown to ask the House to pass a Bill, the necessity for which is supported by anonymous anecdotes.'

In self-defence Balfour explained that the actions of the Land League had even been condemned by the Irish judges. Labby retorted: 'Everyone knows that an Irish judge is made a judge because he is a partisan.' As for the judicial harangues against the League, 'there was this peculiarity about them: they were all made at a time when there happened to be a vacancy in the Court of Common Pleas'. Turning to his old ally Chamberlain, whose descent had been proportionate to his previous position of graçe, Labby sneered: 'He does not care for coercion one way or the other, so that his miserable vanity is satisfied.' The inhabitants of Ulster were not in sympathy with the nationalist aims of their Catholic countrymen, and it is doubtful whether Labby's reference to the Orange-men helped to promote an alliance between the opposing sects: 'These men are, as far as I can gather, steady, sensible, practical, law-abiding men; but once a year they are seized with a sort of erotic season. From about the commencement to the middle of July it is dangerous for a Catholic to come in their way. This is called the celebrating of the Boyne. After the 15th of July they become once more perfectly reasonable human beings.' But he also spotted the absurdity of the nationalist extremists. One evening a recently elected Irish member was busy cursing the English with the fine frenzy of youth, closing with a prophecy: 'The Cossacks of Russia will yet stable their horses in the British House of Commons.' Labby turned to William O'Brien and asked: 'What sort of young man is this you've sent over to us? It isn't that he's against law and order – we're all against law and order – but, you know, he's such a blawsted awss!'

A demonstration of protest against the Coercion Bill was held in Hyde Park, when most of the nationalist leaders spoke, but the crowd was chiefly interested in an English M.P., for nearly everyone was asking 'Where's Labby?' and his platform was the most popular. All through the troubles that followed the passing of this measure he advocated resistance to it and during a visit to Ireland he witnessed an episode at Mitchelstown, where a lawful assembly was broken up by the police, who fired into it, killing three men and mortally wounding two. Labby gave a full account of the incident in the House and another in *Truth*, writing of Brownrigg, the officer responsible for the outrage:

> 'The ferocity, the insolence, the brutality of this man never were exceeded. . . . I strongly recommend him for promotion. He is a man after the hearts of our Tory despots, for he seemed to me to unite in his person every characteristic that goes to make up an official ruffian, armed with a little brief authority. . . . If he has furnished Mr. Balfour with an account of what took place, he adds to his other virtues the capacity of being one of the best liars that the world has produced, for the statement of Mr. Balfour in the House of Commons . . . is one long tissue of deliberate falsehoods.'

Neither the police nor the politicians of to-day are dealt with by journalists in quite that spirit.

More of Parnell's supposed letters encouraging violence appeared in *The Times*, and Labby, who had gone into the matter carefully, decided that all of them had been forged by a man called Pigott. He got into touch with Pigott, who at last, after several lengthy conferences, admitted that the letters were forged. At the request of Parnell a parliamentary commission was appointed, the sittings of which were prolonged for several months. Pigott collapsed under the deadly cross-examination of Sir Charles Russell, who had been provided with all the necessary facts by Labby. After his exhibition in the witness-box Pigott called on Labby and made a full confession of guilt; he then retired to Madrid and blew his brains out.

The fury of the anti-Parnellites with Labby for his responsibility in exposing the forgeries was considerable; several tories threatened to shoot him, and as he made fun of his credulous adversaries week after week in *Truth* he became extremely unpopular with those who had been taken in by the hoax, one of whom, probably acting for many, determined to teach him a lesson. The method of instruction, though not original, was annoying. One morning there arrived at Labby's house the following: a representative from the cremation company to arrange for the disposal of his remains, a marriage cake from Buzzard, a bed from Shoolbred, furniture of all sorts from Maple, Druce and Barker, tons of coal from half a dozen firms, a coat from one shop, several caps from another, a billiard-table from Thurston, carpets from Swan and Edgar, pictures, beer, spirits, wine and a large quantity of other goods from various West End houses, including an umbilical belt for hernia from a city shop. He was also favoured with many prescriptions for many diseases from many physicians, and was advised that cabins on steamers for India and the United States had been reserved for him. Further, presents were sent in his name to eminent statesmen: a salmon to Mr. Gladstone, a Stilton cheese to Sir William Harcourt, a travelling-bag to Mr. Asquith, a haunch of venison to Sir George Trevelyan, etc.; and cards had been sent out to scores of people inviting them to dine with him at his London and country houses.

Thus did he suffer in the cause of Ireland, exposing his scars in the columns of *Truth*, so that everybody could enjoy the joke.

During these years of strain Labby became more

and more closely associated with Parnell; in fact, he was the only Englishman to be treated with any degree of confidence by the Irish leader, probably because he was by descent a Frenchman. Labby did not think highly of Parnell's intelligence, always advising his colleagues to put a definite clear-cut programme before Parnell, 'otherwise he'll maunder about Grattan's parliament, of which he knows nothing'. But there was sound sense in this advice, for Parnell thoroughly distrusted English politicians and played them off one against the other. 'He never makes a bargain without intending to get out of it,' said Labby; 'he has either a natural love of treachery or considers that promises are not binding when made to a Saxon.' Parnell was, however, a 'character' and provided Labby with considerable amusement. Praise had gone to his head and he believed that he was the only person who could save Ireland. He saw himself as the leading character in a thrilling patriotic drama, and he had a childlike love of mystery. He liked disguising himself; he used often to conceal his place of residence when there was no need to do so; he carried a revolver in his pocket, explaining that he was in hourly danger of assassination; he moved from place to place under various aliases. Sometimes he called on Labby in the dead of night, dressed in an old white coat with the collar over his ears, a slouched hat drawn over his eyes, a black bag in his hand; and once, when seeing him off from the front door, the hall light having been extinguished at his request, Labby asked:

'Shall I call a cab for you?'

'No, I will walk.'

'Where do you live?'

'Over there,' replied Parnell, sweeping his arm towards the outer darkness, and vanishing noiselessly.

Labby joined his friends in the library and announced: 'I do believe that I've just parted from "Jack

the Ripper"; anyhow Parnell is the only man who
answers to the description.'

Apart from the incalculable value of Labby's assistance in the Pigott business and as a link between
himself and Gladstone, Parnell found it difficult to
resist a man who could suggest a conference in terms
like these:

> 'Come to my house.   Nobody minds me.   It don't
> matter who comes to see me.   Everybody knows
> that everybody comes to see me.   If the Pope, the
> Czar of Russia and Bismarck were to be seen on my
> doorstep arm-in-arm, nobody would infer anything.'

All the same Parnell did not trust Labby with the
great secret of his life, his infatuation for Mrs. O'Shea,
and Labby was forced to assume, from his constant
changes of address, that his loves were numerous:
'Parnell has disappeared with an Egeria of some kind
and his colleagues are hunting for him,' Labby reported to Lord Rosebery, and a few days later came
another bulletin: 'Parnell has retired to warm salt-
water baths with a new Egeria, but his colleagues
do not exactly know where.'   These frequent absences
irritated the other Irish leaders and received unfavourable comment from the English liberals: 'Parnell's
disappearance is being seriously considered in the
Moral-Reform Club,' reported Labby.

When O'Shea filed his petition for divorce and cited
Parnell as co-respondent, Labby tried hard to stem
the wave of puritan morality which he felt sure would
submerge the Liberal Party.   'As a party we liberals
have nothing to do with Mr. Parnell's private affairs.
We want measures, not women,' he declared; and in
*Truth* he wrote: 'If I knew that my banker had broken
the seventh commandment, it would not lead me to
fear that he would make away with my balance.'   In
the smoking-room of the Reform Club he treated the
matter from a different angle.   Asked what he thought

of the fact that O'Shea had commenced his suit after years of patience, he replied: 'When I think of Parnell and O'Shea I recall the Latin phrase *Otium cum dignitate*,' the first word being then pronounced *osheeum*. And when O'Shea had won his case and the papers had done full justice to the facts, Labby was highly entertained: 'Fancy! We were told by members of his party that these mysterious disappearances of their great chief were only evidence of his tireless and secret devotion to the Irish cause, while all the while he was hiding in the kitchen with Mrs. O'Shea.'

Eventually Parnell suffered in Labby's estimation because, like Chamberlain, he turned on Gladstone, split a party, and in effect harmed the radical programme. The moment it became clear that, as a result of the scandal caused by the divorce, the nonconformist conscience would stir itself as never before, there was but one sensible course open to Parnell: retirement from the leadership of the Irish Party. Gladstone, whose political existence depended on the nonconformist vote, suggested that he should do so. But Parnell, like many another politician before him, was fonder of himself than of his cause; he rounded on Gladstone, published confidential conversations that had taken place between them and declared that the G.O.M. was conspiring against Home Rule and could not be trusted.

Realising that Parnell had the radical vote solidly against him and that the cause of Home Rule would suffer from his continued leadership, Labby spoke and wrote against Parnell, who now behaved as if his personal affairs were of more importance than the affairs of Ireland. 'Parnell is suffering from cerebral excitement and consequently is not responsible for his actions,' was Labby's charitable and truthful view of a man who fancied himself as a sort of Mahdi and tried to start a crusade in his country against the hypocrisies and treacheries of everyone who was not a Parnellite.

Labby diagnosed the leader's case with care week by week in *Truth*: Parnell was the victim of hallucinations; he was suffering from a mental malady; so persistent was his illusion that he was more important than Ireland that he forgot everything he had ever said or done that conflicted with it; he imagined he had a divine right to leadership; he would probably declare, all in good time, that he had never even heard of Mrs. O'Shea; anything might be expected of him, for, wrote Labby,

'I have not the slightest doubt that Mr. Parnell is mad. . . . Never since the world began was there such an egotist.'

Labby wanted Ireland to get Home Rule and he came to the definite conclusion that, with Parnell and without the English vote, she would not get it; but that, without Parnell and with the English vote, she would. Though much too optimistic, such was his belief, and he supported it by tongue and pen. 'With me, in politics, principles are everything; men are mere counters. I should denounce my best friend if he stood in the way of the triumph of my political principles, and I should make common cause with my greatest enemy if I thought that he could give efficient aid to make them triumph.' We need seek no further for an explanation of Labby's failure as a party politician.

### III

Let us finally try to picture Labby as his political contemporaries saw him, both standing up in the chamber and sitting down in the smoking-room. In each posture he was something of a paradox. No one took him quite seriously yet everyone felt he was quite serious. He did not divide his personality and so never appeared to be grave with this man, gay with that, solemn in one place, jocular in another, Jekyll here, Hyde there. That would have been at least understandable. The trouble was that with him Jekyll and Hyde walked arm-in-arm. He simply could not be depended upon to say the right thing in the right place. During a debate on Irish affairs Henry Chaplin informed the House that the leading thinkers and writers of Europe were opposed to Home Rule. 'I think I might perhaps quote the opinion of another foreigner, Mr. De Molinari, who I understand is a distinguished Belgian. He said a few years ago – ' At this point Labby rose and interrupted with much gravity: 'Mr. Speaker, this is a matter of great importance, and it is essential that the House should get the name correctly. Am I right in thinking that the right hon. gentleman said Mr. Apollinaris?' In cold print this may not appear to exhaust the possibilities of humour, but in a tense debate, with party feeling running high, its effect was catastrophic. It took the House some time to recover and Chaplin ceased to quote the sayings of distinguished foreigners. The story is useful here because it accentuates the main feature of Labby's political and social make-up: his hatred of humbug. Was it of the least importance that some historian had decided against the principle of Home Rule? Professorial aeration!

So frequently did he upset the dignity of debate that he was sometimes called to order by the Speaker, who accused him of trifling with the House. In the course of a speech on the Budget he suddenly turned to an under-secretary, who combined a large general grocery business with statecraft, and asked: 'If you add this tuppence to the pound, what will my right hon. friend be able to do me a good sound tea for?' Again, in a discussion as to whether the House should sit on Saturdays, he remarked that the extra day's work was mostly opposed by married men, on the ground that they had 'to go into the country at week-ends in

order to do something'. He was not in any sense an
'outdoor man' and when a number of M.P.s complained of the atmosphere of the Commons, due to
bad ventilation, he declared: 'For the sake of my
health I would rather spend a month in the House
than six months on the Brighton front.' Neither the
opinions nor the abilities of his fellow-members impressed him. 'A man of the upper class perhaps has
more education than an artisan, but his mind is
entirely warped by belonging to a privileged class,'
he told them. Further: 'I think we owe a great debt
of gratitude to the newspaper reporters for not reporting us fully. What would the public say of us if
they did? We stammer and stutter and use the wrong
words and frequently do not finish our phrases and
are rarely grammatical. . . . I wish gentlemen in the
gallery would report a few speeches verbatim in order
to convince my hon. friends of the miserable figures
they cut.'

He once accused Lord Salisbury of lying, was called
upon to withdraw the statement, declined to do so
and was suspended for a week. Gladstone, who considered that a member of the Commons was entitled
to say what he liked about a member of the Lords,
offered to bring the question before the House. Labby,
though grateful, refused the offer and on his return
to the scene of conflict he complained that the House
of Commons was particularly hard on the members for
Northampton: 'My hon. friend (Mr. Bradlaugh) was
suspended for disbelieving in God and I am suspended
for disbelieving in man.'

He could always be depended upon to lighten the
heaviest subject. A Bill was introduced to regularise
cremation and there was much opposition to it. Sir
William Harcourt, then Home Secretary, said he objected to the practice not only on religious grounds
but because it afforded greater facilities than burial
for the concealment of violent deeds and stated his

intention of voting against the Bill. Labby favoured incineration and replied to Harcourt:

'The Home Secretary has told us that he would feel afraid he might be poisoned if other people were burned. "My relations would immediately poison me," he says; "one cousin would poison me, another cousin would burn me, and neither cousin would hang for it." Well, I think that is within the range of practical politics. . . . But the Home Secretary also says "Look at Christianity! When Christianity came they ceased to burn the dead." I should like to point out to him that many sects of the Church have always been in favour of burning, for they used to burn heretics on both sides, even before they were dead. Then the right hon. gentleman tells us that it is a question of sentiment, or of feeling. I do not know who has that feeling. So far as I am concerned, it is a matter of absolute indifference to me whether I am buried or burnt or anatomised or anathematised.'

Harcourt was the last of the famous whigs and did not relish the light touch that Labby imparted to parliamentary discussions; he was a man of elephantine proportions, known in the House as 'Jumbo'; when he did not get his way he sulked, and even Gladstone felt a little uncomfortable when Harcourt was glaring at him in displeasure. He had a caustic tongue and all the radicals except Labby stood in awe of him; he inspired more fear than affection, and gave favours without gaining followers. He regarded Labby as a public nuisance, who instigated and organised obstruction from a sheer love of mischief. 'Can't you get up a crisis for us?' he growled at the Christian member when some debate was more than usually tame.

Labby had not been in parliament long before he had mastered the art of obstruction. At first adopted

G*

solely to prevent coercive measures against the Irish,
he later applied his knowledge to achieve any end he
had in view and when someone complained of his
tactics he retorted that obstruction was carried on
with the consent and approval of the House. He was
in politics a most persistent person. Once he had
taken a thing up it was not easy to make him drop it.
He fought in session after session for the conversion
of Constitution Hill into a public thoroughfare, fought
against the influence of the Queen and the whole
official world, and scored a victory. Another series
of skirmishes with the powers were engaged in his own
behalf. He used to walk from the House along the
Horse Guards side of St. James's Park, via the Duke of
York's steps, to the Reform Club. In winter the
stretch from Storey's Gate to the Mall was a morass
and Labby constantly begged the First Commissioner
of Works to provide a proper footpath, the First Commissioner always pleading poverty. One night, in
Committee, Labby organised opposition to a particular
estimate. It came on during the dinner-hour and
so long as his men were standing by the Government
majority was uncertain. In the middle of the debate
the Government Whip begged him not to carry the
matter into the Division Lobby.

'All right,' said Labby, 'on one condition. You go
and get the First Commissioner to promise to lay down
an asphalt pavement from Storey's Gate to the Mall,
and I'll draw off my men.'

The pledge was given, Labby withdrew his opposition, the pathway was put down, Labby's trousers
were no longer caked with mud in bad weather, and
the public have ever since enjoyed the result of his
private-spirited action.

In no sense of the word was he an orator. Words did
not leap to his tongue. He spoke deliberately, lucidly,
and often very effectively, in an even, drawling,
raucous voice, and as he was nearly always amusing

the House was seldom empty when he was 'up'. His words seemed to be addressed to the gentlemen of the press in the reporters' gallery, for he took no more notice of his fellow-members than if they had been so many rows of dummy figures. He usually spoke from odd notes which he had jotted down on slips of paper, dropping each slip as he finished with it into his hat. He was extremely untidy in his habits, his pockets being crammed with all sorts of oddments, and very often his notes got muddled up or mislaid. This did not 'rattle' him in the least: he just left a theme half-completed in the air and took up another, possibly returning to the one he had abandoned if he happened to come across the relative note later on. He was always in complete command of himself; his self-assurance, which had nothing of self-assertion in it, was perhaps his most valuable, as it was certainly his most aggravating, quality in debate. Physically, though short, he had dignity, for his body was well-proportioned and his movements were graceful. Mentally, his poise was perfect, and to his opponents insufferable: he could not be 'drawn'. When he was being attacked he smiled with provoking blandness, and the detached serenity of his own attacks maddened his victims.

A tory, Colonel Sanderson, once did his utmost to 'draw' Labby by calling him a 'political gargoyle'. Labby did not stir. 'I say that the hon. gentleman, the member for Northampton, is a political gargoyle,' repeated the colonel. Labby remained quiescent. A few days later they ran into one another and Labby asked the colonel what he had meant by calling him a political gargoyle. 'It's rather late in the day to ask me that,' replied the baffled colonel, 'but if you look in the dictionary you will find that it means a grotesque gutter-spout.' Labby looked at him sadly. 'You're a very clever fellow, colonel. That would have been a capital point – if you had made it.'

In spite of the anger he so easily aroused in debate,
Labby was on excellent terms with men of all parties.
It was difficult to dislike him personally; his manner
was so friendly and ingratiating, his conversation so
entertaining, his help and advice so ready, that his
popularity was considerable on both sides of the House.
'I have been asked by the Government to speak to-
morrow on the compound householder,' a young tory
lawyer informed him, 'and I mean to say that I
cannot.' 'My good friend,' replied Labby, 'you are
mad. The Solicitor-Generalship is vacant; if you
speak by request, you will probably get it. The compound householder is such a recondite subject that
very few understand it. Get it up this evening as you
would a brief.' But the next day the young lawyer
did not speak, a fellow named Baliol Brett did, and
though no one paid much attention to the speech he
became Solicitor-General and eventually Lord Esher.
However, Labby determined to do his tory friend a
good turn and, knowing that he was nervous of
speaking in the House proposed to cure him. A
matter was coming up for discussion which involved
a good deal of law. 'If you like I will get up and
speak against the Government view,' said Labby.
'You must jeer at me. I will complain of this and
suggest that as you are an eminent lawyer you should
express your objections articulately. Then you, having prepared your speech, must get up and crush me.'
The lawyer agreed and everything was arranged.
When Labby started to lay down the law, the lawyer
laughed. Labby looked indignant and continued his
speech, which was punctuated by the lawyer with
sarcastic 'hear hears'. At last Labby protested, invited his critic to reply, and sat down. The speech
by the young tory marked him as 'a coming man'.

Whigs, tories, liberals, radicals – as politicians
Labby used or abused them according to their beliefs,
as human beings he did not distinguish between them.

In fact, one of his greatest friends was a leading tory: Lord Randolph Churchill. They made a curious pair. Their characters were to be seen in their conversational style, in the impetuous lunges of Churchill, the languid parries of Labby. They chaffed one another unceasingly, across dinner-tables, across the floor of the House. Churchill was a misfit: a rebel among aristocrats, an aristocrat among rebels. Fiery, imperious, self-assertive, impatient, quick-tempered, he desired above all things power and the admiration of the world. Labby was his political complement; they were unlike one another in every respect, which was probably the cause of their liking one another, for they did not compete. Labby, however, discovered a virtue they possessed in common: 'I think Churchill is one of the most serious politicians in the House of Commons – the most serious, I should say, after myself. He has been devoting himself for several years back with the most indomitable perseverance and energy to the task of finding out what his political opinions are.' Such was their friendship that when the Fourth Party[1] copied the custom of the ministerial and opposition leaders and had whitebait dinners at the Ship Hotel, Greenwich, after the parliamentary sessions, Labby was their only guest.

Although he was able to make most of his opponents squirm, Labby's shafts of ridicule seemed to glance off Churchill's armour of friendship. When some clergyman advised his flock to vote for 'Churchill and Heaven', the alternative being 'Gladstone and Hell', Labby remarked in public: 'Churchill and the Church would have been neater, I think, and perhaps slightly less like oil and water.' But that was only the political game and when Randolph was faced with a personal crisis Labby was the only man who gave him the sane

[1] An independent tory group, which consisted of Sir Henry Drummond Wolff, Sir John Gorst and Mr. A. J. Balfour, under the leadership of Lord Randolph Churchill.

advice of a loyal friend. Churchill was Chancellor of the Exchequer and Leader of the House of Commons in Salisbury's Government, but his restless nature impelled him to force Salisbury's hand and so achieve dominance in the cabinet by threatening to resign on the ground that he disapproved of the increased Estimates for the Army and Navy. Labby felt certain that Churchill was riding for a fall and told him so: 'In your own interests think it over. This would have been all very well if you had not been Leader of the House, or if you had been Leader for some years. In the former case, you might have upset your friends and been Leader; in the latter case you would have become a fetish.' Churchill was making the same mistake as Chamberlain had made: he was ignoring the power of the party machine. Also Churchill had selected a bad occasion, for even liberals at that moment favoured an increased expenditure on armaments. 'Yours is a waiting game,' counselled Labby. 'Sacrifice everything to becoming a fetish; then and only then you can do as you like.' But Labby's excellent advice, given against the interests of the party he served and solely in Randolph's personal interest, was not heeded. Salisbury accepted the resignation of Churchill, whose political crash was a major sensation.

In those days M.P.s took the business of government very seriously, and the chamber often resembled the feeding-hour at the Zoo for noise, a school playground on breaking-up day for disorderliness. Labby did not indulge in these howls and scrimmages. He preferred to sit quietly in his place and make a note of the scene for *Truth*. One such episode occurred in the middle of '93. It was started by Joseph Chamberlain, who compared Gladstone to Herod. Gladstone's followers then shrieked 'Judas!' at Chamberlain. The tories complained that 'Judas!' was unparliamentary, though, as Labby pointed out, 'Herod' was decidedly worse. A free fight followed the inability of M.P.s to reach an agreement on the relative demerits of these scriptural characters, and while it was in progress Labby, above the battle, made his note:

'On the Opposition Bench . . . sat Mr. Carson.[1] He had already attracted attention owing to the yells in which he had been indulging to beguile the time and to relieve his feelings. He is by no means an ugly man, but his expression is suggestive of Law Courts, and not exactly of those portions of them which are occupied by the Bench or by the Bar; indeed, Nature has so fashioned his face that any theatrical manager to whom he applied for an engagement would at once cast him for the part of Iago, if he contemplated producing *Othello*.'

Labby always sat on the end seat of the front opposition bench immediately below the gangway, which he managed to secure through the offices of some friend (usually Sir Charles Dilke) who happened to be present at prayer-time, when members could reserve their seats by placing cards upon them. The Christian member did not indulge in prayers.

Such was his craving for a cigarette that unless his presence was imperative he never remained in his seat for more than a quarter of an hour at a time, dashing out for a whiff of smoke, rushing back for a whiff of politics, out again, in again, and so on. He was a slave to cigarettes and smoked perpetually, even while feeding. Nothing but an important debate could keep him from the weed for twenty minutes together, and even during the grave deliberations of the Upper House on Home Rule, in the midst of Lord Derby's important pronouncement, his passion got the better of him. 'I'm off,' he whispered to a friend; 'I shall do what the noble Lord is doing – read his speech.' But he was also a slave to duty and no M.P. has ever attended the House so assiduously.

[1] Afterwards Lord Carson.

He was to be seen and heard at his best in the smoking-room of the House of Commons where, seated in an American rocking-chair, smoking interminable cigarettes, and surrounded by a crowd of fellow-members, he would tell stories and discourse on political conspiracies and hit off in biting phrases the peculiarities and absurdities of all the leaders, irrespective of party. An equally favoured spot was the smoking-room of the Reform Club, where he would sit on one side of the fireplace, beneath the windows that look across Pall Mall to the east side of St. James's Square. In both places he had a ready, eager audience, and before he had lit his first cigarette he was the centre of a group. Naturally his fame as a conversationalist grew with the years, and after the disappearance of Oscar Wilde he was fairly generally regarded as the best talker in England. Perhaps his finest flights were those in which he recounted, with a wealth of amusing comment, his past exploits in diplomacy, in Mexico, in the siege of Paris; but the amount of fancy he mixed with fact was sometimes too considerable for politicians, who are not among the most imaginative of beings, and one of them said: 'I do not mind having my leg pulled but I dislike to feel the process too distinctly.'

His voice, when not raised in public speech, was pleasant, and its drawling delivery gave piquancy to his cynical comments on men and affairs, his humorous revelations of plots and counter-plots. 'Do not, I implore you, allow the intellect to recede from the features,' an earnest photographer is reported to have said to someone who was adopting the look of a complacent idiot common to most sitters. Labby never allowed his intellect to recede from his features or his speech, both of which he rigidly controlled. No one could tell what he was thinking while he was speaking. Not a muscle of his face moved; he gave the appearance of knowing everything, of being surprised by nothing; his dark eyes, half closed, were mysterious, his immobility was sphinx-like; he toyed delicately with a cigarette, and occasionally he chuckled in a manner that some thought devilish.

He was what would now be described as a 'debunker'. That is to say, he told the truth, as he saw it, about everybody and everything, including himself. Whenever he attributed a good motive to a man, he instantly qualified it with a satirical comment on the fellow's sanity. 'So-and-so is a solid man – yes, that's the word – solid, respectable, possessing all the good old domestic and political virtues – including imbecility.' A young disciple went up to congratulate him on a trenchant speech he had just delivered on behalf of some oppressed nationality. He shrugged his shoulders, smiled genially and said, 'Oh, it was very good business!' This effectually damped the enthusiasm of his disciple, who had previously pictured him as Don Quixote and ever afterwards thought of him as Sancho Panza. After denouncing Gladstone's coercion policy in Ireland, he quelled the crusading spirit of another follower in these words: 'I only speak and vote with you in this ridiculous minority against coercion because nothing we can say or do will have any serious effect. You no doubt feel strongly about it, and so in a way do I. But I certainly should not care to risk the position of the Party on the issue, and if there were any danger of upsetting the Government by our protest I should probably vote the other way.' One day a card was brought to him in the smoking-room from someone who wanted a seat in the gallery. When he had attended to it and returned to his rocking-chair, he was asked whether the request came from one of his supporters in Northampton. 'What?' he replied, 'do you think that any elector who had money enough to pay his fare to London and back would be such a fool as to vote for me?'

It may have been a fellow-feeling that made him
paint himself as black as he painted everyone else, or
it may have been a hatred of sham so profound that
he could not bear to side for a moment with the senti-
mentalists. The fact remains that he typified in his
own person the violent reaction of an honest man
from the general dishonesty of political life and the
particular hypocrisy of his age. Nothing could induce
him to own up to a generous or disinterested action.
Joseph Chamberlain once caught him out befriending
some unlucky individual at considerable trouble and
cost to himself, but Labby was ready with an explanation: 'A political tool, my dear fellow; the man may
be serviceable; I pay him enough to use him when I
want to, without shame or scruple.' That was his
favourite attitude in any circumstance. After a
rubber of whist his partner said that his play, though
successful, had been risky because one of his adversaries
might have held such-and-such a card. 'I agree,' he
said, 'but then I took the precaution of looking over
my adversary's hand.'

He was quite impartial in his estimate of men; they
were all pretty much alike, whatever their political
colour. A few of his dicta, flung out in the course of
conversation, may be quoted here:

'The mere denial of the existence of God does not
entitle a man's opinion to be taken without scrutiny on
matters of greater importance.'

'Of course I think our party is right, but whether
we are or not we've got all the bunkum on our
side.'

'When all praise you, this will be proof positive that
there is something wrong.'

'The tories will go in for any enterprise which they
think will land them on the Treasury Bench – and so
will the radicals.'

'Chamberlain is very honest and straightforward,
they say, and he has a conscience, he says. . . .'

'Gladstone is simply wild to get in and will certainly go mad if he's not allowed to make a move.'

Occasionally he disappointed the group that surrounded him, especially when something more than usually important was going on behind the scenes and much was expected from him.

'I don't exactly claim to be an inspired prophet,' he remarked at the peak of some crisis in which he had been playing a large and secret part, 'but I do observe that what I predict does somehow always come to pass.'

'But you haven't predicted anything in this case,' said one of his breathless auditors.

'No; so you'll find that what I haven't predicted, what I keep to myself, will in this case come to pass.'

A noticeable quality in Labby was his politeness, due to an ever-present sensitiveness to the feelings of others. Except in the give-and-take of political warfare, his geniality was never-failing. He could not bear to give pain, except to those who inflicted it, and it is reported that he once ran out of a room rather than face a maidservant he had summoned by too vigorous a pull at the bell. Leaving the House with a friend after a tiring sitting, they passed Herbert Gladstone. 'So you're free from the old tyrant at last?' asked Labby, meaning the Speaker. Herbert did not reply and Labby turned anxiously to his companion with: 'I hope he didn't think I meant his father.' On all occasions he displayed a marked courtesy to friends, strangers and servants alike. Two House of Commons officials strolled into the smoking-room without realising that it was for members only. Knowing that, if they discovered their mistake, they would be ill at ease, and anxious to make them feel at home, Labby left his chair, went over to them and chatted pleasantly until they had to go. He even survived with a serene countenance a strain on his forbearance that must have caused him acute suffering.

'Most people have read Milton's *Paradise Lost*, but I wonder if anybody has read *Paradise Regained*?' he asked John Bright, who promptly began with the opening line and recited the greater part of the poem. When he stopped there was a silence, broken at last by Labby, who said gratefully: 'D'you know, this is my only experience of Paradise Regained.'

Like Abraham Lincoln, Labby enjoyed repeating or inventing coarse stories, which were not always amusing, but which added to his popularity in the smoking-room. These have not come down to us, and so we do not know the precise shade of coarseness that appealed to his sense of humour, but most of them were probably as innocuous as this:

'Don't you remember the story of Millie Moidore when she got married and left the stage and re-formed? One day her husband thought she had relapsed a little and accused her. She owned up handsomely and said, "You know I hadn't seen him for ever so long and one must oblige *such* an old friend".'

Labby used to say that every story that had survived the publication of the Nicomachean Ethics was but a variant of one of the Seven Originals told to Eve by the Serpent in the Garden of Eden. He seems to have forgotten that they were told to a lady.

# CHAPTER IX

## PRIVATE AND IMPERSONAL

LABBY was a lonely man. Anyone who despises the trumpery distinctions and hollow applause which are the motives of most endeavour and for which nearly all men struggle cannot help feeling an alien on earth. Yet he was far from being an unhappy man. He never ceased to be amused by the strange antics of his fellow human beings, and though he could not help feeling a vague pity for them he was healthy enough to perceive that, in the general spectacle of life, there was more to laugh at than to cry over. His private life was pleasant because it was conducted in that unruffled impersonal manner so characteristic of him. He was much too considerate of other people ever not to do exactly what he wanted to do, knowing well that a dissatisfied man is a bad citizen and a poor companion. He was that apparently abnormal product, a perfectly normal man, who wished people to do just as they pleased, never interfered with others and would not let others interfere with him. A Freudian would have found the question of his 'complexes' rather too complex and would have given him up as a hopeless case on the ground that he was not 'a case'. On the other hand, Labby would almost certainly have regarded the Freudian as 'a case'.

His domestic life was entirely free from 'scenes'; his private habits and doings and conversations with friends could have been published without much editing in *Truth*, and indeed many of them were.

It might almost be said that his private life would not have been different if it had been passed in public. His relationship with his wife was of the friendliest description, but there was little sentiment in it; they were fond of one another, understood one another perfectly, but they were not dependent upon one another. Labby was not the kind of man to fall head over ears in love with anyone, and from the beginning there was more affection than passion in their marriage. Probably it was Henrietta Hodson's frankness and capability that first attracted him. She certainly had much personal charm, a musical voice and a pretty if pugnacious face; but his fancy was taken by her business sense, her determination, her dominating personality.

She opened the Royalty Theatre in 1870, managing it with considerable ability and introducing one or two novelties to the West End, such as the unseen orchestra. She even emerged with honours from a battle royal with the redoubtable William Gilbert, having publicly accused him of pretty well everything short of murder without serious consequences to herself. Labby, by the way, shared her dislike of Gilbert, about whom comments which must have seriously upset his digestion frequently appeared in *Truth*. Perhaps Henrietta Hodson's most remarkable achievement was her 'creation' of Mrs. Langtry as an actress. Though she retired from the stage in the 'seventies she never lost interest in it and it always gave her the greatest pleasure to impose her personality on actresses who lacked individuality. She caught up Mrs. Langtry, a great social beauty of the time, and forced her to appear in a charity performance at Twickenham Town Hall. She then drilled her so well that she was able to give a passably good performance of Kate Hardcastle in *She Stoops to Conquer*. In fact, Mrs. Langtry surrendered herself to this plump, good-natured, high-spirited, determined creature, whose square jaw and curly grey hair were outward signs of an inward will-power, and to whose patience and resource she owed her career as an actress. Eventually Henrietta insisted on arranging a tour for Mrs. Langtry in the United States and actually obtained for her the same terms as had been paid to Sarah Bernhardt. Henrietta also stated her intention of accompanying her protégée to America. Labby smiled and said, 'You'll be back soon, as you're bound to quarrel with one another.' But Henrietta had a reason for going.

'She had often told me "Labby" had no sentiment,' related Mrs. Langtry, 'and that it was by providing for his comfort that she held him. Now she was bent on showing him *le revers de la médaille*. She dismissed the cook and most of the servants, muffled all the rooms in brown holland, and cut the buttons off his shirts, etc., before she left.'

Labby was faintly amused by these preparations, prophesied a speedy return home for his wife, and during her absence lived quite happily on sandwiches and sausages. The quarrel soon occurred, as he had foreseen, and Henrietta, who had probably been left out of the numerous invitations sent to Mrs. Langtry, returned home in a peevish frame of mind. Labby was delighted to see her again, but the lack of surprise in his welcome was irritating. It is more than probable that he was largely responsible for her becoming a Roman Catholic. His undeviating equability, his amused and slightly disdainful toleration, his cynical knowingness, his unwavering scepticism, must have been quite sufficient to precipitate an ardent nature like hers into a Faith in which she could find nothing at all that distantly reminded her of him. Characteristically he had not the least objection to her conversion. It was merely another of the comical vagaries of life. Like many agnostics he felt that, if people had to embrace a religion at all, the Roman Catholic was the pick of the bunch; and when in 1886 his daughter was old enough to go to school, the following colloquy took place between himself and his wife:

'Henrietta, does it occur to you that when our girl grows up she can hardly find a match in England acceptable to us?'

'Yes.'

'Well, it follows she must marry on the Continent.'

'Very good.'

'So she should then be brought up a Catholic?'

'I suppose so.'

'Is there any convent in the neighbourhood to which we could send her?'

'Yes, the convent in Kensington Square.'

'Let her go there to-morrow morning.'

And it was so. This daughter, Dora, whom Labby worshipped, inherited her father's dark eyes with their mischievous twinkle and became in time the Marchesa di Rudini[1], one of the loveliest women in Rome.

The homes of the Laboucheres were all within easy reach of the House of Commons and the offices of *Truth*. For about a dozen years they lived at No. 10 Queen Anne's Gate, moving in the late 'eighties to a tall gloomy house near Victoria Station, No. 24 Grosvenor Gardens, where the Pigott and Parnell conferences took place, and then to their final London home in 1889, No. 5 Old Palace Yard. This last residence was secured by Labby in a rather curious manner. One day he happened to meet the First Commissioner of Works, Shaw-Lefevre, who gleefully announced that he had his eye on certain premises which would enable him to realise his cherished plan of building an annexe to Westminster Abbey in which famous men could henceforth be buried. It would become a sort of Valhalla, a sepulchral aisle, and would

[1] She is now Princess Ruspoli.

relieve the Abbey of further congestion. There was a difference of a few hundred pounds between his offer and the amount required by the owner of the premises, the Duke of Marlborough, but he felt sure they would soon arrive at an amicable agreement. Labby displayed considerable sympathy with the project, asked where the house was, how much had been offered and demanded, and then went off to inspect the position. He discovered that it was the very place for him, slap opposite the entrance to the House of Lords, paid a visit to the owner, sprang the full sum required, and became possessor. 'Shaw-Lefevre seemed rather angry when he called and found the house had been sold,' Labby recounted in tones of mild surprise. 'I pointed out to him that as the place was so close to the Houses of Parliament, it was better to have a live M.P. in it than a dead statesman or poet.'

The house stood in need of much repair and workmen were called in. They took so long over their job that, during one of his visits to see how things were progressing, Labby advised them to consult their own tastes in furnishing the premises, since it was clearly their intention to settle down there permanently. As soon as it became known that Labby was about to reside within the precincts of Westminster Abbey, Sir Frederick Bridge wrote a parody of 'Sally in our Alley' which appeared in *Punch* under the heading of 'Labby in Our Abbey':

> Of all the Rads that are so smart
> There's none like crafty Labby,
> He learns the secret of each heart,
> And lives near our Abbey;
> There is no lawyer in the land
> That's half as sharp as Labby,
> He is a demon in the art,
> And guileless as a babby!

For 'Bomba Balfour' (a) in the week
There seems to be no worse day
Than is the one that comes between
A Tuesday and a Thursday,(b)
For then we read each foul misdeed
'Unmanly, mean and shabby',
Exposed to view in type so true
By penetrating Labby.

Lord Salisbury and the Tories, all
Flout, gibe and jeer at Labby,
Though but for him 'tis said they'd be
A sleepy set and flabby;
And 'ere their seven long years are out,(c)
Could they be rid of Labby,
'Snug lying' they might find for him;
But not in our Abbey!(*)

The dinners and receptions given by the Laboucheres at 5 Old Palace Yard were notable throughout the 'nineties. The splendid dresses and gorgeous uniforms of the dinner-guests contrasted strangely with the rather seedy smoking-jacket of their host, and the exquisite dishes and admirable wines set before them with the plate of cold ham, piece of dry bread and glass of water which satisfied him. He was ascetic by nature, actually preferring a beef sandwich to a perfectly-cooked dish, a public bus to a private carriage, a third-class to a first-class compartment. His breakfast usually consisted of two cups of tea and an egg, which he gulped down as quickly as possible in order to enjoy his cigarettes and the papers. His liking for beef sandwiches was due to the accident of his arriving home unexpectedly one evening and

(a) Arthur Balfour was then Chief Secretary for Ireland.
(b) *Truth* was published on Wednesdays.
(c) A reference to the Septennial Act.
(*) Reprinted by permission of the Proprietors of *Punch*.

demanding something to eat.  The butler, finding
nothing in the house, sent to the nearest public-house
for some slices of ham and beef, 'which I enjoyed so
much that I seriously thought of dismissing my cook',
said Labby.  He seldom used his carriage, which was
hired from a livery stable, nearly always travelling
by bus or underground.  Once he was standing on
the platform in the midst of a discussion with some
financial magnate when the train came in.

'We'll finish our talk in here,' said the magnate,
drawing Labby towards a first-class compartment.

'No, no; if you want to talk to me you must travel
third,' said Labby; and they did.

The receptions at No. 5 Old Palace Yard were sometimes informal to a point of discomfort.  They were
mixed gatherings, in which famous actors rubbed
shoulders with famous politicians, eminent vocalists
with eminent barristers, in which bishops, surgeons,
soul-curers, body-curers, thought-readers, jam-makers,
engineers, financiers, diplomats, journalists, soldiers,
sailors, gentiles and Jews, made up a social potpourri
that was unlike anything else in London.  There were
no formalities; people were not introduced to one
another; anyone could talk to anyone; and as a result
no one's reputation was safe.  It was a modern School
for Scandal, in which the spirit of outspokenness had
been released by their host, the editor of *Truth*.
Rumour was allowed full rein and so sensational were
some of the revelations that, in self-preservation, no
one dared refuse an invitation.

Mrs. Labouchere was always discovering artists who
were going to set the Thames on fire and at these receptions there was usually a new violinist or a new
vocalist who would be expected to electrify the guests.
Once she got a large crowd together to hear a young
'find' of hers named Clara Butt, and the wife of a
famous dramatic critic, Mrs. Clement Scott, was one
of the crowd.  It was Mrs. Scott's first experience of a

Laboucherean reception, and knowing no one she sought out a quiet spot, half-hidden by ferns, and waited for the show to begin. Unfortunately, her attempt to escape the crowd had been observed by a male guest and she was subjected to the company of a most impertinent man, who planted himself on a seat by her side and began in a loud voice to abuse Mrs. Labouchere for her excessively tedious parties: her taste in friends was rotten, he said; in fact, she showed no taste whatever in her friends; it was positively indecent to inflict such bores on intelligent people; as for the singers she got together, well, just listen to the one who was about to open her mouth and send forth sound and fury, signifying nothing except want of brains; and so on and so on. Mrs. Scott was limp with the effort of trying to be polite to this ill-mannered fellow and trying at the same time to dissociate herself from him. As he went on talking at the top of his voice and as he was saying the rudest conceivable things about their hostess and their fellow-guests, it became plain to Mrs. Scott that the room was giving them more than half an ear, and she was wondering whether to make a bolt for it and never come near the place again when, to her horror, she saw Mrs. Labouchere bearing down upon them. Her brain was reeling. What on earth could she say? It had not been her fault. Apparently Mrs. Labouchere realised this because she addressed her remarks to Mrs. Scott's detestable companion:

'Shut up, Labby! Do be quiet and behave yourself properly.'

At that moment Miss Butt began to sing.

Except perhaps with Mrs. Scott, Labby was extremely popular with women, who flitted around him at these receptions and were always begging him to tell them stories. 'He's a Jacobin,' said a certain duchess; 'I should hate him if he didn't tell such amusing naughty stories. But I know he would put

on the red cap in a minute and sentence us cheerfully
to the guillotine. He wants to do away with *us*!'
He was not only popular for telling naughty stories.
Whenever it was known that he would make a speech,
the ladies' gallery of the Commons was packed. His
assumed lack of interest in people aroused their interest
in him. He would lounge into a drawing-room with
an expressionless face, as if he had no thought of anything but how to kill time, and with a single glance
through half-closed eyes he seemed to take in the individuality of everyone present. 'How d'ye do?' his lips
would say, but not his other features. 'I say, Labby,
why don't we ever see you at So-and-so's?' someone
would ask: 'do you never leave London?' His answer
would throw no light on the problem: 'I never frequent
the country-houses of the great. It may be because
I am not asked, and it may be because I do not care
to go – that is my affair.'

Except when abroad most of the time he was away
from London was spent at his house on the Thames,
Pope's Villa, Twickenham. Here the Laboucheres
used to go for week-ends during the fine weather and
for several weeks every summer. Its chief historic
interest was that it had once been the residence of the
poet, Pope, but Labby poured cold water on that belief,
as he did on so many others. When someone became
ecstatic over its literary associations, he broke in:

'But this isn't Pope's real villa.'

'Oh!'

'Good heavens, no! Pope built a villa on this site,
but it was destroyed and a worthy Swiss built the present house. Naturally, when the family are absent
the servants show the bedroom to sightseers as the
identical room in which the poet died and reap a considerable benefit from the lie. It would be unfair on
them and needlessly cruel to the sightseers if we interfered with this charming old-fashioned custom. When
Pope built the grotto he received from admirers all

over the world bits of malachite, chrysophrase, blood-
stone, onyx, sardonyx, the matrix of opal, turquoise
and many semi-precious stones, and with these he
adorned the place.  But there are only two bits left;
the remainder have been plucked by enterprising
tourists, American probably, as they have practical
and acquisitive minds.'

Guests would arrive at about noon on Sundays in
summer, sit on the lawn till lunch was ready, return
to the lawn for coffee, wander about the grounds
doing what they liked all the afternoon, go through the
grotto to the other side of the garden for tea, roam
about smoking cigarettes and talking until dinner –
Labby himself always the centre of a laughing circle
– and then back to the house for a wash and brush-up,
morning dress being always the rule for the convenience of everybody.  After dinner a moonlight or
starlight drive home to London.  Crowds of M.P.s as
well as city magnates would come to these entertainments, and standing once at the door of the Villa,
looking down upon the large company that had
assembled, Labby remarked to O'Shea: 'I think we
have every rascal in London here.'

Sometimes Mrs. Labouchere provided her guests
with pastoral performances of *A Midsummer Night's
Dream* or *The Tempest*, which she produced and stage-
managed with great care, and in the later performances of which their daughter appeared as Puck and
Ariel.  These productions were of great beauty and
many people have left their memories of the exquisite
setting, with countless electric lights among the trees,
and the well-coached cast of players.  After such performances the guests were entertained to dinner in a
large hall, where flowers, palms and various-sized
tables were dispersed about the floor.  Labby did not
look forward to these meals, as, apart from the fact
that he never ate them, he had to drink the health of
the producer, his wife, in champagne, experiencing

great difficulty in getting through the business without looking as if he had just been poisoned.

He was fond of Pope's Villa, especially when he had it to himself and it did not matter what the cooking was like. Except when Mrs. Labouchere was expecting a crowd, the cooking was 'awful, always', according to Mrs. Langtry; so bad indeed that the Duke of Marlborough once confessed his inability to eat the dishes placed before him. 'Ah!' replied his unabashed host, 'I make a point of having a bad cook because I do not wish to grow fat.' Another reason that he liked Pope's Villa was that his little daughter Dora loved him to row her about the Thames, and as he never grudged her his time or leisure, however busy he was or however important his social engagements, he frequently spent Saturday afternoons rowing her up and down the river, chatting easily and reasonably with her as if she were already grown up.

He would not have dreamt of taking this exercise for his own pleasure or benefit. He had an utter contempt for most of the things that English people like or admire. He abhorred sport of all kinds, especially blood-sports, and the notion that one was doing some sort of good to oneself by straining one's heart while exercising one's limbs was dismissed by him as too childish for discussion. 'Why on earth does anyone take the trouble to climb a mountain?' he asked. 'I never could understand how anybody could take an interest in such a stupid beast as a horse,' was another of his remarks. When a golf-course was opened near his favourite spot in the Italian Lakes, Cadenabbia, he wanted to know 'what business have these people with their clubs and knickerbockers in a place like this? They are out of the picture and bore everybody with their talk. I don't think I shall come here again.' But he had to admit ruefully:

'The age is given to athleticism. I suppose some

people like it. I do not and therefore I never hit
balls with a stick or kick one with my foot, nor do
I do much in the way of walking. All this is a habit
acquired in youth, and the body so adapts itself to
the habit that it cannot be shaken off. Never take
exercise and you will never want to! is a golden
maxim.'

Most of his holidays were spent in discovering new
health resorts, either in England or on the Continent.
We hear of him often at Brighton, at Bayreuth (where
he was embraced on both cheeks by Wagner for some
trifling service), at Homburg, and frequently at
Marienbad:

'I always take the waters when I am at a place of
this kind, for if they do no good they do no harm.
What these particular waters are composed of, I have
not the slightest notion.' And again: 'I really believe that in the course of my life I have drunk every
healing well in Europe. I never consult a doctor,
but on my arrival at a watering-place I buy a book
which tells me how much is to be quaffed, what I
am to eat and what not to eat. The whole thing is
much like turning a horse out to grass.'

His happiest holidays were spent idling at Cadenabbia
on Lake Como:

'Of course there is a pleasure in doing absolutely
nothing. This pleasure I am indulging in at
present. . . . I am one of those who agree with the
traveller who, on being told that there was nothing
to see in some town at which he had arrived, said
"Then I remain here for a fortnight. . . ." There
are some books in the hotel, mostly novels. I take
up Vol. 1 of one of the books and if I cannot find
Vol. 2 go on with Vol. 2 of some other novel equally
exciting. From morn to night I do absolutely
nothing. I sit under a tree with my book and

occasionally vary the scene by being rowed about on the Lake. I talk to anyone who talks to me and we both get through our conversation without saying anything. I have not heard one word of politics since I have been here; indeed I should feel justified in pushing anyone into the Lake who even remotely alluded to the Irish Question, for there is a time and season for everything. During the first few days that I was here, I came to the conclusion that politics and newspapers and any serious business in life are vanity and vexation, and that a wise man would do well to give up all these things and to remain here for the rest of his life. But such is human nature that I have not been long here before the *dolce far niente* palls a little. Finally one takes the train journeys back to England and plunges into the Irish Question, the Eight Hours Question, and generally into all sorts of valuable reforms which probably would come about in due course of time if I remained for the rest of my life reading odd volumes of novels, talking about nothing to persons who talk about nothing, being rowed on the Lake listening to itinerant musicians, and eating the delicious little fish that come out of the Lake.'[1]

From this it will appear that his taste in literature was fairly catholic, but when he really wanted to enjoy himself he picked up a volume by Miss Braddon, whom he placed 'amongst the greatest benefactors of the present generation. When I read a novel I have no desire to be instructed or to be improved. I wish to be amused, and there is not one of Miss Braddon's books which does not enlist the interest of the reader. They are sensational, as all good stories ought to be.'

Outside politics Labby had three intimate friends who claim notice in his biography. He had helped all three in their struggling days and maintained a

[1] *Truth*, September 24, 1891.

real affection for them to the end. The first of these, James McNeill Whistler, he met at Washington in the 'fifties. When Whistler came to London they met again and Labby was probably the only friend Whistler never quarrelled with. Had Labby been quarrelsome by nature there was good cause for trouble when he bought Whistler's picture of Connie Gilchrist, 'The Gold Girl', at an auction, and then lent it to the artist who wanted to make a slight alteration. 'That was ten years ago,' said Labby to someone who wanted to know what had happened to the portrait. 'He is still not sufficiently satisfied with it to return my picture and I don't expect ever to see it again; he does not think that payment for one of his works entitles the purchaser to possession of it.'

But Whistler's friendship was worth more to Labby than a hundred portraits, and the tables of many hostesses in the 'eighties were kept on a roar by the grave demeanour and mock-serious conversation of these two. They talked in American, French and English, and each brought out the best in the other. Whistler's strength lay in his attack, Labby's in his defence. The smashing deliveries of Whistler were countered by the deft rallies of Labby. Whistler forced the pace, Labby steadied it. The painter's wit was daring, the politician's was cunning; Whistler was hammer, Labby was tongs. It was however the politician who forced the pace when words gave way to action. Whistler fell in love with the widow of Godwin, the architect, but did not dare to ask her to marry him because he was afraid his mistress would make hostile demonstrations. Both Whistler and Mrs. Godwin were thoroughly bohemian and since they were obviously in love with one another Labby thought it absurd that they should not get married at once. So, during a dinner with a few friends at Earl's Court, he put the matter before them in a business-like manner:

'Jimmy,' he said, 'will you marry Mrs. Godwin?'

'Certainly,' replied Whistler.

'Mrs. Godwin,' he said, 'will you marry Jimmy?'

'Certainly,' replied Mrs. Godwin.

'When?' demanded Labby.

'Oh, some day,' said Whistler.

'That won't do,' declared Labby; 'we must have a date.'

It was at last agreed that Labby should fix the day, choose the church, provide a clergyman and give the bride away. The chaplain of the House of Commons promised to perform the ceremony, which was arranged to take place a few days after the dinner at St. Mary Abbott's, Kensington. The day before the marriage Labby happened to meet the bride in the street.

'Don't forget to-morrow,' he said.

'No,' she replied; 'I am just going to buy my trousseau.'

'A little late for that, isn't it?'

'No. I am only going to buy a new toothbrush and a new sponge, as one ought to have new ones when one marries.'

After the ceremony they went to Whistler's studio, where a banquet was prepared. There were no chairs, so the guests sat on packing-cases. When Labby left them Whistler and his wife had not quite decided whether they would go to Paris that evening or remain in the studio.

Though he was not always able to arrange happy marriages, Labby often helped men of talent to recognition. Pellegrini, who became famous as a caricaturist, was encouraged by him to do a series of public men. 'I got him into the House of Commons under the gallery to inspect a few specimens,' explained Labby. Presumably the specimens appealed to Pellegrini, for he quickly made his name.

Once only did Labby show any grave lack of sympathy with an artist and his failure was due to the essential normality of his nature. He had known Oscar Wilde for years and, while thinking him extremely clever and witty, had noticed in him an almost diseased craving for notoriety. Consequently, when the Wilde scandal burst upon the town, Labby wrote in *Truth*:

'It would not surprise me if he were deriving a keen enjoyment from a position which most people, whether really innocent or guilty, would prefer to die rather than occupy. He must have known in what a glass house he lived when he challenged investigation in a court of justice. After he had done this, he went abroad. Why did he not stay abroad? The possibilities of a prison may not be pleasing to him, but I believe that the notoriety that has overtaken him has such a charm for him that it outweighs everything else.'

When Wilde was found guilty, Labby thought that the sentence of two years hard labour was inadequate:

'Wilde and Taylor were tried on a clause in the Criminal Law Amendment Act which I had inserted[1] in order to render it possible for the law to take cognisance of proceedings like theirs. I took the clause *mutatis mutandis* from the French Code. As I had drafted it the maximum sentence was seven years. The then Home Secretary and Attorney-General, both most experienced men, suggested to me that in such cases convictions are always difficult and that it would be better were the maximum to be two years. Hence the insufficiency of the severest sentence that the law allows.'

In judging Labby's attitude we must remember that the Victorians regarded homosexuality as a crime, not as a disease, and that his real feeling about Wilde's punishment was simply this:

[1] In 1885.

'In view of the mischief that such a man does, the sentence he has received compares but lightly with those almost every day awarded for infinitely less pernicious crimes.'

That was the essence of the thing. When men were daily sent to prison for stealing food for their starving families, it was absurd to feel sympathy with a man who had asked for trouble and got what he asked for. Incidentally it must have been strange for Labby to find himself so entirely on the popular side, and for once he lost his balance; like a man who, leaning hard against the wind, topples over when it veers.

The second of Labby's intimate friends to be noticed is Sir Henry Irving, who made one of his earliest appearances in London under Labby's management. Since he was less easily imposed upon than any critic or any man of his time, it is interesting to recall that Labby was not an admirer of Irving as an actor but had a great admiration and affection for him as a man. At the Queen's Theatre, Long Acre, back in the 'sixties, Irving had walked the stage like a normal human being and had spoken distinctly; why he neither walked nor talked like any human being after he had achieved fame, especially as he was perfectly natural off the stage, Labby could never understand. Mannerisms did not matter so much in parts like Louis XI, which Labby thought his best performance, but his Hamlet was 'very mediocre' and his Romeo 'thoroughly bad'. According to Labby 'he never passed the line where art ends and genius begins. It may sound a paradox in considering the merits of an actor, but his fault was that he was always acting.'

What Labby really liked in Irving was his kindness and generosity and the fact that success did not spoil him. No one who appealed to him for help did so in vain; he spent little on himself, much on charity and hospitality. Knowing that his great ambition was to

raise the social status of the stage, Labby once proposed
to Gladstone that a knighthood should be conferred on
Irving. Gladstone was completely taken aback.
Knight an actor? However he discussed the question
with Lord Granville and eventually told Labby that
he would recommend Irving for the title if the actor
agreed. But when Labby told Irving what he had
done, the actor declined the distinction on the ground
that it might render him ridiculous. Since Irving
accepted a knighthood from Lord Rosebery at a
later date, it is safe to conclude that his first refusal
was not unconnected with the manner of Labby's
approach. We can almost hear the words:

'The G.O.M. wants to know if you'd like to be
tapped on the shoulders by the G.O.W.? I told
him you were anxious to turn actors into gentlemen
– God alone knows why! they're much funnier as
they are – and that if you were knighted the whole
theatrical profession would instantly become respectable, and of course dull. Well, I needn't tell
you what nonsense it all is, but such is life, don't
you know, and there we are, so to speak. Shall I
tell him you are dying to be tapped?'

Irving used often to call on Labby after the shows
were over at the Lyceum and St. Stephens and sit up
talking till 5 or 6 in the morning, neither of them
anxious to go to bed. Only a few weeks before
Irving's death they were dining together and the
actor, after railing against the craze for silly plays and
musical comedies, tried but failed to convert the
politician to a belief in municipal theatres.

The third of Labby's famous friends to be mentioned
was Charles Russell, afterwards Lord Russell of
Killowen, who became Lord Chief Justice of England
in 1894. Russell once informed Labby that he traced
his success in life from the time he was first briefed for
*Truth*, and though Labby disclaimed any credit for

this the fact remains that Russell was unknown to the general public until at the age of 45 he made the most of the chance given him by Labby's solicitor, Sir George Lewis. After that his rise to fame was rapid, in spite of the fact (or because of it) that he would not plead a cause he felt to be wrong. Thus, when he took up a case, he did so with a passionate conviction that right was on his side and his emotion was not simulated. He possessed a hasty temper, which made him unpopular with his juniors, and sometimes his outbursts of rage were quite alarming, but he was capable on occasion of suddenly checking himself in the full flow of his fury and continuing so coolly that people blinked in amazement. Although Labby now and then disagreed with Russell and drew upon himself 'all the terrors of that flashing eye and sarcastic tongue', they enjoyed one another's company so much that they frequently went to the same holiday-resort. Once they were enjoying a game of cards with two friends under the veranda of a hotel at Marienbad, when a seedy-looking individual passed by and after regarding them curiously for a while addressed them in German. Labby was the only member of the party who could speak the language and promptly entered into conversation with the man, who shortly produced a pack of cards and offered it to Labby. Meanwhile Russell's temper had been rising and he told Labby to buy the pack at once and get rid of the fellow. Labby obeyed and after the man had gone he was asked what they had talked about. At first he refused to say, but upon being pressed he owned up: 'Well, the fact is he said to me that he did not like the look of my companions, especially the Lord Chief Justice here, and he feared I was a pigeon; so, being connected with the police, he insisted on my playing with a fresh pack of cards.' This was a slight adaptation of the actual facts, the seedy-looking individual having been a revenue-officer whose job it was to see that people played cards in public only with packs on which the state-duty had been paid.

We may fitly close this chapter with a story that Russell used to tell. An American friend, who had been extremely kind to him during his visit to the United States, arrived in London in the early 'eighties. Russell, anxious to pay him every possible attention, felt sure that he would like above all things to meet some celebrated Englishmen and made out a list: Gladstone, Bright, Salisbury, Randolph Churchill, Parnell, Chamberlain, the Speaker, the Lord Chancellor, the leaders of the Bar, some famous bishops, generals, admirals, artists and so on.

'If I cannot myself introduce you to any of these men, I think I can promise to get an introduction for you,' said Russell, handing his friend the list.

'Well,' replied the American, 'there is only one man I want to meet, and if you can get me an introduction to him I shall feel very much obliged.'

'Certainly I will do my best,' said Russell, cudgelling his brains in an effort to think of some famous personality he had omitted from the list or some extraordinary and quite inaccessible figure.

'The only man I want to meet is Mr. Henry Labouchere,' announced the American.

# CHAPTER X

## FOR QUEEN OR COUNTRY?

A COMMON saying among poor people runs: 'It's easy to be honest if you're rich.' But so strong is the social pressure brought to bear on wealthy people, so flattering the attentions of the aristocracy and the ruling classes, that a rich man might reasonably retort: 'How easy to be honest when you're poor!' It requires uncommon courage and genuine independence of mind for a wealthy man, one who belongs from birth to the ruling caste or whose success in life ensures his absorption by it, to stand outside the established order and criticise it; for it seems a sort of disloyalty to strike at the props of one's own existence; but a poor man has nothing to lose and everything to gain by criticising a state of affairs which keeps him in poverty. Hence the scarcity of rich rebels.

As a rule the rich rebel is a genius, one whose originality of mind and strength of character prevent him from seeing things in a conventional way and accepting them because other people do so; and as mediocrity, the mean which forms the basis of all societies, feels insecure in the presence of a genius, it treats him as a joke to be laughed at or as a freak to be avoided. If a genius were taken seriously, the Establishment would be shaken; and if a genius were given position or prestige, the Establishment would be undermined. Samuel Butler discovered that the Church was not the only organisation that had an Establishment. Science had one too, with its priests and high-priests, its excommunications and anathemas. The world of painting also has its Royal Academy, medicine its Association, while economics, politics, letters, law, the army and the navy have their sacred inner rings which it is the ambition of everyone in the outer circles to placate or penetrate, though the genius knows instinctively that he must stand alone, unbuttressed by his professional Establishment.

Labby in politics had no more chance of official recognition than Butler in science, and no more chance of sitting on the Treasury Bench than Sydney Smith had of sitting on the bench of bishops. He saw through the Establishment of politics and saw that it was bad, and said so, and went on saying so. He would certainly have liked to shatter it to bits and remould it nearer to the heart's desire; but as that was out of the question, he laughed at it and did his best with it. He was altogether too exceptional a person to be ignored; so the Establishment laughed at him and decided at a very early date to keep him at a safe distance. Although the Establishment draws the line at genius, which is uncontrollable, it does not object to talent, because the occasional indiscretions of talent do no harm and in a way reflect glory on the Establishment, which must surely be a very sound and wonderful institution to find room for such gifted and outspoken members. Thus talented 'insiders', a Churchill in politics, an Inge in the Church, are permitted and even encouraged to tilt the applecart; they can be relied upon never to upset it; and their criticism is called sound and sincere. But Labby in politics, Sydney Smith in the Church, Butler in science, were geniuses and 'outsiders' from the start, and their criticisms, because they went to the roots of the structures concerned, were called flippant and profane. Broadly it may be said that Establishments flourish on the criticism of talent and perish from the ridicule of genius. Occasionally a genius like

Cromwell, by making his imagination the servant of his will, gains an entry into the Establishment, but when this happens he usually ends by being the Establishment.

The outrageous thing about Labby was that he not only ridiculed his own political Establishment, but he attacked from an unusual angle the Establishment of Establishments – the Crown. He said it was too expensive. Here again we must bear in mind his belief that money was strictly limited and that, if diverted from the royal purse, it could be devoted to the needs of the poor. Taxation is still based on this belief and so we cannot yet afford to laugh at his illusion.

His personal attitude towards the Reigning House was quite clear:

'I do not feel the slightest loyalty towards the Royal Family; indeed I do not understand the meaning of the term "Royal Family". My loyalty to the Queen is a feeling of respect for the visible emblem of the laws that we ourselves have made, and I honour her because of her sterling qualities and for the good sense she has shown during her reign.'

He also liked the simplicity of her habits and was pleased by her contempt for those who tried to buy social distinctions. 'I had a more sincere admiration for her than most of the flunkeys who bowed and scraped before her,' he wrote when she died, and we may well believe it, though his manner of showing his admiration was not conventional enough to convince the Queen of its sincerity. For example his attitude in the House towards royal expenses might easily have misled her. 'There is a family for whom we have great respect, but it is not necessary that they should be excessively rich to command that respect,' he said, and whenever sums of money were granted to members of the Royal Family he got up and protested. Some of his protests may be recorded here.

He objected to the excessive cost of keeping four royal
yachts afloat, and also to the fact that 'some German
Prince or other' was always put in command of a royal
yacht. He objected to the cost of conveying royal
personages across the Channel in special steam-packets,
and to the expenses for the upkeep of Royal Palaces
which were not used: Kew Palace should be done away
with altogether, he said; Kensington Palace should be
turned into a temperance restaurant; and Holyrood
Palace should be allowed to fall into ruin.

'A palace in ruin is a far more beautiful object
than a palace not in ruin. The House should not
interfere with the work of time, which would convert
this palace into a beautiful ruin where hon. gentlemen could go by moonlight and meditate.'

When the Duke of Edinburgh became the Duke of
Saxe-Coburg, Labby instantly demanded that the
annuity granted him by the British parliament should
be reduced. This was too much for the Queen who
promptly telegraphed to Gladstone her wish that 'his
friends' should rally round her in such a crisis and
oppose 'that frightful Mr. Labouchere's motion'.
Concerning the shooting rights of another Royal
Duke in Richmond Park, Labby suggested that some
arrangement should be made 'with that eminent
warrior the Duke of Cambridge, so that H.R.H. may
disport himself elsewhere than in a park intended for
the recreation of the public'.[1]

He favoured the abolition of the Order of the Bath,
and indeed the Order of Everything Else, as they were
relics of barbarous ages: 'I cannot understand how
anybody can give a straw for these wretched honours.'
But what particularly annoyed him was that the
country should have to pay when someone received
the Order of the Garter: 'The Garter is not an Order

[1] He also referred to the Duke of Cambridge 'standing at the head
of the troops, his drawn salary in his hand'.

given for merit but one given to peers whom it is advisable to bribe and as a species of millinery to Royalty.' He had not the smallest objection to anyone having the Garter; it would improve the appearance of many M.P.s and make many princes and tinkers happy; all he objected to was that because a young gentleman (H.R.H. Prince Albert Victor Christian Edward) was rewarded with the Garter, for the sole reason that he had done the world the benefit of coming into it, the country should be called upon to pay a sum of £548 9s. 4d.

Then, too, he did not see why Her Majesty should send some special representative to take part 'as a species of glorified beadle' in coronation ceremonies abroad; for in his opinion the inauguration of the President of a Republic was a far nobler thing than the coronation of an Emperor. He described the Duke of Connaught's Leave Bill [1] as 'an obsequious and servile Bill brought in to suit the private convenience of a Royal Prince' and he asked 'If any Governor-General or Commander-in-Chief who was not a Royal Prince wished to come home and see his mother, would anybody bring in a Bill to enable him to do so?' Having thus dealt with the Queen's favourite son, he opposed a vote of £30,000 as dowry to her favourite daughter, Princess Beatrice, saying that the Queen ought to be able to support herself and her family with comfort on an annual income of £700,000. If Her Majesty wished to raise money, she might let the shooting in Windsor Forest; if she wished to curtail expenses, she might do away with the Royal Buckhounds:

'The right hon. gentleman will hardly contend that the honour and dignity of the Crown is involved in having a number of tame dogs to run after a tame stag and in giving a peer £1,700 a year to gallop after these animals.'

[1] The Duke came home to attend the Queen's Jubilee.

The Golden Jubilee gave Labby further opportunities of displaying his loyalty to his constituents, if not to the Crown. 'Why should anyone be knighted because Her Majesty has reigned fifty years?' he asked, and why this profuse scattering of medals to tories, ladies of the bedchamber 'and other such ladies', and even, he was informed, to cooks and kitchen-maids? He opposed the 'reckless and ridiculous' expenditure on the Jubilee festivities and speaking of the ceremony in Westminster Abbey he said: 'You are going to convert the noble aisle into a species of race-course stand under the auspices of some West End upholsterer.' The usual laudatory prose poems were chanted by M.P.s on this occasion and Labby commenced a reply to one of them with: 'Mr. Chairman, there are some speeches which one always expects to finish with *Rule Britannia*!'

But it was in connection with the grants to the Queen's grandchildren that Labby's 'sincere admiration' of Her Majesty had to be taken on trust, and to enter into the Queen's feelings we must forget her position and think of her simply as any old lady whose investments were being tampered with by an unscrupulous and unsympathetic stranger. 'The extreme limit of our obligation is to provide for the children of the sovereign,' he declared, 'and a little reflection will show the necessity for such a limit. George III had thirteen children and if each of his children had had as many it is an interesting little sum to ascertain the number of descendants that would have to be provided for now.' He repeated his assertion that the Queen was quite rich enough to make handsome allowances to her grandchildren, and remarked: 'Sufficient for the reign are the grandchildren thereof.' When the Prince of Wales[1] inquired of Labby:

[1] Afterwards King Edward VII.

'Do you suppose I should drown my children like puppy dogs as soon as they are born?'

'No, sir,' Labby replied, 'but your Royal Highness should live within your income.'

If the Queen really could not support her grandchildren out of her income, Labby suggested that she should sell her three estates, Osborne, Claremont and Balmoral, which would fetch a large sum of money if cut up into lots. Much to the Queen's disgust he was a member of the committee which considered the provision for her grandchildren and took the opportunity of raising the question of her personal fortune.

'Is Osborne included in this estimate of Her Majesty's private estate?' he asked W. H. Smith.

'No, because large country-houses fetch nothing nowadays,' replied Smith.

'Indeed?' queried Labby. 'Well, I am willing to offer you £100,000 for the Osborne estate, and will bet you at the same time that I would make a handsome profit out of the transaction by selling the house as a hydropathic establishment and the grounds for building sites.'

Apparently neither the offer nor the bet was considered a sporting one.

On the subject of the Royal Grants Labby had very few followers in the House. Even the Irish deserted him and voted with Gladstone for the Grants, to the unbounded joy of the tories. 'Go in and get your cheer,' said Labby to an Irish M.P.; 'it will probably be the last tory cheer you'll ever get.'

Although he had no respect for a crowned head, Labby sometimes thought well of the head beneath the crown, but it so happened that his references in the House to Queen Victoria's predecessors were not of a kind to warm her heart. He described Henry VIII as 'an unmitigated ruffian' and the only ruler he praised was one she had a natural disposition to dislike: Cromwell, he affirmed, was 'a man of genius' and 'the greatest ruler this nation has ever known'. What made matters infinitely worse was that the Queen held him responsible for everything that appeared in *Truth*. Needless to say Labby did not write one twentieth part of what was attributed to him, but as he retained the nominal editorship for many years he was credited with pretty well every paragraph in the paper.

From the pages of *Truth*, then, Queen Victoria culled certain phrases that left an indelible impression on her mind. One of them was about the Prince Consort:

> 'With all his good qualities Prince Albert was quite incapable of conceiving a real regard for any servant whatever with the one solitary exception of Löhlein, his valet, who had been with him since boyhood. Like most other persons of "exalted rank" Prince Albert looked with ineffable disdain on those beneath him.'

It did not help matters when the writer added that one of the Queen's most admirable qualities was her regard for the humble dependants around her, such as John Brown. There was another jarring reference to the Consort, who had composed the music for a hymn which was sung at a royal wedding in 1880:

> 'If this is really a specimen of what the Prince thought a hymn should be, it is well that his multifarious occupations left him little time for such work.'

Then there were two articles on the marriage of Princess Beatrice to Prince Henry of Battenberg which must have infuriated the Queen, who, according to the writer, was 'sick to death of the whole business'. The entire Royal Family was against the marriage, which was generally regarded as a mèsalliance, stated the writer. The description of the wedding at Whippingham Church, Osborne, in 1885 was certainly in Labby's style:

'The Prince of Wales seemed ill at ease and out of sorts; so also did the Queen, who looked exceedingly cross. . . . The bride looked very flushed and rather nervous. . . . Decided absence of beauty among the group of bridesmaids. . . . The Archbishop (Dr. Benson) introduced a novelty at the end of the service – to the horror of the congregation, who by this time were tired to death and longing for luncheon – in the shape of an address by himself. . . . The Queen had consented to this innovation on condition that the homily should not exceed two or three sentences, and it only occupied a few minutes; but Her Majesty commenced to tap with her foot in a very ominous way and the Prince of Wales was evidently fidgety and eager for the ceremony to end.' . . . (After the service) 'The Queen, who had become more cheerful and amiable, followed with the Prince of Wales, who seemed sulky and did not appear to respond with any enthusiasm to his mother's observations. . . . The Grand Duke of Hesse looks old and haggard. . . . The Duke of Edinburgh looked even more sour and supercilious than usual and the sullen expression which has become habitual to the Duchess appeared to be accentuated for the occasion. . . . Princess Louise looked well but has a very flighty manner. Lord Lorne was in tartans, but certainly looked very common. . . . Prince George of Wales seemed thoroughly well pleased with himself. He is a very ordinary looking lad but apparently has more "go" about him than his brother. . . .'

When these happy royal gatherings take place nowadays the descriptions which appear in the press are pitched in a different key. The final reference was to a future King of England, George V, and when the Duke of Clarence died Labby remarked that Prince George ought to follow the example of the Czar of Russia and marry the lady to whom his elder brother had been engaged. 'I commend this arrangement to the consideration of those whom it may concern at Sandringham and Windsor,' said he. 'Such a settlement would undoubtedly be popular and add the last touch of romance to a domestic story that has enthralled the world.' If the arrangement owed anything to his suggestion, England owes much to Labby.

*Truth* also commented with great severity on the Queen's

'intense selfishness in persisting in holding two Drawing-Rooms in March instead of four in May. . . . These functions will be continued till some member of the Royal Family is killed by exposure.'

And Her Majesty was taken to task for other delinquencies:

'Nothing can exceed the stupidity of Royalty and those who are habitually about them. They expect everybody and everything to give way to their crazy whims and caprices. The Queen's train reached Perth on Friday evening at the busy hour, and yet an idiotic order was telegraphed from Balmoral "to exclude the public from the platform". But why should Her Majesty be so ostentatiously ungracious to her subjects at Perth?'

The Queen regarded none of these comments as proofs of Labby's 'sincere admiration' for herself, and when in a burst of high spirits he parodied the National Anthem to give point to his strictures on the Royal Grants, she failed to catch the infection of his fun:

> Grandchildren not a few,
> With great-grandchildren too,
> She blest has been.
> We've been their sureties,
> Paid them gratuities,
> Pensions, annuities,
> God save the Queen!

At a later date Labby expressed surprise that the Queen had not appreciated the good-nature behind his 'genial banter', but he ought to have known that Victoria was not imbued with the true spirit of burlesque and could hardly have been expected to scream with laughter over japes which would have produced the heartiest guffaws from her predecessor Queen Elizabeth, after she had flayed the perpetrator alive. Asked by a friend why he never stopped attacking the Royal Family, he answered:

'One must find some very solid institution to be able to attack it in comfort. If the love of royalty were not so firmly established in the middle-class English breast, I should not dream of attacking it, for the institution might topple over, and then what should I do? I should have all the trouble of finding something else to tilt against.'

If Labby's feeling for Queen Victoria stopped at admiration, it went as far as liking for her eldest son, who also liked him. For many years they were on terms of friendship. Labby's realistic view of life appealed to the Prince and his stories were an endless source of amusement. It must have been pleasant for the Prince to meet a man who treated him quite unaffectedly as an equal, who showed neither the respect of self-abasement nor the disrespect of self-assertion. Their friendly intercourse was terminated abruptly by the appearance of a story in *Truth* for which the Prince held Labby responsible. As a fact Labby had not seen it before it appeared in print, but since he made a point of shielding all his contributors he was unable to put matters right with the Prince by explaining what had occurred. For years they were not on speaking terms, though the Prince must have softened toward Labby when the Tranby Croft scandal shook the social fabric of the nation and the nonconformists descried a Day of Wrath because the heir apparent had played cards in questionable company, for on that occasion Labby wrote in *Truth*:

> 'Never will I join in a dead set against anyone, be he prince or peasant, for doing what very probably under similar circumstances I should have done myself; or raise my hands in pious horror at a Prince playing at cards when I have played cards myself a thousand times.'

About a year later, in 1892, both Labby and the Prince were at Homburg, rather elaborately cutting one another whenever they happened to meet. The Prince suddenly tired of this game and asked Sir George Lewis to effect a reconciliation. Lewis did so and in the course of their first talk together Labby learnt something from the Prince the point of which we shall appreciate better after a glance at the political events of the hour.

Lord Salisbury's Administration lasted from 1886 to 1892 and throughout that time the tory ministers had kept the Queen well posted with the iniquities of Labby. 'Your Majesty would naturally object to Mr. Labouchere as a minister, if Mr. Gladstone should dare to propose him,' remarked Lord Salisbury; while the First Lord of the Treasury, *Pinafore* Smith, informed the Queen on different occasions that Labby's language was offensively cynical, that he was as mischievous as he possibly could be, and that he regarded everything which proceeded from Her Majesty's servants with suspicion. In 1889 she received an unexpected blow: 'I am quite horrified to see the name of that horrible lying Labouchere and of the rebel Parnell on the Committee for the Royal Grants,' she telegraphed in cipher to Lord Salisbury. 'I protest vehemently against both. It is quite indecent to have such people on such a Committee.' Lord Salisbury reassured her: they were chosen by their parties and would form an insignificant minority.

In 1891 the country was getting tired of tory government and Labby explained the position of the Liberal Party to a friend: 'Gladstone in his dotage is pulled this way by one and that way by another. They don't expect a dissolution until next year, but hope to keep the old man alive like the Tycoon of Japan, even after he is dead.' At the General Election of 1892 Gladstone was returned to power and Queen Victoria was appalled by his hint that he was thinking of giving cabinet rank to Sir Charles Dilke and Mr. Henry Labouchere. She wasted no time in letting him know that she could not possibly receive Sir Charles Dilke 'on account of his dreadful private character'. As for Mr. Labouchere, he was 'not a fit and proper person to be recommended to her for any of the chief offices of the Government or for any appointment which would bring him into personal communication with the Queen as a member of Her Majesty's most honourable Privy Council'. Gladstone relinquished Dilke without a murmur, but he was seriously concerned over Labby, who after all had stuck to him at a time when everyone else of importance was deserting him and who had been of great personal service to him. Labby was, in fact, the only man of note who had been quite disinterestedly loyal and whose future loyalty could be absolutely depended upon. Gladstone was in a quandary and discussed the matter with Lord Rosebery, Lord Rendel and a few other personal friends. He was on terms of real intimacy with Rosebery, to whom he had once confided, 'The Queen alone is enough to kill any man!', and set great store by his judgment.

Rosebery pronounced strongly against Labby; one could not trust him; the Government would be a public laughing-stock if he were in the cabinet. Rendel and others backed up Rosebery. Labby had no influence or following, they declared, and no one took him seriously. They spoke the common

language, the Esperanto, of the Establishment. Besides,
they pointed out, he had not asked for a post, so why
offer him one? It was true that he had not even
hinted he would like a place in the cabinet, but in
Gladstone's eyes that was the best reason for offering
him one. What clinched the argument against
Labby's inclusion in the Government was his editorship of *Truth*. It was obviously unfair that a cabinet
minister should also be the proprietor of a paper.
Gladstone was apparently the only person in England
who was unaware of Labby's connection with *Truth*,
for he received the information with surprise. Having
digested it, he went to see the Queen, who spoke of
*Truth* as an insuperable obstacle and repeated that
she could hold no personal communication with Mr.
Labouchere. After allaying her anxiety concerning
his moral conduct, for the rumour of a deferred
marriage had reached her, Gladstone admitted that
Mr. Labouchere would not make a good cabinet
minister, but thought that if he gave up *Truth* he ought
to be offered a subordinate post. This – the statement by Gladstone that he would not make a good
cabinet minister – was what the Prince told Labby
at Homburg. Naturally he was incensed and two
months elapsed before he discovered the truth:
namely, that Gladstone was reporting Rosebery's
opinion to the Queen, not his own.

After leaving the Queen, Gladstone got into touch
with several of Labby's friends, all of whom agreed
that he would not give up *Truth*, and when Labby
arrived in London in the middle of August he received
a call from Mr. Timothy Healy, who broke the news
that the Queen's attitude made it difficult for Mr.
Gladstone to offer him a post in the cabinet. Healy
begged him to extricate the Prime Minister from an
awkward position by writing a letter saying that he did
not wish to join the Government as he would be more
useful to his party as a free lance. If he would do this

Healy assured him that Mr. Gladstone would always consult him on public matters. Naturally Labby declined to write such a letter, which, apart from his dislike of such humbug, would have let down his radical friends. 'I may be a political leper,' he said in *Truth*, 'but I could hardly be expected to admit it.' A few dignified letters then passed between the G.O.M. and Labby, in which the latter's admiration and affection for the great liberal leader showed no signs of cooling, though he was overheard in the House of Commons smoking-room at about this time referring to Gladstone as 'a superannuated old goose!'

Labby accepted the situation with his usual good humour. He had not asked for a post in the Government and he had not expected one. 'So that the good old ship *Democracy* sails prosperously into Joppa,' he said, 'I care not whether my berth is in the officers' quarters or in the forecastle. Jones or Jonah, it is all the same to me, and if I thought that my being thrown overboard would render the success of the voyage more certain, overboard I would go with pleasure – all the more as I can swim.' Nevertheless he would probably have liked the opportunity of refusing an offer to join the Government, and he did not at that time think that Gladstone had dealt squarely with him. But the whole incident was soon forgotten. 'He never bore malice,' according to Lord Gladstone, and it must have given him some pleasure to know that for the first time in his life the G.O.M. had been compelled to dip into *Truth*.

He left England for a holiday at Cadenabbia, passing through Homburg where recent happenings prompted a recollection:

'I remember years ago I used to sit by a very agreeable man at the *table d'hôte* here. We got up quite an acquaintance. When he left he asked me to call on him in some unpronounceable place where he resided. I had taken it into my head that he was a waiter on holiday, so I asked him at what hotel I should find him. "I am," he replied, "the Sovereign of my country." Unfortunately I forgot the name of his country; otherwise I might have visited him and possibly he would have made me a chamberlain or a gold or silver or brass stick. . . . I feel proud, not I hope unduly, to think that there is a Sovereign somewhere in whose eyes I find favour.'

The fates were not being kind to him this year, for even a holiday at Cadenabbia had its drawbacks.

'A man who is owned by a dog has a troublous time. I am owned by a child, who is owned by a dog. I have a daughter. This daughter insisted on my buying her a puppy which she saw in the arms of some dog stealer when we were at Homburg. My advice to parents is, Never allow your parental feelings to lead you to buy your daughter a dog, and then to travel about with daughter and dog. This puppy is the bane of my existence. Railway companies do not issue through tickets for dogs. The unfortunate traveller has to jump out every hour or so to buy a fresh ticket. I tried to hide the beast away without a ticket, but it always betrayed me by barking when the guard looked in. I tried to leave it at a station, but the creature (who adds blind fidelity to its other objectionable qualities) always turned up before the train started, affectionately barking and wagging its tail. The puppy, being an infant, is often sick, generally at the most undesirable moments for this sort of thing to happen. When it is not sick it is either hungry or thirsty, and it is very particular about its food. I find bones surreptitiously secreted in my pockets. I am told that they are for the puppy, and if I throw them away I am regarded as a heartless monster. Yesterday he ate a portion of my sponge. I did not interfere with him, for I had heard that sponges were fatal to dogs. It disagreed with him, but, alas, he recovered. I take him out with me in boats, in the hope that he will leap into the lake, but he sticks to the boat. I am reduced to such a condition on account of this cur that I sympathise with Bill Sikes in his objection to being followed everywhere by his faithful dog. Am I doomed, I ask, to be for ever pestered with this animal? Will he never be lost, will he never be run over, will he recover from the distemper if fortune favours me by his having this malady? Never, I repeat, buy your daughter a dog, and travel with daughter and dog.'[1]

Although Labby himself had received the royal rebuff with a phlegm which people who could not understand him thought affected, his wife had been seriously perturbed by it, and now began to agitate for some recognition of her husband's services. Possibly she was tired of being plain 'Mrs. Labby'. Possibly she was angry because he lacked ambition. Possibly she knew that he had more intelligence than all the other politicians put together and wanted to see him publicly acknowledged. Whatever the cause, she got it into her head that he must be the British Ambassador at Washington, and when some visitors to Cadenabbia from the United States assured her that such an appointment would be extremely popular in that country, she would not rest until her husband had written to a friend of Lord Rosebery, who was Foreign Secretary in Gladstone's Administration, saying that he would accept the Legation at Washington, retire from parliament, and come to an agreement about the succession to Mr. Gladstone; otherwise there would be trouble ahead for Rosebery. Now from any

[1] *Truth*, September, 1892.

other man this would have looked uncommonly like blackmail. But there was absolutely no humbug about Labby, who meant it as a plain statement of fact. If Rosebery gave him Washington, he would anyhow be out of the way; but if he remained in parliament, Rosebery would be subjected to the violent criticism he must expect from one who wholly opposed his imperial policy.

For many years Rosebery and Labby had been friends – of a kind. Labby amused Rosebery, who once said, 'If I were a rich man I would pay Labouchere £1,000 a year to write me a letter every morning.' Rosebery also amused Labby, but not quite in the same way, for Labby had the gift of being able to excite Rosebery to a frenzy of annoyance. Rosebery was a man whose heart responded to what his head rejected. Lacking mental balance and spiritual contentment, he was a creature of moods and, like Reuben, unstable as water. Labby was not subject to moods and though he liked water he was not at all like it. The consequence was that when Rosebery was in a cheerful frame of mind he enjoyed the company of Labby, but when in a mood of despondency the mere sight of Labby made him scream, for he could not bear the truth about things when he was feeling below par.

Back in the early 'seventies they had spent many jolly evenings together in the company of actresses at the Star and Garter Hotel, Richmond. But when Rosebery put on his Hamlet mood and became aloof and self-important and touchy, Labby's quips were more than he could stand. In addition to their temperamental divergence Labby had already opposed Rosebery on two crucial points: his policy over Uganda and his succession to Gladstone as liberal leader. At the Cabinet Council concerning Uganda Rosebery was alone in favour of a British Protectorate, but Gladstone weakly permitted him to put in a clause which maintained the military occupation for three months, and Rosebery at once got up a press agitation in favour of annexation. 'He is an ambitious young man,' Labby told a friend, 'and wants to be Prime Minister, playing the part Palmerston formerly played with the help of the tories against his own party. We shall have to join against him and get up a cry *Delendum est Rosebery*.' Labby promptly began to attack Rosebery in *Truth*, while Rosebery, who probably thought that Labby was not playing fairly, told Queen Victoria discreditable tales about him.

This was not the most propitious moment for the request of a favour by Labby or the granting of one by Rosebery, especially as the request was accompanied by a threat, and Rosebery's friend, to whom Labby had written, pointed out in reply that a more appropriate occasion might have been selected. But Labby thought that was all nonsense. 'Rosebery's gain would be clear,' he said. 'I have no personal dislike to him – quite the reverse. But he is much too clever a peer to have as P.M. to my thinking.' As a radical he would naturally have to oppose the appointment of a Prime Minister who was in the House of Lords. But if he were in America it would be no affair of his; and he renewed his menace: 'I am quite prepared to use the arms put into my hands for my own advantage, not being of a modest or retiring habit of mind.'

His wife must have kept him up to the scratch, for he displayed a thoroughness and a forcefulness of purpose during these negotiations which were not at all in keeping with his character, except when fighting for his party. He approached John Morley on the subject, saying that he wanted the matter settled before parliament met, because he would get into a mess with his radical friends if he were to shirk the Uganda question, while if he showed antagonism to Rosebery and then received the appointment later it would look like a case of buying and selling. He was, he said 'a dangerous nuisance'. Morley spoke of insuperable difficulties which in reality were 'blessings in disguise', on which Labby observed: 'I don't quite believe in disguised blessings; in fact, I never heard of them except in a tract and in Balfour's speeches when he put the Nationalist M.P.s in prison.' Morley hinted at the attacks on Rosebery in *Truth*. Labby retorted:

> 'Rosebery takes one side in foreign politics, I take the other. Of course I fight for my side. There is nothing personal in this. I did not adopt my opinions in order to attack Rosebery; but I have always held them and always fought for them.'

Finally he wrote personally to Rosebery saying that his wife had got it into her head that Washington was an Elysium, that he himself in the damp atmosphere of England suffered from rheumatism in the neck and throat which made sitting in the House like the torments of the damned, that if he went to Washington he would stay there, like St. John in Patmos, and give up parliamentary life, and that, so far from its being a case of buying and selling, he would lose heavily on the transaction, for *Truth* brought him in more than twice a cabinet minister's salary. In reply Rosebery promised to talk the matter over again with Gladstone, Harcourt and Morley. 'That is very kind of you,' returned Labby, 'but all the ministers named have already spoken of insuperable difficulties, while each individually has favoured the appointment. . . . A cabinet, in fact, is the firm of Jawkins and Spendlow on a large scale.' Rosebery seemed to fear that people would accuse him of getting rid of a dangerous opponent, but Labby reassured him: 'You are overestimating my opposition. The safety of any Foreign Secretary is that not ten men in the House know anything about foreign politics or want to know anything.'

With regard to his qualifications for the post at Washington, 'a man must be an utter fool who does not get on with the Americans,' said Labby. 'This is done by never expressing an opinion on party issues; by occasionally making a speech at a dinner about the language of Shakespeare; by feeding Senators and others; by carrying out instructions like a machine; and by generally professing that, if there are two countries made to love each other, they are England and America.'

Meanwhile, knowing her husband's laziness and lack of push and uningratiating epistolary style, Mrs. Labouchere determined to act on her own behalf without telling him of her intention. She asked Rosebery for an interview of 'not more than ten minutes'. He of course granted it and was amazed at the contrast between the brilliant actress of the 'seventies and the very plainly attired lady who sat before him. She pleaded her husband's cause with a persistence that would have highly entertained Labby, taking forty-five minutes to enumerate his merits. She also had a long talk with Gladstone on the same topic. But her time was wasted. Rosebery could not forget the digs he had received from *Truth*, could not separate personalities from policies. He wrote to Labby saying that he had been so thoroughly abused in *Truth* that he could not offer any office to Labby, who could not accept any office from him. Labby replied: 'If rheumatism will keep off, I shall get as much enjoyment out of the House of Commons as in writing you dispatches about seals from Washington.'

But Mrs. Labouchere would not allow the matter to drop. She begged her husband to renew his efforts, and herself sent off a frantic letter to Rosebery ending with the words 'Washington, Washington, Washington!' To please his wife Labby made another effort, but not before he had done something else to nullify it. When asking favours it is the custom to suspend overt acts of hostility against the person of whom they are asked. Not so with Labby. He wrote an article in *Truth* bitterly assailing Rosebery's Uganda policy. He then wrote to Rosebery renewing his request for Washington. Rosebery promised to refer the matter to Gladstone, Morley and Harcourt. Upon which Labby wrote to Morley and Harcourt, explaining to the former that he wished to spend the last nine years of his life in the American capital. Why nine? Well, when he was in Homburg last summer, he got a pair of boots which fitted him so well and pleased him so much that he consulted the tables in Whitaker to find out his expectation of life, read that his allotted span covered another nine years, and ordered a sufficient number of the same kind of boots to last that period.

Somehow it got about that Labby was doing his utmost to obtain the American Ambassadorship and many of his political opponents, welcoming the chance to be rid of him, dropped hints in favour of the appointment. Among others Lord Acton strongly advised Rosebery to propose Labby to President Cleveland. But Rosebery had some old scores to pay off, and, not being in the House of Commons, was not so anxious as some of his fellow-liberals to see the last of Labby. Above all, he and the rest of the cabinet dreaded the effect on Anglo-American relations of having such a rebel, such an 'outsider', at Washington. The Establishment must be maintained, as Henry V implied in the course of a long speech to Sir John Falstaff, and Labby, because he looked 'quite through the deeds of men', was permanently labelled 'very dangerous'.

The final refusal would not have hurt Labby if he had not discovered that his wife had made personal appeals to Rosebery. That cut him to the quick. He never refused his wife anything that she asked; and that she should have been refused a favour she was asking for him brought his personal feelings into

play for the second and last time in his life. He came
to dislike Rosebery as much as he disliked Chamberlain; the first had slighted his domestic loyalty, the
second his political loyalty. Thus a certain amount of
venom salted his political antagonism to Rosebery
and he was soon to enjoy the only kind of revenge
that appealed to his sense of humour.

Early in '93 Gladstone introduced his Home Rule
Bill, which, after a series of scenes such as can only be
witnessed in the House of Commons or Colney Hatch,
was passed by the people's representatives but rejected
by the peers. At this point Gladstone should have resigned and gone the Laboucherean whole-hog for the
abolition of the House of Lords, but the tendency of
his mind was really conservative and, moreover, he
could not relinquish office so soon. 'As to Gladstone,'
Labby told a friend, 'the question of evacuating Egypt
is one merely of his parliamentary majority. "Can
you show me a majority?" the old man says when
questioned about it; he cares nothing any longer for any
political question, even Ireland, only to stay in power.'

Gladstone lingered on in office for another year,
during which an imperialistic section of the Liberal
Party under the leadership of Rosebery and Asquith
was countered by a combination of Labouchere and
Harcourt. 'Hell would be pleasant compared to the
present situation,' remarked Harcourt, whose anti-
imperialistic feelings forced him for the first time in his
life to ally himself with a radical. Harcourt at this
stage might have saved the Liberal Party from a
decade's oblivion if he had taken the trouble to conceal
his feelings, but he could not endure fools and nearly
everyone who came into touch with him quickly
developed a sense of inferiority. Labby, who did not
at all mind being made to feel an ass, liked 'Jumbo' and
would no doubt have continued to intrigue with him
against the Rosebery gang; but Harcourt did not
fancy a life in the wilderness with Labby, and when

Gladstone resigned in March, '94 and Rosebery became Prime Minister Harcourt again became Chancellor of the Exchequer.

Almost immediately Labby enjoyed the best joke of his political career and brought down so much ridicule on Rosebery's head that if the latter had been a much less sensitive man than he was he would still have been fired with resentment. On March 13, 1894, Labby moved an amendment to the Address which practically abolished the power of the Lords. He stage-managed the business very cunningly. First he advised a large number of tories to absent themselves on the ground that they could neither give a Liberal Government their vote of confidence nor give a radical amendment their support. Next he persuaded those liberals and radicals who favoured the abolition of the Upper House to be in their seats. Finally, after delivering an attack on Lord Rosebery, he moved his amendment at the dinner-hour, in a House of under 300 members. His amendment was carried by a majority of two, and although Rosebery's Government lasted until June '95 it never heard the last of the joke. Harcourt rebuked Labby for levity and got out of the difficulty by moving a new Address; but Rosebery, who was made to look a fool within a fortnight of taking office, was deeply offended and in the years ahead must often have regretted that he had not sent Labby to Washington. It was but poor consolation to send him to Coventry, which Rosebery did for the rest of his life. Labby, however, had the advantage of talking to anyone who was not on speaking terms with him in the columns of *Truth*, and Rosebery had further cause for regret when he read the following:

'By universal consent Lord Rosebery would have been fitted for the highest place in the land – if only he had never occupied it!'

Of course Queen Victoria regarded the success of Labby's amendment as a personal insult. But she had long ago exhausted her stock of adjectives on this man, and there was something of anticlimax in her comment on his latest action: 'A regular revolutionist!'

# CHAPTER XI

## WAR AND PEACE

### I

VERY few people sweeten in the process of living. The poison of life accumulates in the majority of men and women, who become more evil as they grow older, until they reach the period when they are too old to be actively evil and sink into a condition of senile sanctity. Labby reversed this process. The longer he lived the more bitterly did he resent injustice, the more sensitive did he become to other people's pain, the more angrily did he attack stupidity, hypocrisy and cant. The colonial policy of Great Britain throughout the last decade of the nineteenth century provided him with a wide field for the exercise of his satire and scorn.

Ever since entering parliament in 1880 he had kept a wary eye on England's behaviour in South Africa, and speaking on the Address in answer to Her Majesty's Speech, January, 1881, he had 'declined to recognise that Her Majesty's Government had any legal authority in the Transvaal', considered the annexation of that country 'one of the grossest frauds ever committed', and hoped the Government would withdraw its troops and acknowledge the Transvaal as an independent republic. When, after the battle of Majuba Hill, Gladstone granted the Boers self-government, Labby described it as 'one of the noblest acts in a noble life'. But when, through the efforts of Cecil Rhodes, the British South Africa Company received a charter in 1889, Labby realised that the forces of 'civilisation' were mobilising for war on the peaceful backward races.

The Company began by obtaining mining concessions from Lobengula, the Matabele chief, and sent an expedition to dig for gold in Mashonaland. 'The expedition proceeded, after the usual flourish about spreading the blessings of Christianity and civilisation, upon what is really a search for alluvial gold,' Labby informed the House. 'I am opposed to the whole system of chartered companies, holding that in regard to these large territories the Government should have the courage of their opinions and if they think there should be annexation assume direct control.' The Chartered Company discovered that it would not pay to delve for gold in Mashonaland and the shares became so much waste paper. 'A more scandalous financial company never existed since the days of the South Sea Bubble,' announced Labby in the House.

But times had changed since the South Sea Bubble; the world had not laboured to achieve machine-guns in vain; and the Chartered Company decided to pick a quarrel with Lobengula in order to look for gold in Matabeleland. The quarrel was easily picked, for white men who have machine-guns and want land are abnormally sensitive. A number of Matabele warriors, who had entered Mashonaland at the Company's request, were accused of certain offences, ordered to return home at once, and, so grave had been their crimes, attacked and killed while obeying the order. The Company's forces, commanded by Dr. Jameson, then invaded Matabeleland in a state of righteous indignation and proceeded to mow down the black savages with Maxim-guns, killing the prisoners to save trouble. The envoys sent by the King to make terms were murdered; Lobengula fled and died before he could be captured; his lands and the live-stock of his people were appropriated by the

Company and the 'soldiers' of the expedition were handsomely rewarded. One million new shares were 'created' by Rhodes and Co.: and in the subsequent boom were unloaded on the British public at anything up to £8 a share.

Labby was not a buyer. His contributions were solely verbal. 'Something should be done to stop these filibustering and massacring expeditions,' he said, and he spoke of 'Mr. Rhodes and his pernicious company', describing the latter as 'a wretched, rotten, bankrupt set of marauders and murderers.'

Unfortunately the gold in Matabeleland was no more abundant than it had been in Mashonaland, and the value of the Company's shares began to drop. What was to be done? Certain Englishmen in Johannesburg came to the rescue. They complained that they were denied the rights of citizenship in the Transvaal Republic, and this was seized upon by Jameson as an excuse for the next move. Labby described the episode in *Truth*:

'In the Transvaal there are extensive paying gold mines, and money which the gang would like to pocket is going elsewhere. Forthwith the Chartered Company's forces are marshalled again. A sudden and obviously factitious agitation springs up at Johannesburg. Rumours of deadly peril to the alien population are put in circulation, goodness knows whence. The women and children are packed off – so it is said, but no one knows why or at whose instigation. Simultaneously a message imploring aid from the quaking citizens reaches Jameson, no one knows how, and in a moment the fighting doctor and his bold buccaneers are once more over the border. There, however, all resemblance between the two coups ends. The Chartered heroes have not to deal this time with naked half-armed savages, but with white men as well armed as themselves, and as well able to use their arms. There are Maxim guns on the other side this time, and Krupp guns as well. Result: after a few hours' fighting, the conquerors of Matabeleland are killed or taken prisoners, and the doughty Jameson and his staff are lodged in Pretoria Gaol. I have no desire to exult over their fate. It is a shameful and abominable business all round, out of which no Englishman can extract a grain of satisfaction. But if ever men died with their blood on their own heads, they are the men who fell in this raid, and if ever prisoners of war deserved scant mercy, Jameson and his comrades are those prisoners. They may thank their stars that they have fallen into the hands of men who are not likely to treat them as they themselves treated the Matabele wounded and prisoners.'[1]

All this happened in the last days of 1895, and the sporting spirit of the English people, which Labby did not share, was soon expressing itself in poetry. On the first day of January, 1896, it was announced in the daily press that 'Her Majesty has been pleased to appoint Alfred Austin, Esq.: to be Poet-Laureate to Her Majesty', and the appointment shortly bore fruit. Voicing the natural feeling of his countrymen that any Englishman who violates the laws of a foreign State is a hero, Mr. Austin celebrated his reception of the bays with some verses which were supposed to express the emotions of one of the raiders. They appeared in *The Times* of January 11, and the following samples will serve to illustrate the popular view of the Jameson Raid:

'There are girls in the gold-reef city,
There are mothers and children too!
And they cry "Hurry up! For pity!"
So what can a brave man do?'

[1] *Truth*, January 9, 1896.

'If even we win, they'll blame us:
If we fail, they will howl and hiss.
But there's many a man lives famous
For daring a wrong like this.'

'I suppose we were wrong, were madmen,
Still I think at the Judgment Day,
When God sifts the good from the bad men,
There'll be something more to say.'

'We were wrong, but we aren't half sorry,
And, as one of the baffled band,
I would rather have had that foray
Than the crushings of all the Rand.'

Not even Kipling could have hit the sentiment of the
moment more exactly, though he might have captured
it more effectively. Labby did not view the raid or
the raiders from the same angle. Of the class of men
who made up these buccaneering exploits, 'I know
them well,' he told the House, 'I have lived amongst
them. They are lazy, lounging drunken planters
of the West India islands.' He was eloquent, too,
concerning the objects of the raid: 'During the last
two or three years a group of exceedingly shady
financiers has carried on a gambling establishment
with the Union Jack flying over it (*laughter*), and
society, the aristocracy of the country, has rallied to
that establishment and punted at it (*renewed laughter*).
The Chartered Company is one of the most scandalous
and disgraceful companies that ever existed (*laughter*),
and considering what companies are that is saying a
great deal (*renewed laughter*).' Clearly the House of
Commons thought the whole business extremely
funny; for every time Labby demanded an investigation into the financial and political action of the
Chartered Company and its complicity with the
Jameson Raid, the House tittered; and when he suggested that the Chartered Company should be debited

with the cost of keeping British troops in South Africa, the nation's representatives were tickled to death.

At the request of Her Majesty's Government President Kruger handed over Jameson and his brother-officers to be dealt with by their own countrymen. Their arrival in England was signalised by extra-ordinary demonstrations of popular feeling, and to prevent Jameson from being mobbed as a national hero and martyr the public were kept in the dark as to his movements. The raiders were sentenced to various terms of imprisonment, upon which Labby, who believed that Cecil Rhodes was the real villain of the piece, remarked to Sir Henry Lucy: 'It is just as if Eve were tried and sentenced in the matter of that apple, while the Serpent was reinstated in his arch-diaconal position.'

He continued to agitate for an inquiry and Joseph Chamberlain, the Colonial Secretary, appointed a committee to go into the matter. In the hope of gagging Labby, Chamberlain made him a member of the committee, which met in the early part of '97. The evidence of Cecil Rhodes was of course the main feature of the inquiry and when Labby, his chief critic, began to question him it seemed like a duel between David and Goliath. But this Goliath was armed from scalp to toe, partly by his own ease and self-assurance and partly by the sympathy of the committee, and the pellets of this David could not so much as dent his armour. Once or twice in the early stages Rhodes was slightly harassed but he quickly recovered. For example, he was complaining that Kruger always gave jobs to foreigners instead of Englishmen, when Labby quoted a statement by Rhodes that all his own mine-owners were American. Rhodes accepted the statement and Labby pounced:

'Then all your managers were Americans?'

'Wait a bit,' said Rhodes, realising that he had blundered.

'They were not Englishmen?' pressed Labby.

'Wait one moment,' said Rhodes, who then explained that all the latest ideas about mining came from America and that in any case he had not given Americans preferential treatment.

A little later Labby had another chance. The Witwatersrand Chamber of Mines had complained that the Government did not sufficiently punish black men who deserted from the service of the mines.

'I gather,' remarked Labby, 'that those who do desert, on the second time, receive twenty-five lashes?'

'I really do not know,' replied Rhodes.

'And the complaint of the gold-owners of this country is that they ought to receive more lashes if they desert, that the law is not sufficiently strong. I only want to point out,' continued Labby, addressing the committee 'that the revolution was not intended by these gentlemen (the Jameson raiders) to help to give those unfortunate people civil rights.'

'The black people, you mean?' queried Rhodes.

'They have none?' asked Labby, quickly turning on Rhodes.

'They are not fitted for them in their raw barbaric state,' replied Rhodes.

'And flogging is a good thing for them?'

'That I do not say at all.'

'Mr. Rhodes has not said that,' echoed the chairman.

'I do not say that flogging is a good thing for them,' added Rhodes, in case the two previous statements had obscured the matter.

Labby's examination of the witnesses was quite valueless because so much vital evidence was withheld. Again and again he had to content himself with some such evasion as 'I am not giving away any confidences' or 'I shall say nothing that might involve third parties'. He was fighting with his hands tied, else he would not have been on the committee. Rhodes had the sympathy of the committee, though of course the members

realised that they would have to register disapproval
of him in their Report. One piece of suppressed evidence was of the utmost importance. Some correspondence between Chamberlain and Hawksley, the
solicitor of the Chartered Company, was alluded to,
and Labby wished to examine Hawksley about it, but
the committee would not permit him to do so. When
the Report of the committee was issued, Hawksley
declared that, if this correspondence were published,
a guilty knowledge of the Jameson conspiracy would
be brought home to Chamberlain; and when the
debate on the Report took place in the Commons,
Hawksley gave a member instructions to read the
correspondence if Chamberlain attacked Rhodes.
Chamberlain did not attack Rhodes.

The committee prepared a Report, which, though
it condemned both Rhodes and the raid, was not strong
enough for Labby, who prepared a minority Report,
in which the raid was stigmatised as 'one of the most
disgraceful episodes in our country's history'. He
complained that witnesses had refused to tell all they
knew, that examination had been gagged, and that
important documents had been withheld. It was his
opinion, too, that the real promoters of the raid,
Rhodes and Beit, 'merit severe punishment'. This
Report was only signed by himself, the other ten members of the committee being satisfied with their less
stringent summary.

Yet there was something about Rhodes as a man
that appealed to Labby. 'I like Rhodes, I like his
porter and sandwiches,' said he, referring to the
pleasant informal way in which Rhodes enjoyed a
simple lunch while giving his evidence. And indeed his
opinion of the South African Colossus changed with the
years. At first he wrote about Rhodes in this strain:

'To me this Empire jerry-builder has always been
a mere vulgar promoter masquerading as a patriot,

I*

and the figure-head of a gang of astute Hebrew financiers with whom he divided profits.'

But after the death of Rhodes he revised that opinion:

'I do not suppose he cared for money except for the power it gave, and though, in the making of it, he had to associate himself with a crew of financial adventurers, he was head and shoulders above them all.'

No man was ever more free from cant than Labby, and this final estimate of Rhodes is a tribute to them both.

Throughout the 'nineties, as imperialism waxed, Labby's popularity waned. He sold his share of the *Daily News* in '92 because it backed the imperialistic section of the Liberal Party. By '96 the extreme Radical Party under his leadership was reduced to about three members in the House of Commons. In April of that year a rumour spread about Northampton that he had been shot, the hope no doubt being father to the rumour, but a newspaper correspondent comforted his anxious constituents with a wire: 'Mr. Labouchere assures me he is not shot.' The Soudan was finally conquered in '98; the backward blacks were everywhere being subjected to the blessings of civilisation under the dominion of the forward whites; ominous clouds were rising over South Africa; the British people were becoming more and more conscious of their place in the sun; and on December 16, 1898, Mr. Wilfred Scawen Blunt wrote in his diary: 'There must be a few lovers of liberty left in England, but for the moment they have no voice more powerful than Labouchere's.' He was indeed very much behind the times. The youth of England were straining at the leash of common sense, soon to be slipped by Joseph Chamberlain. In July, 1899, young Winston Churchill went up the river with some friends in a launch. They passed the lawn of Pope's Villa.

'Look, there is Labouchere!' cried Lady Jeune, pointing to the figure of a man seated upright in a chair at the brink of the river.

'A bundle of old rags!' said Joseph Chamberlain, with such an expression of hatred and contempt that Winston Churchill was impressed by its intensity.

Chamberlain was right, for Labby had never turned his political coat, which had been worn to rags; while Joseph's coat was always of the latest cut and most fashionable colour.

In August '99 Labby was doing his best to avert war in South Africa by advising the Boers to spin out negotiations in order to give the British public time to forget some inflammatory speeches made by Chamberlain. Labby had never doubted that war would be the inevitable outcome of the Jameson Raid, that the imperialist gang would never rest until the slur of that surrender had been wiped out; and so the moment Chamberlain began to make things difficult for President Kruger in the negotiations over the franchise for the Uitlanders of Johannesburg, Labby knew that the Colonial Secretary was out for blood. But his advice to the Boers was useless because Chamberlain forced the pace, making full preparations for war while the negotiations were still in progress and telling the Transvaal Government that it must accept the final offer of Her Majesty's Government. On October 9, in self-defence, the Boers delivered their Ultimatum and war broke out two days later.

When the British parliament met on October 17 to vote supplies, Labby at once demanded arbitration and suggested that the American President, William M'Kinley, should act as arbitrator. 'I believe if we were to arbitrate in this particular cause,' he declared, 'we should give such an impetus to the whole principle of arbitration that it would go very far to put an end to war in the future.' He told the House that the Transvaal Government was not responsible for the war: 'I say that we are responsible for it and that it was the absolute act of the Colonial Secretary himself.' Three days later he informed the House that the vote of ten millions was a mere beginning, because the war would cost the country at least a hundred millions before it was over. The House considered this the best joke of the century, rocked with laughter and rang with ironical cheers. They expected General Buller to be in Pretoria by Christmas (and so did General Buller) and they could scarcely have been more amused if they had been told that the actual cost of the war would be about 223 millions.

Labby never missed an opportunity of denouncing the war as a crime and of urging an immediate cessation of hostilities. 'I wash my hands entirely of it,' he said, but apparently he could not get them clean because he washed them again and again. The moment Lord Roberts reached Bloemfontein, Labby advised parliament to give the Orange Free State back to its inhabitants; when Lord Roberts arrived at Pretoria, Labby hoped that the British Government would 'allow these unfortunate Transvaalers to have some district in Africa where they can still call themselves a Republic'. Frequently he praised the Boers in language that was not appreciated by the heroes in the House: 'I regard the Boers as brave men and I would honour any man who resists no matter what force when it is a question of the independence of his native land.' The Boers, he said, should have the fullest autonomy: 'Self-government is not a privilege, it is a right. . . . Every man, so soon as he becomes a citizen of this Empire, has that right.' So bitter was his criticism of the Government, so strongly did he side with the Boers, even advising them to continue their resistance in the hope of foreign intervention, that Joseph Chamberlain accused him of 'moral treason'. But Labby had an answer to that. The Government was making the name of England hated throughout the civilised globe. 'I prefer my country to my party,' he affirmed. Great Britain would decline as a power because of this senseless and iniquitous war. 'I wish to ask the right hon. gentleman upon what ground he says I am pro-Boer. I am a pro-Englander.'

The right hon. gentleman was, needless to say, Joseph Chamberlain, and when the 'khaki' election of 1900 took place Labby was only asked to give one pledge by an elector: 'Will you promise to keep your eye on Joe?' He promised, and kept the promise both in the House and in *Truth*. 'Out of his own mouth let him be judged,' wrote Labby in the course of a long article on the history of the Chamberlain diplomacy, quoting a speech made by the Colonial Secretary in the House after the Jameson Raid: 'To go to war with President Kruger in order to force upon him reforms in the internal affairs of his state, with which successive Secretaries of State standing in this place have repudiated all right of interference, that would have been a course of action as immoral as it would have been unwise.' In another number of his paper Labby gave full details of the connection of Joseph Chamberlain and his relations with the group of Birmingham companies holding contracts with the Admiralty and the War Office, details which were set forth by Mr. Lloyd George in the House of Commons.

Chamberlain, seething inwardly, maintained an outward composure under the slashing attacks of his old radical colleague. With his sharp, bleak, birdlike face, arms and legs crossed, sitting bolt upright, his features as cold and set as his monocle, the Colonial Secretary, like a bird at roost, pointed towards the stormy quarter, receiving gust after gust of Laboucherean invective, unruffled and immovable. He could afford to treat his opponent with derision, for the country was behind him and even the liberals were scared of Labby. Harcourt was afraid of being seen in his company and Campbell-Bannerman excused himself for being 'a casual and not a regular correspondent' of Labby's on the ground that 'it is right to be taught even by the devil'. Besides, Labby had the bee of finance in his bonnet and hurt his case by extraordinary statements. Englishmen could never be brought to believe, with the member for Northampton, 'that they have been fooled into this war by the vilest body of financiers that ever existed in this world'.

The feeling of the country towards Labby underwent a marked change after the outbreak of war. He had always been regarded as something of a joker, but this was not a laughing matter and he was repeatedly warned that his form of humour had ceased to be funny. Perhaps it may be said that he was as popular as a man could be whose opinions were almost universally detested, but he was subjected to considerable personal abuse in every paper and from every platform in the country. 'I do not waste my time in answering abuse,' said he; 'I am accustomed to it and I thrive under it like a field that benefits by the manure that is carted on to it.' The yells of 'traitor' that greeted him whenever he rose to speak, and the tendency to lynch him displayed by loyalists of both parties, left him cold. The socialist, Hyndman, was amazed at his sang-froid during an anti-war demonstration at Northampton. Labby, J. M. Robertson and Hyndman tried to make themselves heard, but they were all howled down. Labby took it quite calmly and did not turn a hair when, escorted by the police and accompanied by the hoots and threats of a hostile mob, he returned to the George Hotel, smoking cigarettes on the way.

He presided over a meeting of Boer sympathisers in Queen's Hall on June 19, 1901, when various 'treasonable' speeches were made and the Transvaal colours were displayed. In his speech he outlined a series of proposals for peace based on an amnesty to Cape rebels, lavish expenditure on the re-establishment of the Boer farmers, and the dismissal of the High Commissioner, described by him as 'that wretched penny-a-liner Lord Milner'. During the meeting a crowd of patriots and pickpockets, who are usually in agreement on these occasions, surrounded the Hall. Labby, forewarned, got away by a side-door, but many of the Boer sympathisers were pelted with stones, knocked on the head, mobbed and relieved of their possessions, all of which probably deepened their sympathy with the Boers.

In spite of his general coolness of demeanour, many people who had known him for years stated that the only subject on which they had ever heard him speak bitterly and with intense feeling was the South African War. Voules and his assistant on *Truth* recorded the fact that the only time they had ever known Labby to lose his temper was when they begged him to moderate his opinions in writing for the paper, because both sales and advertisements were steadily declining as a result of his views on the Boer War. He not only lost his temper but thumped the table in his rage and used bad language, also for the first time in their experience of him: 'If I choose to ruin my own blasted paper, I shall do so, and I'll see Chamberlain and the rest of you in hell before I stop saying what I want to say!' or words to that effect.

But such explosions were few and far between. He seldom lost his sense of humour. When asked why a meeting of the Liberal Party was called at the Reform Club in 1901, he explained: 'To make an honest woman of Campbell-Bannerman,' who had recently shown signs of 'thinking imperially'. And when, following a series of British victories, a pro-Boer radical politician said that he wondered if he should not be right to give up his championship of the Boers, Labby exclaimed: 'For heaven's sake don't do anything of the sort! You'd far better stick to your present line. It will pay in the long run.'

For two and a half years the war went on and Labby was able to say: 'I retract not one word that I have published in *Truth*, or spoken in parliament, or written in any letter, or uttered in any shape or form about the Chamberlain diplomacy and the Chamberlain war.'

Since then we have had a greater and more futile war, but curiously enough it is the example we set the rest of Europe in the Boer War that will affect the future of civilisation far more than anything we did or failed to do in the Great War; for Mussolini has bettered the instruction of Chamberlain, and the laugh would now be with Labby if only he were alive to enjoy it.

## II

Through all these years of political storm and stress *Truth* had been making a fortune for Labouchere by exposing fortune-makers. Charity swindlers, professional blackmailers, girl-floggers, shady hospitals, shadier Friendly Societies, army contractors, moneylenders, quack doctors, religious humbugs, fraudulent company promoters, every class of shark had been exposed (and taught to be more cunning). Abuses in the army, the navy, the civil service and the church had been ventilated, and every week a column had been set aside for comment on miscarriages of justice, the cruelty and stupidity of unpaid magistrates receiving particular attention. Scores of libel actions had been brought against Labby; and although in the first twenty years of the paper's existence he had only defended six cases unsuccessfully, he had lost at least twenty thousand pounds during that period because of his inability to obtain costs either from those who were defeated or from those who, like Horatio

Bottomley, abandoned proceedings before the cases came into court. *Truth* had also opened funds for the various needs of poor children and had compiled an annual 'Who's Who of Imposters'.

As already remarked, after the first two or three years Labby lost interest in the paper and the entire control passed into the hands of Voules, but Labby regularly wrote political stuff for it and the general public could never get it out of their heads that he was personally responsible for every line, especially every line of libel. One of Voules's victims called at Pope's Villa to challenge Labby to a duel. The servant delivered the challenge and Labby instantly returned: 'Will you please thank the gentleman very much, but I am not fighting to-day. Ask him to call again.' The injured person went away, apparently quite satisfied. Sometimes he received complaints from friends who had been pilloried in his paper. One of these, Hugh Childers, wrote to deny a story in *Truth* that he had lost some official papers in a music-hall. Labby replied:

'I did not even know that there had been a "photographic portrait" of you until I received your note. I had requested the gentleman who was writing these "portraits" to do so in a good-natured vein, and as regards Liberals in a somewhat eulogistic one. I am exceedingly sorry that he should have allowed his fancy to run riot, but this is the fault of all periodical writers. Facts are their stumbling-block. They are ready to sit down at a desk and write for any length of time, but they will never give themselves the trouble to verify anything which they fancy that they have heard.'

To another friend, G. W. E. Russell, who complained of a personal attack, Labby sent a word of advice: 'Never be drawn. Let a licentious and scurrilous press say what it likes and sit tight.'

He followed his own advice whenever he was personally attacked, but then he was in a strong position: 'I have made it impossible for anyone to vilify me. I have told such dreadful things against myself that no one can invent anything worse.' Perhaps the oddest and most attractive thing about Labby was that he wrote and said whatever came into his mind without considering for a moment its possible effect. His writing has the style and freedom of 'thinking aloud'. He did not wish to hurt people about whom he was speaking or writing; he merely wished everyone to enjoy the joke about them (or himself). No other editor in the history of journalism could ever have written quite like this of a distinguished contemporary within a month of launching his paper:

'I see that Mr. Tom Taylor, the editor of *Punch*, has inserted in that periodical a cumbersome impertinence respecting this Journal. The idea of anyone writing to *Punch* to contradict a statement made in another newspaper is exquisitely humorous; but alas! Mr. Taylor has no sense of humour. I remember once walking with him from Parliament Street to Long Acre. He commenced to tell me a joke in Whitehall, and when we had reached Long Acre, where I had to leave him, he had not arrived at the "point". As we traversed the crossing, he paused, and monotonously took up the thread of his joke as we found ourselves again on the footway. I have often wondered how many miles of steady walking would have brought that joke to its climax.'[1]

He thought the press an excellent medium for propaganda and was responsible for the conception of the *Star* as a radical evening paper, getting a number of wealthy liberals to raise the necessary capital for it and making T. P. O'Connor its first editor. But he had an absolute contempt for press-made reputations:

[1] *Truth*, January 25, 1877.

'When I see a man praised and lauded in the press I distrust him, for I know how this sort of puffing is worked. If I could find a public man whom the entire daily press of London were persistently to declare a knave and an idiot, this would greatly tell in his favour with me. . . . I remember years ago finding myself with a French newspaper writer whom I slightly knew. The conversation turned on Garibaldi. "Do you know him?" I asked. "Know him?" he replied, "I invented him!" And I make no doubt that he and other pressmen of his kidney honestly believed they had hatched an egg into an eagle.'

He was strangely indifferent to his own compositions. 'You need not sentimentalise about my stuff,' he wrote to R. A. Bennett, who succeeded Voules, 'I send it to you to do what you like with.' He did not mind whether his writings were published or not; after relieving himself in words he took no further interest in the matter; indeed he seldom read anything of his after correcting the proofs and once made inquiries concerning an article in *Truth* about which a friend had spoken to him, only to find that it had been written by himself, but not having read it in the paper he did not recognise it by the title which the editor had given it. He liked writing as other people liked walking, for the sake of the exercise.

'I am the only person, I believe, on the press who does not care in the least whether his lucubrations do or do not appear in print. It has always appeared to me that the making of an article requires two persons, one to write it, the other to cut it down – and generally to cut out what the first man most admires.'

He wrote very rapidly, making no corrections until he received the proofs, when, instead of correcting

them, he would often start to re-write the article.
More exercise. Often he wrote articles and forget
to post them; sometimes he wrote articles and lost
or destroyed them; occasionally he sent second
editions of articles, because he could not remember
whether he had posted or mislaid the first editions.
He could write anywhere, in buses, in trains, while
watching a play, while listening to music, during
children's parties at his home, and incessantly during
debates in the House of Commons. Fortunately for
him, Voules 'vetted' everything he wrote, saving him
from many more libel cases than those he fought; and
fortunately for Voules, who had a large financial
interest in the paper, Labby had no objection to being
'vetted'.

One of the libel cases Voules failed to prevent was
due to Labby's carelessness. Archibald Forbes, the
well-known war correspondent, sent in a paragraph
containing a phrase about a famous general which
Labby thought rather strong. With the approval of
Forbes, he drew his pen through it, or thought he had
done so. But the printer mistook the erased sentence
for an underlined sentence and printed it in italics.
What was risky in ordinary print was outrageous in
italics and the general, highly offended, brought an
action for libel. Labby would not wriggle out of the
responsibility by explaining the mistake and paid up
like a man.

Being free from vanity he was quite ready to apologise to anybody he had unwittingly hurt or irritated,
and, being naturally kind-hearted, it was the easiest
thing in the world to get round him. He was incapable
of hostile sentiment towards any man he met face to
face, provided the man was in a pleasant humour.
'Labby has been got at again' was a constant saying
in the office of *Truth*, for he promptly stopped attacking
anyone who had the wit to buttonhole him and discuss
matters in a good-natured spirit. A moneylender who

had been attacked in *Truth* arrived at the office and
insisted on seeing the editor. Voules was away so
Labby interviewed him. 'What threatened at first
to be a heated wrangle developed into a friendly inter-
change of views,' related R. A. Bennett, 'in which
Labouchere, showing a keen scientific interest in
moneylending operations, explained to his visitor
exactly where he was at fault in the management of
his business, and gave him a few practical hints which
might assist him to make larger profits without exposing himself to unfavourable remark.' It was almost
impossible not to like him in person, however much
he might irritate one in print. John Kensit, the famous Protestant propagandist, was several times exposed
to ridicule in *Truth* and at last made an unsuccessful
effort to commit Labby for contempt. While the
case was being argued they sat next to one another
in the well of the court and by the conclusion of the
hearing they were on the best of terms.

'Good-bye, Mr. Labouchere,' said Kensit, 'this has
been quite a pleasant meeting.'

'I hope you have enjoyed it as much as I have,'
replied Labby, shaking hands cordially; 'I am sorry
that you have got to pay for it.'

When other people attacked him he did not seem to
mind. From youth to age his judgment was not
fogged by resentment. The don who had accused
him of cribbing at Cambridge, and was therefore
responsible for his expulsion, was hailed by him as an
old and valued acquaintance when they met at
Homburg shortly after. Abusive post-cards, sent to
him as editor of *Truth*, were dismissed in a phrase:
'They're cheaper and better than writs.' And even
the publication of a series of articles, quoting letters
which seemed to implicate him in shady financial
transactions, did not make him put off his plans for
a· holiday in order to deal with the charge. The
articles were sent after him; he lost them and had to

be supplied afresh; and then, because he found the subject tedious, he tried to get his editor or his solicitor to deal with it. He never did anything that bored him if he could get someone else to do it for him. For instance he could not understand accounts and never looked at a *Truth* balance-sheet, getting Voules to explain the position to him in the simplest possible terms. He would arrive at the office, produce his pass-book and ask the office-boy or anyone who happened to be handy what he had in the bank, saying that he did not know which was the debit and which the credit side. Usually his current account ran into tens of thousands of pounds; it was never less than £20,000. 'I have always had a sort of craze for keeping a big bank balance,' he admitted: 'It is like an old woman putting shillings into a stocking.'

Possibly his fortune was his misfortune; certainly his indolence, his carelessness and his inability to persevere with anything except radical propaganda, were due to the fact that he was born with a golden spoon in his mouth. He went about with his pockets full of miscellaneous matter which was never sorted out and most of which got lost in the process of repeated pullings-out. He was extremely heedless with letters, tearing them half-across when there seemed to be too many and tossing them into the wastepaper-basket, whence several were once extracted and offered to the addressee on cash terms. On the other hand he could be too careful of certain things. He walked the London streets in the 'nineties looking like a dilapidated bagman because he hated discarding his old and comfortable clothes. He had a favourite jacket the origin of which no one could remember, the firm that supplied it having long ceased to be. 'It's a bit the worse for wear,' he would explain to anyone in the office, putting his arm into a recess between the cloth and the lining which hung in tatters; 'my wife won't let me go out in it, but I'm rather fond of it and I hide it from her – He-he-he!'

The Mephistophelian chuckle implied that his wife would have to rise very early in the morning to get the better of him. The staff of *Truth* declared they could smell this ancient jacket coming upstairs.

One morning he arrived at the office in a presentable garment; he was irritable, jerked his body about in acute discomfort, and presently removed the new coat and sat in his shirt-sleeves. Mrs. Labouchere, he explained, had laid hands on his old jacket, which had disappeared. A week later, to everyone's horror, the old smell manifested itself on the stairs and Labby was back in the old jacket, bubbling with glee. 'I've done her! I've found it!' he exclaimed; and from the appearance of the cloth the general opinion was that he had found it in the dustbin.

His visits throughout the 'nineties to the office of *Truth* in Carteret Street, conveniently close to his own home and the Houses of Parliament, usually took place on Monday or Tuesday mornings. Having handed the entire business over to Voules, he merely called to correct the proofs of his political stuff and to talk to anyone who happened to be in a talkative mood about any subject under the sun except the business of the paper. While at the office he would order lunch, which consisted of a chop just warmed through. He ate the chop without bread, salt or pepper, without a drop of drink, but with a cigarette. Holding the chop in one hand, a cigarette in the other, he sometimes paused to crack a joke, which Voules, sitting opposite him on the other side of the table, failed to appreciate because of its somewhat bizarre setting. Having finished the chop Labby took out his teeth, laid them on the table beside him and began to correct his proofs. Voules did his utmost to accept the situation with the tolerance Labby himself would have displayed, but sometimes it was too much for him and he would dash into the next room, saying to the sub-editor:

'I can't sit there any longer with those confounded teeth grinning at me. They get on my nerves.'

Either Labby had a curiously shaped mouth or he was too impatient over the fitting; whatever the cause, no dentist seemed able to furnish him with an ideal set of teeth, and as soon as he felt the slightest discomfort he pulled them out and set to work on them with the first implement that came to hand, prodding them with the office scissors or battering them with the office ruler.

'Have you got a hammer in the office?' he asked Voules one day.

A hammer was sent for and inside five minutes Labby had completely destroyed about fifty pounds' worth of good dentist's work. This did not seem to worry him; but then nothing seemed to worry him. His imperturbability was unshakable.

'Voules, would you just touch your bell?' he drawled while correcting proofs one morning; 'the place is on fire and someone had better put it out.'

As he was speaking the wastepaper-basket, into which he had been throwing matches, burst into flames.

Voules, almost in a panic, rushed out for help. Half the staff came bounding in with expedients. Labby did not move out of the way, kept his pen in his hand, his cigarette in his mouth, and made no attempt to help. He just sat looking on till all was over, and then went on with his proof-correcting.

Most people extract every ounce of drama out of every crisis, major or minor, in which they are engaged. If it had been possible to convince Labby that the world was about to come to an end, he would not have displayed greater concern than a lift of the eyebrows. Early in '93 Voules had a serious illness and his assistant Bennett went to tell Labby that it was doubtful whether he could recover. Since the whole future of *Truth* was at stake, it might have been supposed that Labby would have manifested some slight interest in that direction.

'You know Voules eats a great deal too much,' was his sole comment.

Bennett looked aghast. Labby continued:

'His doctor should – ' he told Bennett what Voules's doctor should do, concluding with 'I will write to him at once.'

Bennett suggested that it might be more useful if he would write something for *Truth*, as they had no editorial article ready for the next number.

'You can do very well for once without an article, can't you?' asked Labby.

Bennett reminded him that there was a great deal of work at the office which someone would have to do in the absence of Voules, among other things about fifty letters a day which required attention.

'I should not bother about answering letters, if I were you,' said Labby, one of whose golden rules was that letters answered themselves if left unanswered.

They then had a chat about the Home Rule Bill.

Labby wrote to Voules telling him on no account to return until he was quite well, as everything would go on all right in his absence; and in order to make certain of this Labby omitted his weekly visit to the office the following Monday morning.

For about twenty years Labby remained nominal editor of *Truth* and though Voules was annoyed that the credit of his own work should go to another he valued the money he made as manager more than the glory he might have had as editor. What perhaps brought things to a head was Labby's airy indifference to the whole business. Their relationship cooled and at last Voules kicked.

'My dear Voules,' said Labby with the measured utterance and quizzical glance which seemed to reduce everything to absurdity, '*I* don't want to be editor. You can call yourself the editor if you like,' and the expression on his face suggested an unspoken addition: 'If you really attach the least value to such an absurd trifle, why on earth didn't you say so before?'

So Voules was appointed official editor, retaining the post for four or five years. In 1902 he behaved in a very foolish manner and it became necessary to remove him from the post. Labby, rather than hurt Voules's feelings by appointing one of his subordinates as editor, suggested running the paper without one.

'You can't seriously propose that the paper is to be carried on without an editor?' said the incredulous Voules.

'My dear Voules,' answered Labby, 'I have now been connected with newspapers over thirty years, and I have never yet discovered what an editor is. If you like I will resume the editorship, but it seems to me quite unnecessary.'

Thus for seven years, until the death of Voules in 1909, the paper remained without an editor. This was a typical instance of Labby's kindness of heart, and his final action in connection with *Truth* was another. Bennett, who became editor in 1909, begged him to convert his proprietorship into a limited company. He refused, saying that he distrusted boards and always believed in finding a man who could manage a business and leaving him to do it. But when Bennett urged that it would be a great kindness to the whole staff, who had been connected with the paper for years, if he would put the business on a permanent footing and save them all from the possible results of a sale of the paper to the first bidder in the event of his death, Labby's response was immediate and generous. A company was soon formed and the future of the staff assured.

Normally he was rather a kind-hearted than a generous man. He did not go round searching for objects on which to exercise his philanthropy; but if he heard of a friend in need he helped liberally. When George

Augustus Sala got into difficulties and made up his face with greasepaint to keep his creditors at bay by giving them the impression that he had scarlet fever, Labby frequently sent him money to stave off financial crises. Watts Phillips, a Victorian dramatist who used to sell his plays outright, was pursued with ill-luck at the end of his life and never appealed in vain to Labby, who provided for his family after his death. And the children of Pigott, a man who had done so much damage to the Liberal Party, had to thank Labby that they were not left to starve when their father committed suicide. He was of course wealthy and could afford the luxury of doing good; but unlike most wealthy people he did good by stealth and his name was never to be seen on subscription lists.

The warmer side of his nature was not exposed to view and the older he grew the more acid were his comments on men and affairs. Wilfred Scawen Blunt lunched with him in January 1902, and heard all about the dissensions and intrigues of the liberal leaders: 'If you were to take them all together and boil them in a pot, Campbell-Bannerman, Asquith, Morley, Rosebery and Grey, you would not get the worth of a mouse out of them,' said Labby. His heterodox views made him no less attractive to women, for that same month there was a big party at Devonshire House, and Sir Almeric Fitzroy noted that 'Labby attached himself to the Duchess, who at first appeared to resent his importunity, but later was fascinated by it and allowed him to talk to her at a length which amused some and scandalised others'.

By the end of the Boer War Labby had passed his seventieth year and secretly determined to retire from active life at the dissolution of parliament. He had always wanted to end his days in Italy and now bought Michael Angelo's Villa near Florence for his final home. He and his family spent a week-end in the summer of 1902 at the Sussex home of Wilfred Blunt,

who was shocked to hear that he was 'improving' the
historic Villa 'to suit it to modern requirements', up-
rooting old trees and planting new ones. 'Old
Michael didn't understand how to make a house comfortable; it's time we should teach him,' said Labby.
According to his daughter, Labby was a model father,
always good-humoured, never scolding her, and Blunt
observed that they were a very happy family. 'I have
known Labby now for forty years and feel a real
affection for him,' ran Blunt's entry in his diary. On
the Saturday night they sat up till 1.30 and Labby told
'quite a hundred stories'. As he was one of those
favoured folk to whom 'things happen' and as he could
always enjoy the humour of any situation, his stories
were never dull. To give an example:

'When I was in the diplomatic service I spent some
months in Italy. Entering a restaurant at Genoa
for breakfast one morning, I saw Alexandre Dumas
seated at a table with a very pretty girl, dressed as a
Circassian boy, who was young enough to be the
great novelist's granddaughter. Dumas told me that
they had just landed from a yacht and were spending
the day in Genoa. He introduced the girl to me
as Emile. After luncheon he proposed that we
should all take a carriage and go and see a show
villa in the neighbourhood. When we reached the
villa we were told that it was not open to the public
on that day. 'Inform your master,' said Dumas
to the servant, 'that Alexandre Dumas is at the
door.' The servant returned and told us that we
could enter. We were ushered into a dining-room,
presenting a typically Italian domestic scene. The
father and mother of the family were present, and
several well-grown boys and girls. Dumas was somewhat taken aback for a moment, but introduced
Emile and me vaguely as "*mes enfants*". As we
were asked to sit down to coffee we made ourselves

at home. Afterwards the owner showed us his garden. He and Dumas walked first. Emile and I wandered about hand-in-hand to denote our brotherly and sisterly affection. The Circassian was in a playful mood, and told me that Dumas was of a jealous disposition, which grandfathers sometimes are. He had one eye on the beauties of the garden and the other on his children. "What are you doing?" said Dumas. I replied that I was embracing my sister. As he could not well object to this, for once, I think, I got the better of the lady's eminent grandfather.'

Labby told stories, too, when he wished to point a moral. He and Hyndman had a public debate on socialism at Northampton, during which, though Labby exposed the weakness of his opponent's case again and again, Hyndman stuck to his thesis; but the audience were not present at the best part of the programme, to which Hyndman alone was treated during breakfast the following morning:

'The fact is, Hyndman, you remind me of the man who had a hundred thousand horse-power martingale for winning at Monte Carlo. He spent all his own fortune on testing his system, persuaded his wife to risk and lose all hers, borrowed of every friend he had to the full extent that they would lend him, and lost all that. Finally he was reduced to the last extreme of penury and was dying of starvation in a garret, when one of his associates who had stuck to him through all his self-inflicted misfortunes went upstairs to see him. The poor foolish fellow was at his last gasp and could scarcely utter a word. But he motioned to his old friend to come near him, croaked out to him hoarsely the words "The system was all right" and then died.'

In 1903 Labby sold Pope's Villa and No. 5 Old Palace Yard (at a profit, of course) and the home of

the family was henceforth in Italy, though he attended
the parliamentary sessions until the end of 1905,
staying in a bachelor's flat in Queen Anne's Mansions.
He watched with much amusement the disunion of
the unionists caused by Chamberlain's Tariff Reform
proposals. As a result of wholesale resignations the
Prime Minister, Arthur Balfour, had to reconstruct
his cabinet, and one day a tory plumped himself
down by Labby in the House, surveyed the Treasury
Bench where Balfour and Akers-Douglas were the
only survivors, and exclaimed:

'What a clean-up! Hardly one of the old lot left!
Never saw such a mop-up, did you, Labby?'

'Not really much difference, my dear fellow,'
answered Labby: 'New men, old acres.'

He observed the arrival of the younger generation
in the political arena with interest and was pleased
to see the son of his old friend Randolph Churchill in
parliament, especially when Winston began to display
the same characteristics as his father. Starting as a
conservative he objected to Chamberlain's food taxes
and crossed the floor of the House; but he did not feel
at home with the liberals and one day in the Reform
Club he became violent over something they had done
or not done and swore he would rejoin the tories.

'Oh, no, you won't,' said Labby.

Another explosion from Winston Churchill ending
with a similar threat.

'No, you won't,' persisted Labby.

'!!!' from Churchill.

'Now listen to me, Winston. A man may rat, but
he cannot re-rat,' was Labby's warning.

It was perfectly clear that the Liberal Party would
be returned to power with a large majority the
moment Balfour resigned and that Campbell-Bannerman would become Prime Minister. Labby comforted Campbell-Bannerman by explaining at once
that he wanted nothing, and as a comsequence

Campbell-Bannerman became quite friendly and open with him. Labby did his best to get Dilke a place in the cabinet, but the moment it was announced that Dilke might be included certain nonconformist leaders protested and Campbell-Bannerman dared not take the risk.

In December, 1905, Labby wrote to his constituents at Northampton announcing his retirement from politics on account of his seventy-four years. He had served them through six parliaments for twenty-five years and few M.P.s can ever have received or deserved so much confidence from their electors. He had sided with them in strikes and fought their battles, often single-handed, in parliament. The news of his resignation came as a great surprise to his colleagues who had just witnessed an example of his energy. All through 1905 the liberals had been very slack and Labby had tried to get a newspaper correspondent to publish 'black lists' of members who did not vote against the Government. The correspondent was against such a ruthless proceeding and said that it would be rough luck on a man who was forcibly absent from a division owing to some domestic affliction. Labby retorted scornfully about the mollycoddles who shirked their duty because a wife had a headache or a brat had the pip! He got his way and the lazy members were 'posted'.

Men of all parties were sorry to hear of his resignation. It was impossible to picture the House of Commons without him; it would be a dull place, and the smoking-rooms of the House and the Reform Club would lose their chief attraction. With the regret went a certain amount of relief; for though Sir Henry Lucy could write 'He was at heart one of the kindest and most genial men in the world . . . absolutely free from envy, hatred or malice,' someone who had been stung by him could speak of 'that gadfly Labouchere' and of his 'curious ophidian look'.

Probably no one was more relieved than the new Prime Minister, Sir Henry Campbell-Bannerman, who, now that Labby was for all practical purposes dead, felt that it would be safe to take him on the Establishment. C.B. sounded King Edward on the point; and His Majesty, assured that Labby was not only dead politically but buried in Italy, expressed great pleasure at the prospect of honouring a corpse. So the Prime Minister wrote to Labby: 'But now, as you are going, would you care to have the House of Commons honour of Privy Councillor? If so it would be to me a genuine pleasure to be the channel of conveying it. You ought to have had it long ago.' No doubt he would have had it long ago if he had retired long ago. The significant words in the Prime Minister's letter, which must have produced a chuckle from the recipient, were 'as you are going'.

Labby was at his home, the Villa Cristina near Florence, when this offer arrived. In the first week of January, 1906, he wrote to Voules saying that he presumed there was an office in London presided over by some eminent official, who could forward information, or cause it to be forwarded, relative to his being sworn as a Privy Councillor. A few days later he received the formal letter of summons and wrote to the Clerk of the Privy Council that it 'has now come to hand, having been sent on to me by a certain Russian, among whose letters it had got mixed up owing to the proverbial carelessness of Italian methods in such matters, particularly at Christmas'.

He was in London for the last time that month, returning to Florence towards the end of February. 'At the Council this morning,' wrote Sir Almeric Fitzroy in his diary on February 16th, 'Labby was sworn and comported himself with characteristic effrontery. He came in a cut-away coat, studiously refrained from kissing the Testament in connection with the Oath of Allegiance, and indulged throughout the ceremony in a series of *sotto voce* remarks which were distinctly audible to me standing on the left of the King.' Labby was seemingly unaware of his faulty etiquette. 'I have not the slightest notion what a Privy Councillor is, except that I had to take half a dozen oaths at a Council, which were mumbled out by some dignitary, and then Fletcher Moulton, who was also being sworn in, and I performed a sort of cake-walk backwards.'

Again he stayed at Queen Anne's Mansions, explaining to the editorial staff of *Truth* how simple it was to live on tenpence a day. In the morning he was brought a cup of tea and a slice of toast (6d.). He lunched in the ABC at the corner of Parliament Street on two cold sausages (4d.). At first the waitresses there bothered him to order bread and butter and asked what he would like to drink; but when he replied that if they were dissatisfied with what satisfied him he would go elsewhere, they left him severely alone with his cold sausages. 'So you see, as I don't often take any dinner, I generally get through the day for tenpence,' he concluded. A fellow-member of the Reform Club happened to notice that whenever he ordered tea he was careful, after emptying the small pot of cream, to rinse it round with tea, so that nothing should be wasted. He certainly had a curious way of enjoying himself when freed from domestic ties.

One morning however he arrived at the office of *Truth* and frankly admitted that he had varied his diet.

'I think I must have had something for dinner that disagreed with me,' he said.

'What did you have?' asked Voules.

'Well, I went over to the Reform Club about nine o'clock and feeling rather hungry I thought I'd have some dinner. I couldn't see anything I fancied except some Christmas pudding. It was rather good so I had a second helping.'

K

'I don't wonder you are a bit off-colour,' remarked Voules.

'But I am not sure it was the pudding,' continued Labby. 'The fact is that, just as I was finishing, a fellow I know in the House came to my table and ordered some oysters. They looked very good so I told the waiter to bring me some. I don't know how many he brought, but we got talking and I finished the lot.'

Later Voules discovered that he had polished off a score of oysters on top of his two helpings of Christmas pudding, and as he was seventy-four years of age Voules wondered whether Mrs. Labouchere ought not to be advised of her husband's excesses.

However, he arrived safely in Florence after this sparto-sybaritic interlude and never again faced the sausages, the oysters and the plum-pudding of London. Life flowed pleasantly away in Italy. He wrote letters, entertained, occasionally saw old friends, kept up an interest in politics, and never stopped smoking cigarettes at ten a penny. His conversation did not become more reticent nor did his sentiments mellow with age. Asked whether he liked a certain woman he replied: 'Oh, yes, I like her well enough, but I shouldn't mind if she dropped down dead in front of me on the carpet.' The British colony at Florence were annoyed because he did not invite them to his fêtes at the Villa Cristina, but he had seen enough of the British in Britain and wanted a change of language, customs and opinions.

Now as before his summers were usually spent at Cadenabbia, of which he was so fond that Lady Bancroft said it ought to be called Cadelabbya. The Bancrofts were constant visitors to Lake Como and Sir Squire Bancroft relates how he and Labby went into a local curiosity shop, picked up a piece of old iron-work and pretended to examine it closely. It was quite worthless, being merely a bit of an old

mowing-machine, and the shopkeeper was amazed
when they went into raptures over it. At last they
asked what he wanted for it. The wily dealer, taken
in by their pantomime, suddenly became cautious and
remarked that it was a very rare specimen. They
agreed and begged him to be quite candid with them:
was it really genuine?

'*Mais oui, oui, oui, c'est vraiment – vraiment véritable – et
bien remarquable!*'

'*Combien?*'

'*Pour vous – mais seulement pour vous – vingt-cinq francs.*'

They suggested the five without the twenty.

Did they wish to rob him, he asked?

No, no! Oh, dear, no! But they would have to
think the matter over.

They left the shop, having enhanced the value of a
piece of old iron and rendered it unsaleable owing to
the fancy price thereafter placed upon it by the
shopman.

In the ordinary way Labby was not much of a
practical joker, though Hyndman reports that he
once took the famous socialist Jaurès to call on Labby,
who made a number of idiotic remarks in execrable
French, which he could speak perfectly, and continually pressed his visitors to remain and listen to his bad
pronunciation and absurd opinions. This was unlike
Labby, usually the essence of courtesy, and so we must
assume that something dogmatic in the attitude of his
socialist callers got on his nerves.

He was a famous figure at Cadenabbia and nearly
everybody talked to him. One visitor even asked him
for advice on a religious matter. The English church
at Cadenabbia was, it appeared, too 'high'. What
should he do? Labby pointed to the opposite shore
and suggested that the visitor should transfer his
patronage to the English church at Bellagio. But
here was another snag: the services at Bellagio were,
it seemed, too 'low'.

'Then there is a third course open to you,' said Labby. 'When the bells of the rival establishments begin to ring, hire a boat, row to the centre of the lake, stop, and say your prayers half-way between the two.'

The mountains, the distant villages, the blue water and the long days of sunshine were very pleasant in that clear soft air, and Labby would sit for hours surveying the scene, sometimes talking, always smoking. His face was now strangely masklike; the skin had hardened and set in wrinkles; but the eyes were still shrewd, bright, mocking.

'Let us get away from this beastly band,' he said to Bennett, the editor of *Truth*, after dinner one evening; 'one can't hear oneself speak.'

So they left the hall of the hotel and sat down outside in the company of the stars.

'I can't think why people want bands when they come here,' continued Labby. 'Wonderful place this for stars! What I like about it is that you can see them in the lake without craning your neck. I sit here and follow Bacon's advice: look at the stars in the pond instead of in the sky, and you won't tumble into the pond. There was a Greek named Pythagoras – or some ass at any rate – who comforted himself with the notion that in the future state he would be able to hear the music of the spheres. Who wants to hear the music of the spheres? Bother that band! What strikes me most about the stars is that they do their work so quietly. Pythagoras picked up his notions in the East – probably from the Jews. They imagined angels with harps and a perpetual concert in Heaven. Good God! Think of having to sit at a concert for all eternity. Wouldn't you pray to be allowed to go to Hell? The only reason that I can see for desiring immortality would be the chance of meeting Pythagoras and the other asses, and having a few words with them. Now Socrates was not an ass. He was for banishing musicians from his republic. No doubt he saw that this would get him a lot of republican votes. Gladstone once said to me – '

The voice had suddenly stopped. The bright eyes were closed. Labby had fallen asleep. He was getting old.

But all was well until the autumn of 1910 when, without any warning, his wife left him. She had given a lively reading from *David Copperfield* to the family circle on the evening of October 30, but by the following night she was dead of apoplexy. The shock unnerved Labby and he was never quite the same again, though his interest in life remained keen. He had always depended on her to pilot the domestic vessel and keep it in repair. 'I am merely a passenger on the ship,' he used to say, and for that matter he had depended upon her to make the chief passenger presentable. Shortly after her death their daughter, now married to an Italian marquis, was shocked by the shabbiness of his clothes and remonstrated with him. On her next visit to the Villa Cristina she was staggered by the gaudiness of his clothes: he looked like a British tourist on the Italian music-halls. She discovered that he had taken counsel with his major-domo.

'Where in Florence can one get a really good suit of clothes at a price within reach of a man of limited means?' he had asked.

The major-domo had a friend in a remote corner of the town, a description of whom appealed to Labby, who commanded the attendance of the Florentine artist, who manufactured the confection which surprised the Marchesa.

Visitors were constant and his conversational powers showed no sign of waning. On the surface he was as cheerful, as easily amused, as ever. Lord Fisher called to see him in the spring of 1911 and received an affectionate greeting.

'Don't put your arm on my shoulder!' shouted the

peppery sailor: 'Read that damned thing there!' and he pointed to a venomous attack on him that had recently appeared in *Truth*.

'My dear fellow,' said Labby, 'where would you have been if you had not been persistently maligned? You owe your position to these attacks. But take my advice: never reply to them, never correct mis-statements. If you try to brush away the filth, you will only soil your own hands.'

He told Fisher that he had none but Italian servants: 'I am always extremely polite to them because the knife comes so easily to them.'

In the autumn of 1911 he paid his last visit to Lake Como, and on his return showed the first signs of physical exhaustion. His daily walk round the garden began to fatigue him and soon he discontinued it. On Christmas-day he presided over a dinner to his grand-nephews and nieces and suffered a slight seizure, which passed off without much effect. In the first week of 1912 he caught a cold, which developed into bronchial catarrh. When he ceased to smoke, his daughter knew that the end was near. He took to his bed and grew steadily weaker, but his mind remained perfectly clear and he discussed the German elections, the latest political crisis in France, the war between Italy and Turkey.

On Sunday afternoon, January the 14th, he was dozing, when a spirit-lamp on the table by his side was knocked over and flared up. His eyes opened: 'Flames?' he murmured: 'Not yet, I think.'

He chuckled and dozed off again; and just before midnight on Monday the 15th his eyes closed for the last time.

He had wished to lie by the side of his wife in the cemetery of San Miniato, but there was a rule that only Catholics could be buried there. An appeal having been made to the authorities, it was discovered that by a curious coincidence the cemetery was just then passing from the possession of some religious body into that of the municipality. The bar against heretics was thus removed, and Labby was placed close to his Catholic wife in consecrated earth.

It should be added that his wish was dictated by affection, not piety, for he never wanted to be taken on the Establishment, even of a better world.

# AUTHORITIES

*Hansard*, 1880–1905.
*Truth*, 1877–1912.
*The World*, 1874–6.
*The Daily News*, 1870–1 and March 1881.
*The London and Provincial Daily Press*, January 16–17, 1912.
*The Times*, January 11, 1896.
*Punch*, November 9, 1889.
*Saturday Review*, January 20, 1912.
*Second Report from the Select Committee on British South Africa*, 1897.
*The Dictionary of National Biography*.


*The Life of Henry Labouchere* by Algar Labouchere Thorold, 1913.
*The Life of Joseph Chamberlain* by J. L. Garvin, vol. 2, 1933, vol. 3, 1934.
*The Life of Sir Charles Dilke* by Stephen Gwynn and Gertrude M. Tuckwell, 2 vols., 1917.
*The Life of Sir Henry Campbell-Bannerman* by J. A. Spender, 2 vols, 1923.
*The Life of Sir William Harcourt* by A. G. Gardiner, 2 vols, 1923.
*The Life of Lord Courtney* by G. P. Gooch, 1920.
*The Life of James McNeill Whistler* by E. R. and J. Pennell, 2 vols. 1908.
*The Life of W. T. Stead* by Frederic Whyte, vol. 2, 1925.
*The Life of Lord Goschen* by the Hon. A. D. Elliot, vol. 2, 1911.
*The Life of Lord Russell of Killowen* by R. Barry O'Brien, 1901.
*The Life and Correspondence of the Right Hon. Hugh C. E. Childers*, vol. 2, 1901.
*The Life and Letters of Mandell Creighton* by His Wife, vol. 2, 1904.
*Lord Randolph Churchill* by Winston S. Churchill, 2 vols., 1906.
*Lord Rosebery* by the Marquess of Crewe, 2 vols., 1931.
*The Letters of Queen Victoria*, second series, vol. 3, edited by G. E. Buckle, 1928.
*The Letters of Queen Victoria*, third series, 3 vols., edited by G. E. Buckle, 1930–2.
*The Queen and Mr. Gladstone*, with a commentary by Philip Guedalla, 1933.

*Private Diaries of the Right Hon. Sir Algernon West*, edited by H. G. Hutchinson, 1922.

*Memoirs* by Sir Almeric Fitzroy, vol. 1.

*Memoirs of an Old Parliamentarian* by the Right Hon. T. P. O'Connor 2 vols., 1929.

*The Life and Adventures of George Augustus Sala* by Himself, 1896.

*The Milner Papers*, vol 2, edited by Cecil Headlam, 1933.

*T. P. O'Connor* by Hamilton Fyfe, 1934.

*Fifty Years of Parliament* by the Earl of Oxford and Asquith, vol. 1, 1926.

*Memories and Reflections* by the Earl of Oxford and Asquith, vol. 1, 1928.

*Letters and Character Sketches from the House of Commons* by Sir Richard Temple, 1912.

*Press Platform and Parliament* by Spencer Leigh Hughes, 1918.

*Portraits of the Seventies* by G. W. E. Russell, 1916.

*Portraits of the Eighties* by Horace G. Hutchinson, 1920.

*My Diaries* by Wilfred Scawen Blunt, 1932.

*Queen Victoria* by E. F. Benson, 1935.

*The Diary of a Journalist* by Sir Henry Lucy, 3 vols., 1920-3.

*Ten Years at the Court of St. James'* by Baron von Eckardstein, 1921.

*The Personal Papers of Lord Rendel*, 1931.

*Further Reminiscences* by H. M. Hyndman, 1912.

*Memories* by Lord Fisher, 1919.

*Victorians, Edwardians and Georgians* by John Boon, vol. 1, 1927.

*Memories of Eight Parliaments* by H. W. Lucy, 1908.

*Sixty Years in the Wilderness* by H. W. Lucy, 2 vols., 1909 and 1912.

*Nearing Jordan* by H. W. Lucy, 1916.

*Charles Stewart Parnell* by Katherine O'Shea, vol. 2, 1914.

*Sir Wilfred Lawson* by G. W. E. Russell, 1909.

*After Thirty Years* by Lord Gladstone, 1929.

*Letters and Leaders of My Day* by T. M. Healy, 2 vols., 1928.

*Club Cases* by Arthur F. Leach, 1879.

*More Pages from my Diary*, 1908-14, by Lord Riddell, 1934.

*My Early Life* by Winston S. Churchill, 1930.

*Fifty Years of Fleet Street* by Sir John R. Robinson, 1904.

*Seventy-two Years at the Bar* by Ernest Bowen-Rowlands, 1924.

*A Speaker's Commentaries* by Lord Ullswater, vol. 1, 1925.

*Letters and Journals of Viscount Esher*, vol. 1, 1934.

*Collections and Recollections* by G. W. E. Russell, 1899.

*Evening Memories* by William O'Brien, 1920.

*Journalistic London* by Joseph Hatton, 1882.

*I Myself* by Mrs. T. P. O'Connor, 1910.

*Past Times and Pastimes* by the Earl of Dunraven, vol. 1, 1922.

*Memories of Midland Politics* by F. A. Channing, 1918.

*Our Book of Memories*, Letters of Justin McCarthy and Mrs. Campbell Praed, 1912.

*The Rebel Rose*, a novel by Justin McCarthy and Mrs. Campbell Praed, 1888.

*Edmund Yates: His Recollections and Experiences*, vol. 2, 1884.

*Recollections of a Diplomatist* by Sir Horace Rumbold, vol. 2, 1902.

*Recollections of Paris* by Capt. the Hon. D. Bingham, 2 vols., 1896.

*The Diary of a Besieged Resident in Paris*, 1871.

*Bar, Stage and Platform* by H. C. Merivale, 1902.

*Reminiscences of a Radical Parson* by the Rev. W. Tuckwell, 1905.

*W. S. Caine* by John Newton, 1907.

*Randlords* by P. H. Emden, 1935.

*Ne Obliviscaris* by Lady Frances Balfour, vol. 2.

*Reminiscences of My Life* by Henry Holiday, 1914.

*Whistler* by James Laver, 1930.

*Glances Back* by G. R. Sims, 1917.

*After Puritanism* by Hugh Kingsmill, 1929.

*The Strange Life of Willy Clarkson* by Harry J. Greenwall, 1936.

*Ellen Terry's Memoirs*, 1933.

*Dame Madge Kendal* by Herself, 1933.

*My Bohemian Days* by H. Furniss, 1919.

*The Confessions of a Caricaturist* by H. Furniss, 2 vols., 1901.

*Forty Years on the Stage* by J. H. Barnes, 1914.

*Recollections of a Savage* by Edwin A. Ward, 1923.

*The Bancrofts* by Themselves, 1909.

*Empty Chairs* by Squire Bancroft, 1925.

*Old Days in Bohemian London* by Mrs. Clement Scott, 1919.

*A Sporting and Dramatic Career* by A. E. T. Watson, 1918.

*My Life*, vol. 2, by Frank Harris, 1925.

*The Days I Knew* by Lillie Langtry, 1925.

# INDEX

315